DATE DUE

MACY

Modern diplomacy /

JZ 1305 .B347 1988   22618

Barston, R. P.

OEMCO

Modern diplomacy

R. P. Barston

Longman
London and New York

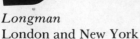

Longman Group UK Limited
Longman House, Burnt Mill, Harlow,
Essex CM20 2JE, England
and Associated Companies throughout the world.

*Published in the United States of America
by Longman Inc., New York*

© Longman Group UK Limited 1988

First published 1988

British Library Cataloguing in Publication Data
Barston, R. P.
    Modern diplomacy.
    1. Diplomacy
    I. Title
    327.2   JX1662

ISBN 0-582-01403-4   CSD
ISBN 0-582-49441-9   PPR

Library of Congress Cataloging-in-Publication Data
Barston, R. P. (Ronald Peter)
    Modern diplomacy.

    Bibliography: p.
    Includes index.
    1. Diplomacy.   2. Diplomatic and consular
service.   I. Title.
JX1662.B347   1988   327.2   87-3943
ISBN 0-582-01403-4
ISBN 0-582-49441-9 (pbk.)

Set in 10/12pt Baskerville Comp/Edit 6400

Produced by Longman Singapore Publishers (Pte) Ltd.
Printed in Singapore.

Contents

List of figures and tables

Acknowledgements

This book has its origins in the teaching of foreign policy analysis over a number of years to students and public sector officials from many countries. Periodic breaks from academic life, particularly on international diplomatic service assignments have brought insights which could not otherwise have been gained. The University of Lancaster has generously provided research assistance throughout the project. A particular debt is owed to a number of individuals, who in different ways, have provided support, including Robert Purnell, Professor P. A. Reynolds and Professor D. C. Watt. Colleagues at the National Institute of Public Administration, Malaysia, including Dr Mohd Shahari, Dr Mazlan, En. Hasmy Agam, En. Anwarudin and Samsudin Osman, provided contact and an inquisitive environment at an early stage of the project. A number of others have been generous of their time in reading parts of the manuscript, including Professor Alan James, Professor A. I. Macbean, Professor V. N. Balasu-bramanyam, Professor William Coplin, Professor Gary Bertsch, Professor Bahgat Korany and Professor Adam Watson. There are, too, others in foreign and other external ministries in several countries who were also prepared to give their time to discuss issues, help with documentation and provide valuable comment, but who cannot be named. Grateful acknowledgement is also due to the staff of a large number of national libraries and international organisations; particular thanks goes to Anne C. M. Salda, Bibliography Librarian at the Joint IMF-World Bank Library Washington; the Southeast Asian Banking Centre Library, Kuala Lumpur; Susan Halls and Joan McPherson, Foreign and Commonwealth Office Librarians and John Illingworth of the University of Lancaster Library. Dr Richard Little and Dr Michael Perrins assisted in the final preparation of the manuscript. Particular thanks are also due to Mrs Susan Anne Riches, who typed the manuscript. Finally, a considerable appreciation is owed to Pamela, Robert and Neill, for support throughout the project.

Preface

Modern diplomacy has undergone a number of major changes in recent years. This book is concerned with exploring these developments as well as how they have affected and in turn reflect the conduct of international relations. There are three main assumptions underlying the approach to the book. In the first place the study of diplomacy ought not to be treated largely from the narrow vantage-point of essentially political issues. The agenda of diplomacy is diverse and complex. The analytical perspective should accordingly be interdisciplinary. This in itself has entailed drawing together specialised material which is not easily accessible or is generally confined within its disciplinary boundaries. Secondly, there have been significant changes in the number of those engaged in diplomacy. The broadening of those involved, to include not only those officially responsible for diplomacy, but a wide range of others, including non-state actors and 'unofficial' diplomats has brought variety, opened up new options and avenues of interaction and, perhaps, introduced elements of uncertainty. A third consideration is based on the very considerable shifts which have taken place especially over the last decade in the content and methods of diplomacy.

The organisation of the book is divided into four main parts after Chapter 1 which provides an overview of the main changes in diplomacy which have occurred since the early 1960s. Following on from this, the book is concerned with changes in organisation and overseas representation; the various forms of diplomatic correspondence and the factors influencing foreign policy assessments. The analysis then proceeds to discuss changes in diplomatic styles and methods followed by a discussion of the key features of the process of international negotiation. Subsequently, diplomacy is explored in three major areas: international financial relations, international trade and security. Treaties, agreements and the growth of informal instruments between states form the core of the enquiry of the final part of the book.

It is hoped that the above goes some way to meeting the needs of those who study or intend to practise diplomacy.

R. P. Barston
Department of Politics
University of Lancaster
November 1986

List of abbreviations

ABM	anti-ballistic missile
ACP	African, Caribbean and Pacific countries
ADB	Asian Development Bank
ANZUS	Australia, New Zealand, United States (Pact)
ASEAN	Association of South-East Asian Nations
BIS	Bank for International Settlements
CAP	Common Agricultural Policy
CARICOM	Caribbean Community
CCD	Conference of the Committee on Disarmament
CFF	Compensatory financing facility (IMF)
CFR	*Code of Federal Regulations*
CMEA	Council for Mutual Economic Assistance
COCOM	Co-ordinating Committee (NATO)
COREPER	Committee of Permanent Representatives (European Community)
CPA	Caracas Programme of Action
CSCE	Conference on Security and Cooperation in Europe
DAC	Development Assistance Committee (OECD)
DTAs	double taxation agreements
ECDC	economic cooperation among developing countries
ECOSOC	United Nations Economic and Social Council
EDC	European Defence Community
EDF	European Development Fund
EEC	European Economic Community (EC)
EEZ	Exclusive Economic Zone
EFF	extended fund facility (IMF)
EIB	European Investment Bank
ENDC	Eighteen Nation Disarmament Committee

ESA	European Space Agency
ESCAP	Economic and Social Commission for Asia and the Pacific (UN)
ETS	*European Treaty Series*
FAO	Food and Agricultural Organisation
FRG	Federal German Republic
G–5	Group of 5
G–10	Group of 10
G–24	Group of 24
G–77	Group of 77
GAB	General Arrangements to Borrow (IMF)
GATT	General Agreement on Tariffs and Trade
GCC	Gulf Cooperation Council
GSA	General Services Administration
GSTP	global system of trade preferences
HCP	*House of Commons Papers*
IBRD	International Bank for Reconstruction and Development (World Bank)
ICAO	International Civil Aviation Organisation
ICJ	International Court of Justice
IDA	International Development Association
ILM	*International Legal Materials*
IMF	International Monetary Fund
IMO	International Maritime Organisation
IPAs	investment protection agreements
IPC	Integrated Programme for Commodities
ITO	International Trade Organisation
JCC	Joint Coordinating Committee
JETRO	Japan External Trade Organisation
Libor	London interbank offered rate
LNTS	*League of Nations Treaty Series*
MFA	Multifibre Arrangement
MBFR	Mutual Balanced Force Reduction
MFN	most favoured nation
MITI	Ministry of International Trade and Industry (Japan)
MYRAs	multi-year re-scheduling agreements
NATO	North Atlantic Treaty Organisation
NGOs	non-governmental organisations
NIEO	New International Economic Order
NLF	National Liberation Front
NPT	Non Proliferation Treaty
OAU	Organisation of African Unity

OECD	Organisation for Economic Cooperation and Development
OMAs	orderly marketing arrangements
ONUC	Opération des Nations Unies (Congo)
OPEC	Organisation of Petroleum Exporting Countries
PLO	Palestine Liberation Organisation
SALT	Strategic Arms Limitation Treaty
SAMA	Saudi Arabian Monetary Agency
SCOR	*Security Council Official Records*
SDI	Strategic Defense Initiative
SDR	special drawing rights
SFF	supplementary financing facility (IMF)
TIAS	*Treaties and Other International Acts Series*
UN	United Nations
UNDP	United Nations Development Programme
UKTS	*United Kingdom Treaty Series*
UNCLOS	United Nations Conference on the Law of the Sea
UNCTAD	United Nations Conference on Trade and Development
UNEF	United Nations Emergency Force
UNEP	United Nations Environment Programme
UNESCO	United Nations Educational, Scientific and Cultural Organisation
UNFICYP	United Nations Force in Cyprus
UNIDO	United Nations Industrial Development Organisation
UNIFIL	United Nations Interim Force in Lebanon
UNOGIL	United Nations Observation Group in Lebanon
UNTS	*UN Treaty Series*
UST	*United States Treaties and Other International Agreements*
VERs	voluntary export restraints
WIPO	World Intellectual Property Organisation
ZOPFAN	zone of peace, freedom and neutrality

To my mother and father

CHAPTER ONE
The changing nature of diplomacy

Diplomacy is concerned with the management of relations between states and between states and other actors. From a state perspective diplomacy is concerned with advising, shaping and implementing foreign policy. As such it is the means by which states through their formal and other representatives, as well as other actors, articulate, coordinate and secure particular or wider interests, using correspondence, private talks, exchanges of view, lobbying, visits, threats and other related activities.

Diplomacy is often thought of as being concerned with peaceful activity, although it may occur for example within war or armed conflict or be used in the orchestration of particular acts of violence, such as seeking overflight clearance for an air strike. The blurring of the line, in fact, between diplomatic activity and violence is one of the developments of note distinguishing modern diplomacy. The point can be made more generally too, in terms of the widening content of diplomacy. At one level the changes in the substantive form of diplomacy are reflected in terms such as 'dollar diplomacy', 'oil diplomacy', 'resource diplomacy' and 'atomic diplomacy'. Certainly what constitutes diplomacy today goes beyond the sometimes rather narrow politico-strategic conception given to the term. Nor is it appropriate to view diplomacy in a restrictive or formal sense as being the preserve of foreign ministries and diplomatic service personnel. Rather, diplomacy may also be undertaken by officials from a wide range of other ministries or agencies with their foreign counterparts, reflecting its technical content; between officials from different international organisations such as the International Monetary Fund (IMF) and the United Nations (UN) Secretariat, or involve foreign corporations and a host government.

1

In this chapter we are concerned with discussing some of the main changes which have taken place in diplomacy since the 1960s – the starting-point for the overall study. Before looking at the changes, some discussion of the task of diplomacy is necessary.

TASKS OF DIPLOMACY

The work of diplomacy can be broken down into six broad areas, within which there are a number of subdivisions. The first and most important of these is representation. This consists of formal representation, including presentation of credentials, protocol and participation in the diplomatic circuit of the national capital or institution. Arguably the most important aspect is substantive representation. This includes the explanation and defence of national policy through embassies and other outlets; negotiations and interpreting the foreign and domestic policies of the receiving government. Second, and related to this, is the function of acting as a listening post. Next to substantive representation, an embassy, if it is functioning correctly, should identify key issues and domestic or external patterns which are emerging, together with their implications, in order to advise or warn the sending government. As Humphrey Trevelyan notes, ' ... apart from negotiating, the ambassador's basic task is to report on the political, economic and social conditions in the country in which he is living, on the policy of its government and on his conversations with political leaders, officials and anyone else who has illuminated the local scene for him'.[1] Above all, timely warning of adverse developments is one of the major functions of an embassy, requiring considerable expertise, judgement and political courage. A third function of diplomacy is laying the groundwork or preparing the basis for a policy or new initiatives. Fourth, in the event of actual or potential bilateral or wider conflict, diplomacy is concerned with reducing friction or oiling the wheels of bilateral or multilateral relations. Fifth, an extension of this, is contributing to order and orderly change. As Adam Watson suggests: 'the central task of diplomacy is not just the management of order, but the management of change, and the maintenance by continued persuasion of order in the midst of change'.[2] The converse of this can also of course be put in that diplomacy may be a vehicle for the continuation of a dispute or conflict. In other words differing state and non-state interests and the absence of generally accepted norms concerning local, regional or international order produce quite substantial differences between parties, in which diplomacy through direct initiatives or third parties simply cannot provide bridging solutions. Finally, at a more general level, an important function of diplomacy is the creation, drafting and amendment of a wide body of international rules of a normative and regulatory kind that provide structure in the international system.

DEVELOPMENT OF DIPLOMACY

In discussing the development of diplomacy an overview of the period will help initially to give some perspective in which to consider certain of the major changes which have taken place. Harold Nicolson's analysis, written in 1961 in *Foreign Affairs* on the theme 'Diplomacy then and now',[3] is coloured especially by the impact of the cold war, the intrusion of ideological conflict into diplomacy and its effect on explanation, and the transformation from the small international élite in old-style diplomacy to a new or 'democratic' conception of international relations requiring public explanation and 'open' diplomacy, despite its growing complexity.[4] A further striking change for Nicolson was in values, especially in the loss of relations based on the 'creation of confidence, [and] the acquisition of credit'.[5] Writing shortly after Nicolson, Livingston Merchant noted the decline in the decision-making power of the ambassador but the widening of his area of competence through economic and commercial diplomacy: the greater use of personal diplomacy and the burden created by multilateral diplomacy, with its accompanying growth in the use of specialists.[6] In reviewing the period up to the late 1970s, Plishke[7] endorsed many of these points, but noted as far as the diplomatic environment was concerned the proliferation of the international community, including the trend towards fragmentation and smallness,[8] and the shift in the locus of decision-making power to national capitals.[9] Writing at the same time, Pranger additionally drew attention to methods, commenting on the growing volume of visits and increases in the number of treaties.[10] Finally, Adam Watson in reviewing diplomacy and the nature of diplomatic dialogue in the 1980s, noted the wide range of ministries now involved in diplomacy; the corresponding decline in the influence of the foreign minister; the increase in the direct involvement of heads of government in the details of foreign policy and diplomacy; and the growth in importance of the news media.[11] For Watson the diplomatic dialogue had 'become more general, less ideological and the two superpowers less dominant except in the new and special field of nuclear military power'.[12]

IMPLICATIONS OF THE CHANGES IN DIPLOMACY

The expansion of the international community – by the early 1960s there were still fewer than 100 independent states, although this rose to 159 by 1985[13] – has affected style, procedures and substance. It has necessarily brought with it divergent regimes and ideologies. Rather than diminishing, the ideological element has, if anything, increased. It necessarily raises the question, can diplomacy in a broad sense 'cope'? Apart from the East–West dimension, numerous national as well as wider ideologies have been introduced, such as those of an economic kind associated with North–South relations, which demand economic redistribution and the transfer of technology. Although these demands declined in the 1980s, being diverted into the promotion of South–South relations between developing countries, they nevertheless were a marked feature of the diplomatic setting of economic confrontation of the previous decade. In that period too occurred the great expansion of multilateral diplomacy, a lot of it economically based, which forms one of the themes examined in this book (see Chs 7 and 8). Apart from this, the growth of units in the international community is reflected in the policies of subnational actors which are projected, often violently, on to the international arena.

A further important feature of the diplomatic setting is the continued growth of groupings. One particular form this has taken is 'associative' diplomacy in which an established grouping such as the European Community seeks to form closer political and economic relations with other states over and above those based on traditional trade agreements. Diplomacy has also been an important vehicle in the growth of regional groupings and the growing decentralisation of the international system.

Moving from these aspects of the changing setting of diplomacy to the agents of diplomacy, two general observations are worth making. The first concerns the enhanced role of personal diplomacy by the head of government.[14] In the main the effect has been to downgrade the importance of the office and influence of the foreign minister, a trend further accentuated, as Adam Watson noted earlier, by the wide range of ministries involved in modern diplomacy.

In the second place the often-put arguments about the decline in the role of the ambassador need to be considerably qualified. Much, of course, depends on the appointee, the post and the practices of the diplomatic service in question. The arguments supporting the decline in influence of ambassadors point to increasing decision-making from the centre, the impact of modern communications and the increasing high-level personal diplomacy discussed above.[15] Furthermore, in some state practice, embassies may not be performing the classically defined diplomatic functions to any significant extent but rather be places of exile, reward or a handling centre for visitors.[16] Against these arguments it can be put that ambassadors do have an important and very often unpublicised role in explaining the policies of the host government to their own government, as well as elaborating the sending government's policies.[17] Ambassadors may also perform major roles at international conferences, sometimes far in excess of the apparent capabilities or importance of the country. Diplomatic power and influence, defined through organisational and negotiating reputation, are quite separate from other elements of power. For example Bulgaria's Ambassador, Yankov, as chairman of the Third Committee of the Third UN Law of the Sea Conference had, through his diplomatic skills, a major impact on the drafting of the new Law of the Sea Convention.[18] In terms of appointments, the choice of an ambassador to a key trading partner or commodity supplier is more likely to be considered on the grounds of effectiveness rather than reward.[19] Ambassadors, too, play many other roles as special envoys, as executive staff in international organisations, and continue subsequently in public international life as consultants and members of corporate boards in international banking and state agencies such as primary commodity boards.

In terms of developments in diplomatic methods, several changes require comment. At the level of superpower relations the overall pattern of bilateral superpower management on strategic nuclear matters has continued since the Cuban missile crisis in October 1962, although the superpower 'condominium' approach, promised in the early 1970s, never materialised.[20] Alongside this has been the marked growth in the past two and a half decades of multilateral diplomacy on social, economic and technical issues. The growth of multilateral conferences has been accompanied by innovations in conference techniques and wider use of consensus decision-making. The ultimate failure, however, of certain forms of multilateral diplomacy,[21] especially connected with Third World demands for a New International Economic Order (NIEO) and economic redistribution within the United Nations Conference on Trade and Development (UNCTAD) context by the early 1980s has led to a resurgence of bilateral diplomacy, especially between developing countries (so-called South–South diplomacy).[22] The rise of bilateralism, particularly in state-directed trade diplomacy,[23] has brought new links between states and non-governmental agencies and innovative arrangements such as complex barter arrangements involving payment in different goods, offsets and other arrangements.[24]

The enhanced negotiating role of the state in defence of domestic economic interests has blurred the line between external economic policy and foreign policy. The extent to which the great Trader States – the United States, Japan, Canada and the European Community – match up and accommodate competing domestic economic interests with other elements of their foreign policies has become increasingly problematic in terms of both national policies and alliance relations, as evidenced by frequent US–European trade conflict and differences over the political use of trade.[25] The Western seven-nation economic summit, a new diplomatic grouping, was in part institutionalised after the 1975 Rambouillet summit, in an attempt to improve Western alliance coordination, which also drew in a somewhat reluctant Japan, itself increasingly in trade conflict with its allies.[26]

A particularly striking feature of the development in diplomatic methods is the tremendous increase in the amount of diplomatic activity in the form of meetings, visits, negotiations and treaties. In 1981, for example, the United States conducted 88 separate negotiations on North–South related topics.[27] Furthermore, between 1980 and 1985 the United States concluded 101 treaties and 1,940 other international agreements.[28] In general, the increased volume and technicality creates overload and places limitations at a multilateral level on the extent to which delegations have instructions, voting participation and hence on the 'quality' of agreements. A noticeable feature in terms of treaties is the increase in the use of informal instruments such as gentlemen's agreements and memoranda of understanding (see Ch. 4). Their use reflects the growth of interdepartmental or agency connections at an international level. The use of informal agreements is largely based on a preference for convenient instruments which avoid the formal constitutional requirements of agreements and remain unpublished. The use of such instruments does nevertheless have implications for the domestic control of foreign policy, such as it is, and norm setting, in view of the frequency with which informal instruments are challenged or revised.

Finally, we can review the preceding arguments by some observations on the changing content of diplomacy. Underlying much of what has been said so far is the impact on diplomacy of the substantial broadening of the diplomatic agenda. Nowadays those involved in diplomacy need to be conversant with an increasingly wider range of matters such as telecommunications, offshore maritime rights, tariff disputes, civil aviation agreements and complex multilateral debt diplomacy. Moreover, states face novel and sometimes quite fundamental threats, which raise questions over the extent to which coordinated diplomatic action can be achieved, and agreements enforced, over such matters as controlling trans-frontier nuclear pollution (e.g. Chernobyl) international financial fraud, counterfeiting of goods and trans-border data flows.[29] Other novel problems such as the dumping of refugees,[30] which although of a lesser order, nevertheless illustrate the variety of issues which continue to crop up. The broadening of the diplomatic agenda has several implications for organisational structure. Writing, for example, in 1981 on the Bureau of Economic and Business Affairs (EB) of the US State Department, Robert K. Olson noted:[31]

> ten years ago top staff members of the State Department were almost exclusively political and in diplomacy the political line had always had clear primacy over the economic, administrative or consular lines. During the 1970s the EB emerged as a powerful and competent department in the State Department on international economic problems as oil, monetary affairs, trade, surged to the top of the international agenda.

The component parts of the central agenda change as new areas are added (e.g. counter-terrorism) although economic issues have come to occupy an increasingly central place in importance in foreign policy and are ones with which many foreign ministries are only slowly coming to terms.

The widening of the diplomatic agenda and the fusion of domestic and foreign policy is particularly evident in the changing participants in diplomacy. These might include East–West economic entrepreneurs,[32] the chief 'private' negotiator in an East–West spy swap[33] or informal mediators in hostage negotiations. Increasingly, individuals are becoming involved in international relations in diplomatic roles, including mediation, in addition to those formally responsible.[34] A further related development is that of the growing impact of the media on the setting and mechanics of diplomacy. The media both intrude and are used by political leaders. Their role in providing rapid satellite-transmitted information and sometimes acting as negotiators was illustrated clearly in the Iran hostage crisis. Media figures can sometimes promote meetings of foreign leaders, for example the deal for Sadat's visit to Jerusalem was concluded when the National Broadcasting Company's (NBC) Walter Cronkite brought both Sadat and Begin together by satellite.[35]

Finally we should note a dilemma for modern diplomacy and that is the spread of intra- and interstate violence. On the whole diplomacy has made increasingly important contributions to managing the technical or 'functional' aspects of international relations. In contrast the cockpits of urban and interstate violence remain only marginally touched by diplomacy.[36]

REFERENCES AND NOTES

1. See Humphrey Trevelyan, *Diplomatic Channels* (Macmillan, London, 1973) p. 85
2. Adam Watson, *Diplomacy: The Dialogue Between States* (Methuen, London, 1984) p. 223.
3. Reprinted with revisions in Harold Nicolson, *Diplomacy*, 3rd edn (Oxford University Press, London, 1963) pp. 244–62.
4. Ibid., p. 245.
5. Ibid., pp. 245–6.
6. Livingston Merchant, 'New Techniques in Diplomacy', in E. A. J. Johnson (ed.), *The Dimensions of Diplomacy* (John Hopkins Press, Baltimore, 1964) pp. 117–35.
7. Elmer Plishke (ed.), *Modern Diplomacy: The Art and the Artisans* (American Enterprise Institute, Washington, DC, 1979).
8. Ibid., pp. 92–8.
9. Ibid., p. 58.
10. Robert J. Pranger, 'Contemporary Diplomacy at Work', in Plishke, op. cit., p. 76. Pranger notes that in 1977 the United States signed approximately 20 new treaties and nearly 500 new agreements with other states and international organisations.
11. Watson, op. cit., p. 126.
12. Watson, op. cit., p. 218.
13. Members of the UN. As of October 1985 the following sovereign states were not members of the UN: Andorra, Taiwan, Kiribati, Democratic Republic of Korea, Republic of Korea, Liechtenstein, Monaco, Nauru, San Marino, Switzerland, Tonga, Tuvalu, Vatican City. See *The Europa Year Book 1986*, Vol. 1 (Europa Publications, London, 1986) p. 4.

14. See for example Peter Calvert, *The Foreign Policy of New States* (Wheatsheaf, Sussex, 1986) pp. 96-8.
15. See Bahgat Korany, *How Foreign Policy Decisions are Made in the Third World* (Westview Press, Boulder, Colo., 1986.)
16. Calvert, op. cit., pp. 90-2.
17. See Panayote E. Dimitras, 'Greece a New Danger', *Foreign Policy*, Nos. 57-60 (1984-85) p. 150 on the role of US Ambassador Stearns in explaining the policies of the new Greek Socialist Government under Papandreou to the United States Government.
18. See on the general work of the Third Committee, R. P. Barston and Patricia Birnie, *The Maritime Dimension* (George Allen and Unwin, London, 1980) pp. 161-2, and R. P. Barston 'The Third UN Law of the Sea Conference', in G. R. Berridge and A. Jennings, *Diplomacy at the UN* (Macmillan, London, 1985) pp. 152-71.
19. See Robert S. Ozaki and Walter Arnold (eds) *Japan's Foreign Relations* (Westview Press, Boulder, Colo., 1985) pp. 142-59, on the use of former Japanese Ambassador Tamuro to build up relations with the Organisation of Arab Petroleum Exporting Countries (OAPEC) after the 1973 oil crisis.
20. Jonathan Steele, *The Limits of Soviet Power* (Penguin, Harmondsworth, 1984) pp. 47-69.
21. Susan Strange, 'The Poverty of Multilateral Economic Diplomacy', in Berridge and Jennings, op. cit., pp. 109-29.
22. See *Strengthening the Weakest Link*, UNCTAD, ST/ECDC/28, 1 Oct. 1985, para. 15.
23. See *Trade and Development Review* (UNCTAD, Geneva, 1986).
24. See UNCTAD, TD/B/C.7/75, 4 Oct. 1985 on economic cooperation among developing countries. Barter trade can take a number of different forms including payments made in other goods, up to agreed amounts, revolving trade accounts, mixed barter and credit arrangements and simple oil for weapons/food transactions.
25. For a classic account of the Trader State agenda see the excellent short paper by Gary Clyde Hufbauer and Jeffry J. Schott, *Trading for Growth: The Next Round of Trade Negotiations* (Institute for International Economics, Washington, DC, 1985). Chapter 3 (pp. 41-81) deals with a possible agenda for General Agreement on Tariffs and Trade (GATT) multilateral trade talks, including safeguards, orderly adjustment and the new trader issues of high technology trade, services, patents, intellectual property rights, trans-border data flows and investment.
26. Cesare Merlini (ed.) *Economic Summits and Western Decision Making* (Croom Helm, London, 1984).
27. Robert K. Olson, *US Foreign Policy and the New International Economic Order* (Westview Press, Boulder, Colo., 1981) p. 103.
28. This compares with 210 treaties and 2,838 other international agreements from 1946 to 1959; and 287 treaties and 5,364 other international agreements from 1960 to 1979. Communication with Department of State, Office of Treaty Affairs.
29. On the negotiations over cooperation between the US, the UK, Japan and France on commercial crime, see *Financial Times*, 17 July 1986.
30. See *The Times*, 16 Aug. 1986 on the cargo ship refugee runner *Aurigae*

which dumped 150 Sri Lankans off Newfoundland. On refugees using Berlin see *The Times*, 26 July 1986.

31. Olson, op. cit., p. 126.
32. The best example is Armand Hammer (Occidental Petroleum Corporation) who has had long-standing links with the Soviet Union going back to at least the 1920s. See C. Levinson, *Vodka-Cola* (Gordon and Cremonesi, London, 1979) p. 252, and M. I. Goldman *Detente and Dollars* (Basic Books, New York, 1975) pp. 248-9.
33. On the Anatoly Shcharansky exchange in Berlin, see *Financial Times*, 12 Feb. 1986, and *Sunday Times*, 9 Feb., 1986, on the role of the German Democratic Republic (GDR) negotiator, Wolfgang Vogel.
34. Oran R. Young, *The Intermediaries* (Princeton University Press, 1967); Maureen R. Berman and Joseph E. Jones, *Unofficial Diplomats* (Columbia University Press, New York, 1977).
35. Bahgat Korany and Ali E. Dessouki (eds) *The Foreign Policy of Arab States* (Westview Press, Boulder, Colo., 1984) p. 139.
36. Adam Watson's assessment, op. cit., esp. at pp. 222-3.

CHAPTER TWO
Foreign policy organisation

CENTRAL ORGANISATION OF FOREIGN POLICY

In general the differences which exist in the central arrangements for conducting foreign policy in various states have been influenced by the expansion in the content of foreign policy, the loosening of central control and the increasingly technical nature of much of external policy. In advanced industrial states especially, the development of an increasingly complex foreign policy agenda including such varied issues as energy, resources, telecommunications, trans-frontier land pollution, as well as the more conventional or traditional political issues, has had several implications for central foreign policy organisation.

The extension of the agenda finds its expression in the international role of ministries which have traditionally been considered as essentially 'domestic'. In other words external policy is no longer necessarily the preserve of the ministry of foreign affairs. The increasing complexity of foreign policy too has also been accompanied, especially in larger states, not only by a proliferation of ministries but a tendency for fragmentation of responsibility. Ministries or agencies acquire foreign policy interests, stakes and perspectives, which are promoted and defended. Departments are not necessarily monolithic, although patterns of thinking can nevertheless be found within various government departments and their subdivisions as well as alliances between departments. During, for example, the later part of the Kennedy administration, elements of the US Defense Department, armed forces and the European Bureau of the Department of State were joined in opposition to an overemphasis on African regional concerns. These groups stressed

11

the importance of maintaining close ties with America's North Atlantic Treaty Organisation (NATO) allies, such as Portugal even if this meant riding roughshod over Black African interests.[1]

The tendency for fragmentation or independent action, especially in advanced industrial states, necessarily places constraints on the central political control of foreign policy. Lack of coordination was well illustrated by the continuation of routine Soviet submarine operations off the Swedish coast, highlighted by the grounding of a Soviet Whiskey-class submarine in November 1981, at a time when another strand of Soviet external policy involved diplomatic moves to promote a regional nuclear-free zone.[2] Fragmentation affects policy-making in other ways. Nor is it always clear what the foreign policy of a state actually is. Objectives may in fact be the subject of drawn-out bureaucratic dispute, aggravated by divisions within an executive,[3] while novel or unexpected international events may cause fragmented or poorly coordinated ministerial responses.

For smaller advanced industrial states, especially in Western Europe, a distinctive feature of the political system is the impact of the open, pluralistic process on the central direction of foreign policy. The problems caused by the expansion in the agenda of foreign policy tend to be less acute through higher degrees of selection and, at an organisational level, greater decentralisation and wider delegation to specialist ministries as in the Netherlands, Sweden and Denmark.

Although Third World systems are often thought of in single leader terms, in practice a variety of systems of central foreign policy organisation can be distinguished, shaped by complex domestic and socio-economic considerations.[4] Korany and Dessouki, for example, in examining the foreign policies of selected Arab states use a presidential, collegiate and oligarchical typology.[5] Korany and Dessouki's study, furthermore, underlines the point that for newer states the type of central organisation should not be considered as being static. Countries may in fact move from one type of central organisation to another, from, for example, bureaucratic to presidential, e.g. Algeria post-Boumedienne, or to a more bureaucratic system as with Egypt post-Sadat.

From the prevalence of presidential systems (i.e. strong central executive, relatively weak bureaucracy and narrow basis of policy formulation) in developing countries a number of effects on foreign policy can be seen. The largest impact is on the style of conducting policy, with a preference for relying on direct negotiation by the head of state and the use of personal diplomacy.[6] Presidential emissaries (not necessarily career diplomats) are also frequently used on assignments. In those presidential-type systems in developing countries which have frequent political instability, the bureaucracy, especially the foreign ministry, tends to be weakened even further by being cut off from interactive decision-making.[7]

Efforts to improve the coordination and direction of foreign policy in the Third World and other states have in the main involved building up agencies under the direct control of or attached institutionally to the office of the head of government or state. Of the developed countries, this type of system has been particularly used by Japan.

Not dissimilar systems have been adopted by a number of newly industrialised countries, e.g. Malaysia, whose foreign policy and external diplomacy are heavily economically orientated. In South Korea, there is considerable departmental autonomy for rapid decision-making, although a clear feature of the organisational style is the central coordinating role performed by the Economic Planning Board, generally headed by the Deputy Prime Minister. In these cases, the foreign ministries are generally relatively weak.

While the agency system described above provides some measure of greater central political control, it almost inevitably leads to or enhances personalisation and the tendency to concentrate foreign policy decision-making and diplomacy at the political centre. This feature is accentuated by the fact that if at all possible foreign companies and organisations prefer to deal directly with the head of state or government of smaller powers, for organisational and other reasons. The effect often is to slow decision-making and create decision bottlenecks, for example over the participants in major projects or the terms of loan agreements.

THE FOREIGN MINISTRY

Foreign ministries as part of the overall machinery for conducting external policy, along with diplomatic posts overseas, differ in structure and importance. In looking at these differences, three areas are of interest. These are the internal organisational structure, the relations between foreign ministries and other ministries and, for newer states, the appropriate organisational structure for the formulation and implementation of development strategies.

At first sight, foreign ministries tend to have certain common organisational characteristics in so far as they generally contain geographic, protocol, legal and administrative divisions. Apart from the question of size, which tends to have a telescopic effect, with divisions or departments covering greater geographic areas the smaller the actor, differences in organisational structure occur partly because of particular foreign policy interests, e.g. the Cyprus Foreign Ministry devotes a separate department to the Cyprus problem. Functional rather than geographic departments may be set up within foreign ministries for several reasons including: the importance attached to a particular international grouping, for example the Organisation of the Islamic Conference (IOC) bringing together Islamic states; the importance of bilateral trade relations, e.g. Finnish–Soviet trade (see Fig. 2.1); special emphasis placed on cultural diplomacy (e.g. in Austria, the Federal German Republic (FRG), France, Sweden); or as a response to new policy issues, such as international energy questions which span several departments. Among the functional departments, for example in the United States Department of State, are those of energy, human rights, international narcotics matters, economic and business affairs, oceans and international environmental and scientific affairs (see Fig. 2.2). Such departments enable a foreign ministry to monitor and follow the work of other agencies and if necessary take the lead.[8] The main potential benefits are the possibility of greater coordination and a broader perspective. The staffing of the more specialist functional departments, e.g. civil aviation, however, generally poses difficulties in view of the traditional training and preferences of diplomatic service personnel. To some extent the problem has been lessened by the secondment of officials from the relevant 'domestic' ministry to functional departments in the foreign ministry. In contrast, socialist states have tended to develop strong international divisions or miniature foreign ministries within domestic ministries. Both approaches bring somewhat different problems for the coordination of diplomacy in terms of the balance between the number of geographic and functional departments, and decentralisation which follows from the development of international divisions within 'domestic' ministries.

Another noticeable difficulty encountered by the foreign ministries in newer, as well as some established states, is the handling of the international economic aspects of foreign policy. As international economic issues moved up the international agenda, many foreign ministries simply found themselves ill-equipped for managing this aspect of international relations in view of their traditional political emphasis or lack of resources. An Economic Division of the Indian

Figure 2.1 Ministry for Foreign Affairs: Finland

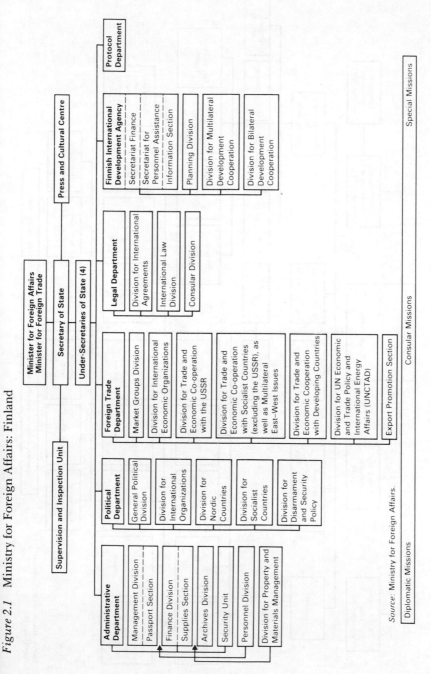

Source: Ministry for Foreign Affairs.

15

Figure 2.2 Department of State: the United States

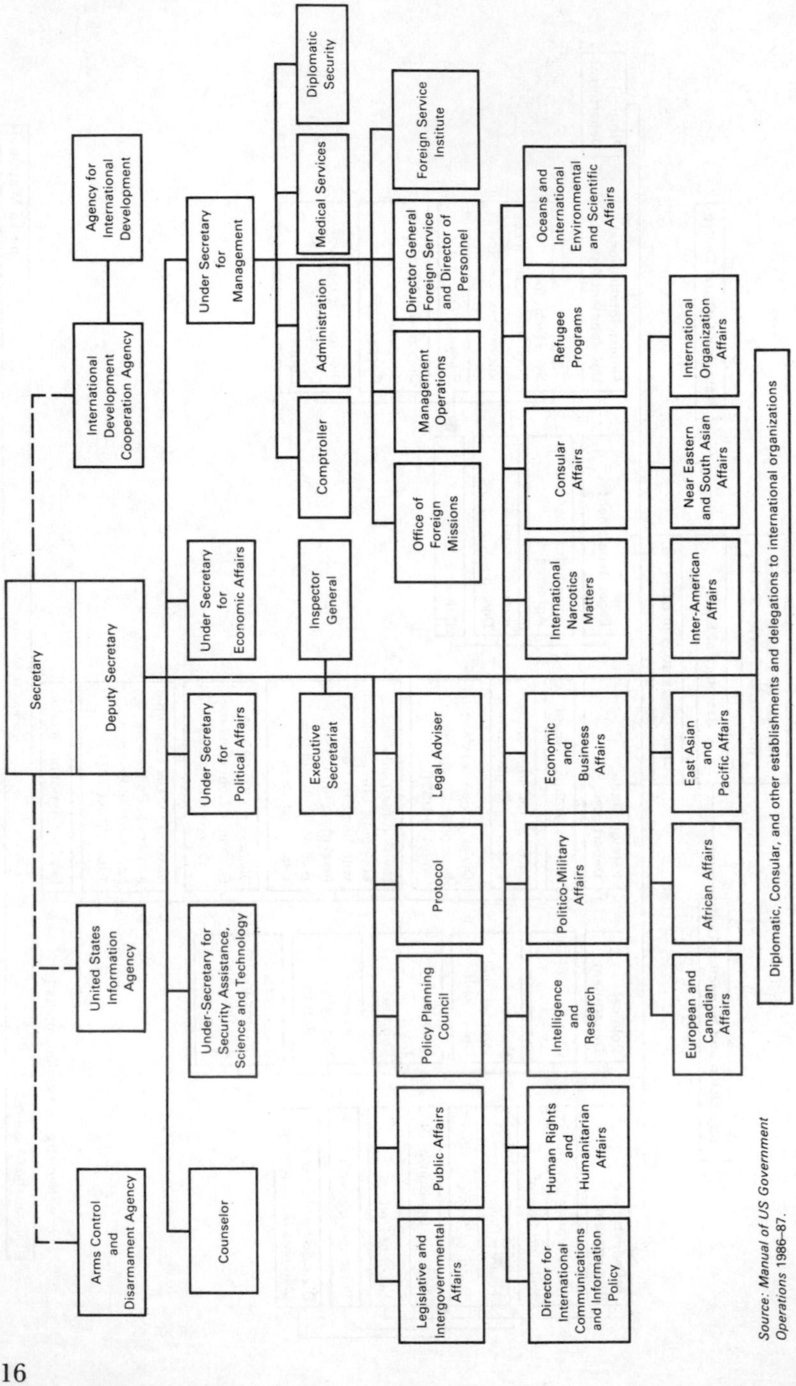

Source: Manual of US Government Operations 1986–87.

16

Ministry of External Affairs was set up in 1947, but three years later the post was left unfilled as part of an economy drive. The division went out of existence for over a decade until it was revived in 1961 as the Economic and Coordination Division.[9] In general, pay and conditions of service have been important constraints on recruitment into the economic divisions of foreign ministries. The same, too, in many respects could be said about the overall recruitment problems of the foreign ministries of new states as well as some established West European states.[10] In order to ensure the paramountcy of the foreign ministry in international financial diplomacy, some countries which play active international financial and commodity roles, such as France, Brazil[11] and Mexico have developed cadres in the foreign ministry through training, secondment and other measures. By the late 1980s most states had established some form of economic division within their foreign ministries.[12]

TRADE

The arrangements for managing trade at a central and representational level have often fitted uneasily into the running of other parts of foreign policy. The uneasy relationship partly derives from problems such as duplication and poor liaison, stemming from dual trade and diplomatic representation overseas and from rivalry about who should be responsible for directing and coordinating overseas trade policy. The primacy of the trade or commerce ministry is justified in terms of expertise, continuity and administrative links with export-financing agencies. In contrast, the arguments in favour of overall responsibility resting with the foreign ministry rely on the capacity of the foreign ministry to provide an overview, coordinate initiatives and its traditional skills of political analysis and persuasion. In practice, while most states retain separate foreign and trade ministries, arrangements for overseas representation vary. Some states have, however, attempted to unify trade promotion in the foreign ministry. In the case of Canada, the External Affairs Ministry was reorganised in 1982, and the department became directly responsible for the promotion of Canadian trade overseas, as the primary federal government contact with foreign governments and international organisations which influence trade.[13] There is also some indication that those states which have previously relied largely on chambers of commerce or other bodies for trade promotion have sought greater involvement by the foreign ministry, in view of the enhanced direct role of governments in trade promotion.[14]

DEVELOPMENT

Development issues are generally at the forefront of the foreign policies of many newer states. Diplomacy is likely to be directed to securing international finance, problems arising from the scheduling of loans, restrictions on key exports, the promotion of regional cooperation and relations with major foreign corporations. While the conduct of foreign policy is often thought of as involving external action, this may well be an inappropriate model for a number of states.[15] Rather, an important part of a country's foreign relations in the main may be conducted *domestically* with a foreign oil corporation, bank or UN local or regional representatives.[16] The economic aspects of development necessarily involve several ministries in this form of internal diplomacy as well as external action. Establishing the boundaries of responsibility and more coordinated rather than *ad hoc* initiatives do present newer states with difficulties due to manpower constraints and the volume of business.[17] In an attempt to overcome some of these difficulties Zimbabwe, in an unusual experiment, merged the Ministry of Finance with the Economic Planning and Development Ministry in 1982.[18] In donor states the difficulty is one of the proliferation of ministries and agencies with some interest or stake in aid, the more especially as aid has become blurred with trade and finance.[19] The other common problem for newer states is the composition of delegations to international conferences. In the context of development diplomacy, ministry of finance, trade or other appropriate officials cannot always be spared. As a result the separation of representation from policy-making tends to have the effect of emphasising the rhetorical aspects of policy, and producing brittle international agreements or arrangements which are subject to frequent reinterpretation.[20]

REPRESENTATION

In general, states establish and maintain overseas representation for four main reasons. Representation is part of the process of either achieving statehood and identity in international relations, or, for established states, essential to being considered a power in the international system. Second, embassies are an important but by no means exclusive means of communication and source of contact with other states and entities, enabling a state to participate in international discourse. Third, embassies are the agencies for promoting, explaining or defending the interests and policies of a country. Four, embassies are a means of acquiring continuous information.

Most states, with the exception of the neutrals, have a core group of countries within their overall diplomatic representation. Those states within that group will be included for historical, alliance, ideological and economic reasons. For newer states the grouping generally will include the former colonial power, and staff would be assigned as a matter of priority to the United Nations, a regional organisation, European capitals, selected neighbouring states and representation set up in the capital of one or more important regional powers. For most states the membership of the core group is likely to remain relatively stable unless the state is undergoing major reorientation of its foreign policy, or is in dispute with the former colonial power. Adjustments in the ranking of countries in the core group, nevertheless, take place through modifications to the staffing, budgetary allocation and tasks of posts, in the light of such factors as changes in the volume of political work, trade opportunities, defence relations and tourism.

Beyond the core group the spread of representation may be influenced by such principles as balance, reciprocity and universality, and, above all, the availability of finance. The principle of universality is generally of importance only for primary powers, and, neutral states. Neutral states, because of their perceived status, have seen it important to have as wide a representation as is practicable. High international representation is common to all neutral states. Austria is represented, for example, in 148 countries through 69 embassies. The idea of balance has been considered important, especially by non-aligned countries to avoid the distribution of embassies becoming excessively weighted in favour of one bloc or region. Pressures to reciprocate representation necessarily reduce freedom of action. States, nevertheless, often do not comply with the principle on political and above all economic grounds.

Apart from the general principles noted above, several other factors can come into play. The opening of further embassies may be part of a policy of prestige. In this sense, diplomatic real estate is seen as part of the accoutrements of power. Conflict between two or more states may lead to the extension of representation. For example, following the outbreak of the Iran-Iraq War both countries have competitively extended their representation as part of the battle for political and diplomatic support. The effect of the war itself on petroleum revenues has influenced the enhanced role of the respective embassies of both countries in facilitating intergovernmental oil sales agreements and other barter trade arrangements.[21] Economic factors are among the more important in leading to increases or reductions in representation. Diplomatic relations may be opened up with another state because it has become important in trade, investment or financial terms. The opening of diplomatic relations between Malaysia and Kuwait, for example, reflected, apart from religious factors, the growing oil relationship between the two countries as well as the Malaysian aim of attracting inward Arab financial investment.[22] Other reasons such as the need for economic intelligence may sometimes influence the decision to establish an embassy. For example, Brazil maintains a significant representation in Kenya, an important coffee producer.[23]

Embassies are not necessarily the sole means of handling the economic aspects of diplomacy. Apart from a separate trade commissioner service used by some states, consular arrangements are used to varying degrees by most states. For example, the Netherlands provides a striking illustration of a small but active economic power, with very high consular coverage, reflecting the widespread range of commercial, technical assistance and maritime operations of its companies and nationals.[24]

Much depends both on the scale of resources and perception of interests in international relations. These might be relatively limited or localized. Jamaica maintains, for example, 10 embassies and high commissions, 4 missions and 6 consular offices. These are supported by some 19 honorary consulates in Europe, Latin America and the United States. Jamaica has no significant diplomatic presence in the Far East, Southeast Asia, much of Africa or the Middle East. In contrast, Zimbabwe, in line with its active foreign policy and geostrategic location, has rapidly expanded its foreign ministry and diplomatic service which at independence was limited to one official mission in Pretoria. By 1985 25 embassies or high commissions, 2 consulates and 1 trade mission had been established, with a total staff of 700, of which 200 are in the Foreign Ministry.[25]

OTHER FORMS OF REPRESENTATION

The growing international involvement of internal ministries has resulted in the proliferation of representative offices overseas. These include development corporations, investment agencies, trade and tourist offices and student liaison bureaux. To these must be added state and para-statal agencies such as banks, airlines and large corporations. In modern diplomacy, the blue neon sign of Toshiba has come to symbolize one aspect of the changing form of representation; the regional office of a major corporation is likely to be as or sometimes more important than its diplomatic counterpart. The growth of representative offices overseas and specialists from home departments in diplomatic posts has contributed to increased bureaucratic rivalry. One aspect of this is the development of multiple information channels for receiving, gathering and evaluating information. In Japan, for example, the information-gathering monopoly of the Foreign Ministry (see Fig. 2.3) is rivalled by the Ministry of International Trade and Industry (MITI) (using the overseas branches of the Japan External Trade Organisation (JETRO)) and links with corporations, the Defence Agency through its attachés and the Ministry of Finance through its personnel attached to Japanese embassies.[26] Another noticeable effect is on the traditional embassy functions of reporting and assessments which can become downgraded through overloading from routine protocol associated with inward visits by representatives of domestic ministries. Third, and most important, are the enhanced problems of coordination and control brought about by the splintering of policy. The independent action by para-statal agencies, a particular feature of the international debt crisis, is discussed in Chapter 7.

REPRESENTATION AND PUBLIC RELATIONS

Information is one of the several specialist posts which have been added to many embassies in recent years.[27] Putting across the correct image of a country, its people and life-style, gathering the support of foreign media and public are major preoccupations. In this way modern diplomacy has changed to being concerned with information, not in a crude propaganda sense of the cold war or the high-tempo marketing style of 'Expo', but in a more limited and fragmentary way. The concern now is with creating confidence in a

21

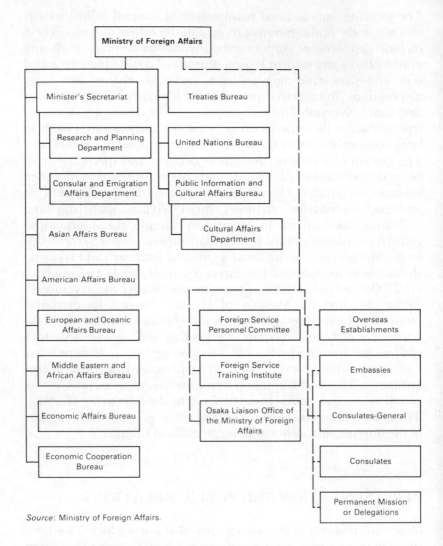

Source: Ministry of Foreign Affairs.

Figure 2.3 Ministry of Foreign Affairs: Japan

country and its products; gaining a paragraph in a major newspaper; correcting a press story. In other words information work is short-term and incremental, more akin to diplomatic journalism than propaganda.

The importance of this aspect of diplomacy can be further seen in that states have frequently augmented their official diplomatic channel by hiring the services of public relations agencies. During the Anglo-Icelandic 'Cod War', Iceland used a London-based public relations firm, Whittaker Hunt, to put across its case.[28] Lobbying by legal and other professional agencies is also a significant aspect of the public relations of states. The area covered by lobbying is wide, including such efforts as the attempts by the Bahamas to counteract its drug-trafficking image;[29] or Thai efforts to amend US tariff legislation during the Thai–US trade dispute (see Ch. 8). Formal and informal developments in information work have to some extent taken the conduct of foreign policy outside its traditional diplomatic framework, by introducing new participants and widening, in certain instances, the arena of debate by bringing, for a short period, greater public attention to an issue.

REFORM

States have traditionally reviewed from time to time the operation and effectiveness of their foreign ministries and diplomatic services.[30] More often than not such inquiries have been occasioned by wider economy moves in the public sector or institutional rivalry. Although the expenditure cost of the foreign ministry and diplomatic service is often low in comparison with other ministries, many items on the foreign ministry budget come under criticism since they are not easy to evaluate in cost-effective terms. Certain regular expenditure components have risen significantly in recent years. In particular, increases in the cost of contributions to international organisations have added significantly to the foreign affairs budgets of smaller powers. The acquisition of diplomatic property has now become a further major budgetary item. The opening of five posts by New Zealand between 1983 and 86 added some $NZ4.6 million to the cost of the overseas service, which rose to $NZ110.2 million.[31] Attempting to offset these types of increases is difficult in some instances in that further reductions in embassy staffing would reduce the staff level below the minimum operational level of three to four personnel.

Reviews have in the main examined five areas: (i) interdepartmental coordination; (ii) the direction given by the foreign ministry to its embassies; (iii) the number, location and function of embassies and other missions; (iv) expenditure; (v) training. Relatively few have made major recommendations aimed at altering the central machinery of government, with the exceptions of those such as the Canadian reorganisation of trade within the Ministry of External Affairs discussed above. Rather, most reviews have recommended improvements in existing arrangements, particularly coordination between the foreign ministry and trade and finance. The Swedish reorganisation in 1985, for example, sought to improve the links between the Ministry for Foreign Affairs, the Swedish Trade Council and private sector business in order to enlarge the role of the former in directing export promotion.[32] The coordination of information policy has been another recurrent issue. In a wide-ranging report on the Indian Foreign Service the Pillai Committee noted that less than half of India's embassies had information officers and proposed closer links between the Ministries of External Affairs and Information.[33]

The other general areas in which recommendations for reform have been put forward have been in the number, size and work of embassies and the training of diplomatic personnel. In a major review of British representational effort overseas in 1969 the Duncan Committee, some twelve months after the merger of the Commonwealth Relations Office with the Foreign Office, looked at expenditure, manpower, diplomatic reporting and the grading of overseas missions.[34] In an attempt to establish some general guidelines for distinguishing between regions of importance for the location of embassies, the Duncan Report identified an inner area of concentration (essentially the Atlantic and developed world) and an outer area. The proposal was rejected in a later review[35] on the grounds that the division was too broad and that an unjustifiably high volume of resources was already devoted to representation in inner area countries. The Duncan Report did, however, have a major influence on altering the emphasis of British posts to greater economic work, including export promotion. By 1985 over 30 per cent of British diplomatic staff abroad were involved in economic work, while only half that number were engaged in political work.[36]

SUMMARY

The differing arrangements states have for managing foreign policy have been influenced particularly by the growth in the volume of international business. As more departments and agencies have become increasingly involved so this has created problems of national coordination and institutional rivalry over the responsibility for the direction of non-traditional areas of policy which are now considered as foreign policy. Trade, international economic policy and technology have been difficult to accommodate and coordinate as foreign ministries, which have generally lacked expertise in these areas, have adapted to the new international agendas. In many respects the issue is more complex for newer states, since development policy is to a large extent foreign and national security policy. The strands of development policy almost automatically, by design or otherwise, have an international dimension. There are, on the other hand, those countries which have only very limited resources which place considerable constraints on conducting any significant external policy. Others simply hope to get by. In some instances, the tradition of a foreign ministry and diplomatic service has remained weak since independence because of recurrent internal instability.[37] Yet for those with a stake in the international system having a foreign policy is something which is increasingly expensive, the product very intangible with few clearly identifiable benefits, but which is nevertheless considered an essential part of continued statehood.

REFERENCES AND NOTES

1. David A. Dickson provides a valuable discussion of bureaucratic influences on US African policy in *United States Foreign Policy Towards Sub-Saharan Africa* (University of America Press, New York, 1985) p. 31 *passim*.
2. *The Times*, 29 Oct., 1981. On the Soviet attitude to a Nordic nuclear-free zone, comprising Finland, Sweden, Norway and Denmark, see *The Times*, 27 June 1981.
3. For an illustration of this point in the context of the differing agency interests in the United States involved in arms control, see Jonathan Dean 'East–West Arms Control Negotiations', in Leon Sloss and M. Scott Davis, *A Game for High Stakes* (Ballinger, Cambridge, Mass., 1986) pp. 102–3.
4. For a discussion of socio-economic influences see Olatunde Ojo, D. K. Orwa and C. M. B. Utete, *African International Relations* (Longman, London, 1985) pp. 18–27.
5. Bahgat Korany and Ali E. Hillal Dessouki, *The Foreign Policies of Arab States* (Westview Press, Boulder, Colo., 1984) p. 327.
6. See Peter Calvert, *The Foreign Policy of New States*, (Wheatsheaf Books, Sussex, 1986) pp. 95–8.
7. For example, the Nigerian Foreign Ministry was not informed of the

decision to expel illegal aliens by the Shagari Government in late 1983. See Olojide Aluko, 'The Expulsion of Illegal Aliens from Nigeria: A Study in Nigerian Decision making', *African Affairs*, Vol. 84, No. 337 (Oct. 1985) p. 559.

8. By the end of Dec. 1977, there were 56 departments in the Foreign and Commonwealth Office. Of these 22 were functional (e.g. Energy, European Integration Department, Financial Relations, Trade Relations and Exports, Maritime Aviation and Environment) and 20 were geographical. The other departments were specialist departments such as the Overseas Labour Adviser, Inspectorate and Legal Advisers.

9. *Report of the Committee on the Indian Foreign Service* (Ministry of External Affairs, New Delhi, 1966) p. 3.

10. The Italian Foreign Ministry has been operating at nearly 20 per cent of its diplomatic service establishment level owing to the competitive pay and conditions offered by the commercial sector. In 1984 the Foreign Ministry was established for 938 diplomats but had 777 on strength. See *Financial Times*, 7 Sept. 1984.

11. Ronald M. Schneider, *Brazil Foreign Policy of a Future World Power* (Westview Press, Boulder, Colo., 1976).

12. See for example *Economic and Technical Cooperation among Developing Countries*, Vol. 1 (Office of the Chairman of the Group of 77, New York, 1984) Annex III, pp. 291-5, and *A Guide to ECDC* (Office of the Chairman of the Group of 77, New York) 27 April 1983, Annexes III, IV, pp. 22-8.

13. *Annual Report 1983-4* (Department of External Affairs, Ottawa, 1984) p. 2255.

14. *The Swedish Budget 1986-7* (Ministry of Finance, Stockholm, 1986) pp. 64-5.

15. Susan Strange, 'Protectionism and World Politics', *International Organisation*, Vol. 39, No. 2 (Spring 1985) pp. 253-4 on the new government–corporation diplomacy.

16. For a discussion of government relations with foreign economic groups, including for example, Ghana and the US-based Volta Aluminium Co. (Valco), see R. I. Onuka and A. Sesay, *The Future of Regionalism in Africa* (Macmillan, Hong Kong, 1985) p. 158 *passim*.

17. The same kind of point is made in the context of the lack of integrated technology policies in many African countries. See Onuka and Sesay, op. cit., p. 166.

18. *Public Service Bulletin* (Harare) Vol. 1, No. 3 (1984) p. 1.

19. For example the need for a review of the administration of the Danish technical cooperation programme in view of its considerable growth was noted in *The Foreign Service of Denmark 1770-1970* (Foreign Ministry, Copenhagen, 1970) pp. 36-8. On the dispute over competence over foreign aid in Japan, see J. W. M. Chapman, R. Drifte and I. T. M. Gow, *Japan's Quest for Comprehensive Security* (Frances Pinter, London, 1983) p. 85.

20. Calvert, op. cit., p. 95.

21. GATT, L/5915, 18 Oct. 1985, pp. 43-4.

22. A Malaysian diplomatic mission was established in Kuwait on 25 May 1974. See *Foreign Affairs*, Malaysia, Vol. 7, No. 2 (June 1974).

23. Wayne A. Selcher, *Brazil's Multilateral Relations* (Westview Press, Boulder, Colo., 1978) p. 221.
24. *Vertegenwoordigingen van het Koninkrijk der Nederlanden in het buitenland* (Staatsuitgeverijs–Gravenhage, Sept. 1984) pp. 97–9.
25. *Public Service Bulletin* (Harare), Vol. 2, No. 2 (July 1985), Supplement, pp. 3–4.
26. Drifte illustrates the institutional rivalry by citing the example of the difficulties caused by the proposal by the US Special Trade Representative for trilateral trade talks being put through the MITI in September 1981. The displeasure and opposition of the Japanese Foreign Ministry delayed the talks until January 1982. See R. Drifte, 'The Foreign Policy System', in Chapman, Drifte and Gow, op. cit., p. 87.
27. Lord Gore Booth (ed.), *Satow's Guide to Diplomatic Practice* (Longman, London, 1979) Appendix VI, p. 487. Of the 2,000 or so officials on the diplomatic lists of 130 countries in London in the mid 1970s, 380 were non-career diplomats working in specialist fields such as commercial, economic and financial, press and cultural relations. Diplomatic service officers also occupied positions in these areas.
28. *Sunday Times*, 20 Aug. 1972. Iceland established a secretary for information at the outset of the fisheries dispute with Britain in 1971. See R. P. Barston and Hjalmar W. Hannesson, 'The Anglo-Icelandic Fisheries Dispute', *International Relations* (David Davies Memorial Institute, London) Vol. IV, No. 6 (Nov. 1974) p. 575.
29. *Financial Times*, 25 June 1985.
30. Prior to the Foreign Service Act of 1961, the Danish Foreign Service and Organisation was reviewed by commissions in 1906, 1919 and 1957. In 1905 Denmark had only 18 career officers in the Foreign Ministry, which rose to 58 by 1919. The great expansion of 1921 was followed by cut-backs in 1927 which reduced the number of career officers from 146 in 1922 to 113 in 1927. The number of diplomatic missions was reduced to 16, covering 35 countries. The 1961 Act, which reaffirmed the principle of a unified home and foreign service, provided for further expansion. At the beginning of 1970, the Foreign Service comprised 280 career officers, and 76 diplomatic missions. See Klaus Kjolsen, *The Foreign Service of Denmark 1770–1970* (Foreign Ministry, 1970) pp. 23–25.
31. *Commentary on the Estimates of the Expenditure of the Government of New Zealand* for year ending 31 March 1986 (Wellington, Government Printer, 1985) pp. 52–3.
32. *The Swedish Budget 1986–7*, p. 66. Coordinators from the Swedish Trade Council were attached to the Foreign Ministry.
33. *Report of the Committee on the Indian Foreign Service*, pp. 56–72.
34. *Report*, Review Committee on Overseas Representation 1968–9, Cmnd. 4107, July 1969.
35. *Review of Overseas Representation* (Report by the Central Policy Review Staff) (HMSO, London, 1977) pp. xiii–xiv.
36. *Minutes of Evidence* by Sir Antony Acland, 3 July 1985, Trade and Industry Committee, House of Commons Papers, no. 335, pt vi, Session 1984–5, p. 87. The Diplomatic Service was given special responsibility for export promotion in the Plowden Report (Cmnd. 2276, Feb. 1964)

and the Trade Commission Service merged with it. See also *Financial Times*, 4 July 1985.

37. P. J. Boyce, *Foreign Affairs for New States* (University of Queensland Press, St Lucia, 1977) pp. 86–98.

CHAPTER THREE

Foreign policy assessments

Foreign policy assessments are concerned with providing explanations of recent past and current foreign policy behaviour. Assessments, too, involve judgements about the likely responses of an actor to proposals, or its probable conduct on a set of issues or problems. The role of the diplomat in this process has been aptly summed up in the following way: ' ... of judging accurately what other people are likely to do in given circumstances, of appreciating accurately the views of others, of representing accurately his own'.[1] Foreign policy itself can be thought of as being made up of three segments. In the first of these are generalised statements containing the broad aims and the overall interests of the state, as articulated in statements, communiques and other public pronouncements. There may, of course, be entirely different, and secret, general and particular interests that are pursued in a 'covert' foreign policy through secret or private diplomacy. In the second place, foreign policy can be thought of as the range of issue areas and preoccupations of a state. These might be European Community questions to do with the Community budget; harmonisation of Organisation for African Unity (OAU) policies on a development programme; bilateral issues in Anglo-American defence cooperation; international currency stability for the major Western powers, or fisheries questions for Iceland. In other words, these and similar types of issue areas constitute the foreign policy 'agenda'. Individual items on the agenda will normally be given some sort of order of importance or priority, which can and will frequently change over time. In the third sector are the specific daily operational problems which make up the routine of the 'external' ministries, such as visits, instructions to a delegation, lobbying on a vote in the UN, overflight clearance, consular problems and so on. This threefold distinction helps to put operational problems, especially of a short-term kind, into the broader context of issue areas and objectives. The threefold categorisation also enables questions to be asked about changes in the types of issue area a country is dealing with and any reordering of its priorities.

Assessment normally takes one of three forms. First there are analyses of short-run events, e.g. the stability of a coalition, the effect of ministerial change, the current state of the economy after a devaluation or the significance of a visit or speech. Second are the longer-range reviews of the national political scene of a country and its foreign policy over a period of, for example, twelve months. The latter are likely to note departures in policy and highlights in bilateral relations. Third are estimates which attempt to give an indication of future patterns, trends of events or likely developments. Assessments of this kind normally ask 'what if' questions, such as what can be expected in terms of defence policy, political relations, investment legislation, taxation if there is a change of government in, for example, four years. Another common set of questions is of a comparative kind on anticipated levels of trade or the likelihood of continued political support on an issue. Apart from these main types, other forms of assessment include the 'devil's advocate' or reversal type and very long-range estimates. This chapter is mainly concerned with the second or review type of assessment and looks at orientation and change in foreign policy. The first part of the chapter provides an overview of the factors influencing the setting and process of foreign policy.

THE FOREIGN POLICY SETTING

The influences on the foreign policy of a country can be initially grouped into domestic and international. These include location, historical background, culture, organisation, the extent of non-governmental interests, degree of domestic stability, economic and leadership influences. External influences include the structural systemic features of the international system, such as the level of violence; the nature and state of local and regional relations; international currency movements; the policies of a powerful extra-regional neighbour or proceedings of an international institution. To these broad categorisations must, of course, be added 'boundary cutting' or transnational influences. These are defined to include the autonomous or semi-autonomous actions of individuals and entities over which a government may have limited knowledge or control. Often transnational influences are thought of in terms of multinational corporations or terrorism, though in practice the range is far greater than this. It includes, for example, radio propaganda, refugees, trans-border smuggling, narcotics, the commercial operations of international companies, repatriated earnings, migrant labour and tourism.[2] Many of these transnational influences are not necessarily new. Some have in fact become instruments of national policy such as the boat people in Southeast Asia[3] or refugees using East Germany as a transit zone to the West in agreement with GDR authorities in a reversal of the Berlin Wall.[4] Other transnational developments are new including rapid developments in high-resolution, satellite-gathered intelligence and data transmission, which have not only altered transnationalism but helped to create further technological stratifications in the international system.[5] Another major development of note is the growth of international capital centres in Europe, the Middle East, Southeast Asia and the Far East. The growth of capital markets and related technology has facilitated the rapid movement of both private and officially sourced capital. These developments are something with which sovereign states have to coexist uneasily.[6] For some states, particularly those weaker ones on the immediate periphery of capital centres, new problems of economic security have been created.[7]

The influences outlined above combine in different configurations to shape the overall foreign policy profile of a state by setting the constraints and opportunities for particular decisions and courses of action. Configurations of course vary considerably. A state may be influenced by relatively few transnational influences because of internal economic weakness but nevertheless have an important strategic location. What is therefore important is to determine the relevant mix of factors in each case. Some may be more or less permanent features of a state's environment, such as location, effective economic territory, climate, resources, land and sea routes and level of development. These might be termed 'intrinsic' factors. Another relatively fixed component of a state's foreign policy environment is the set of treaties, agreements and other formal legal instruments a regime inherits on coming to power. Acceptance of agreements provides continuity and is with some exceptions part of the practice of most established states. Regimes in new states are likely to exercise greater selectivity over inherited agreements. Selectivity is one of the distinguishing features of the conduct of their external policy, though the degree of volatility has been overstated.[8]

Other factors are less pervasive and can be termed 'contingent'. These include personality factors, the effectiveness of the foreign policy machinery, the extent of bureaucratic or public opposition and the type of issue being dealt with.

CHARACTERISTICS OF FOREIGN POLICY

In assessing the foreign policy of another country it is normally possible to construct a profile based on the core and secondary interests. That is there is likely to be a pattern of central interests involving selected states and issues, the range of which will vary according to the capability, location and perceived role of the country in question. Secondary interests are distinguished by the intermittent time and organisational attention devoted to them, along with their 'sectoral' or limited nature. Some, however, may be long-standing, especially territorial disputes and take considerable time to resolve, as in the case of the Beagle Channel dispute between Argentina and Chile.

Second, a major paradox of foreign policy is the contrast between the smooth inter-connectedness of declared objectives and the disjointedness of routine problem-solving. Foreign policy in practice often appears rather brittle – the product of brief diplomatic visits, hasty cables and rapid exchanges of views – as it continually moves from item to item, rather like a scanner on a radar screen. Third, unlike other areas of public policy, foreign policy is made under extreme time constraints.[9] This tends to accentuate the tendency to deal with issues in a short-term manner.

Longer-range assessments need to disentangle the short-term preoccupations and actions and impose some kind of framework of explanation without becoming unnecessarily distracted by the short-term or immediate actions. Decisions, which are the component parts of policy, have a context. It is essential therefore to analyse whether a similar move or decision has been made by that country before or whether it is an apparent departure in policy. Again, an assessment of the importance of a high-level visit must take into account not only the level at which it was conducted, the extent to which the visit was perhaps largely ceremonial and the scope of the agenda, but measure it against what, if anything, was achieved in the last analogous visit. In journalistic assessments, preoccupation with the day-to-day aspects of foreign policy inevitably affects the metaphors of explanation. For example, the metaphor of the United States 'playing the China card' is often used in the context of Sino-American relations. Assessments of Soviet policy tend to focus on leadership politics, attempting to see splits between 'conservatives' and 'reformers'. Metaphors of this type have the effect of obscuring other more probable or complex reasons for behaviour such as organisational, bureaucratic, historical or external influences. Foreign policy is often conducted at multiple levels. The audience can be internal or external, regional or international, public or private. Assessing why countries, organisations and other entities act is one of the major and fascinating tasks of diplomacy. Finally, more than any other area of policy, foreign policy is both more easily reversed and subject to change.

ORIENTATION

In considering why states and other entities act in particular kinds of ways the concept of orientation offers a useful starting-point. Orientation can be defined· as the pattern of governmental and politically significant private attitudes, actions and transactions, which go to make up the alignment of a country. The more important of these are élite views, political groupings, alliance membership and trade patterns. States, in other words, interact in varying degrees with other members of the international community on political, economic, military, cultural, social and many other levels. These interactions generally show certain patterns, which indicate, reinforce or suggest the foreign policy directions and preferences of a country.

Several different foreign policy profiles can be constructed.[10] These can be as varied as the profiles for a complex advanced Western European state, an Asian Islamic republic, micro-state, through to isolation. Some states in fact have very low international involvement, e.g. Malagasy, Mongolia, Burundi, Haiti. On occasion this may change due to regional military conflict as in the case of the impact of the Iran–Iraq War on Oman. Other orientations might be essentially local, with interactions focusing on immediate neighbours, e.g. Thailand, Bolivia, Mali. More complex orientations necessarily involve membership of regional and international political and economic groupings, defence and other arrangements. These may not always be 'uniform' in that there may be divergent political and trade orientations, e.g. Angola[11] or defence and trade orientations may differ, e.g. Malaysia, with its 'Look East' economic policy directed towards Japan and South Korea and its mixed Western and non-aligned defence posture.[12]

LEVELS OF INTERACTION AND AGGREGATION

In any discussion of changes in orientation and the development of a country's foreign policy, it is necessary to look at the various levels of interaction which that state has with other actors. How far are the political and economic transactions largely autonomous of one another? Are there frequent disruptions in political relations or economic disputes? Do cultural questions spill over into political relations? The answers to these and similar questions give an indication whether an orientation is changing, taking on some new form, or whether disruptions are episodic and with no general effect on the overall orientation.

The process by which levels of interactions or transactions become linked or related can be termed 'aggregation'. Aggregation may consist of either internally directed domestic measures (e.g. the promotion of political relations by inward investment schemes, export subsidies, withdrawal of special privileges) or be externally directed or influenced. States which have pursued isolationist or withdrawal policies, e.g. Burma, Oman, will exhibit high degrees of aggregation in the process of attempting to control entry and limit political contacts. Examples of externally influenced aggregation are economic sanctions, e.g. the sanctions of the United States on the Soviet Union after the invasion of Afghanistan, or reprisals such as the People's Republic of China's retaliation against American exports to China following the decision to cut China's textile quotas in 1983.[13]

The degree of aggregation can vary considerably. In the European Economic Community (EEC) the interlocking of budgetary, agricultural and social policies in periodic 'wine lake' and 'lamb war' disputes is a marked feature of Community politics and style. Also noticeable in Community methods is the very wide range of trade-offs between different subject areas which are found in negotiations. For example in negotiations in the agricultural sector, solutions might be found involving compromise packages on wine and farming. In contrast, the Association of South-East Asian Nations (ASEAN) is a regional organisation distinguished by quite distinct areas of interaction and low levels of aggregation. Although initially conceived of as an economic organisation at its founding in 1967, pulling together the economies of the five original members (Malaysia, Indonesia, Thailand, Philippines, Singapore) these early aspirations have been gradually replaced by foreign policy rather than development questions.[14] While ASEAN developed institutional machinery and a committee structure which resembled that of the European Community (although there is no provision for a commission) ASEAN institutions have tended to remain largely autonomous of one another. ASEAN's economic diplomacy, too, became increasingly replaced by political preoccupations as the member states considered how to deal with the opportunities (and problems) created by the defeat of South Vietnam, the impending withdrawal of the US and its recognition of the People's Republic of China. Following the Vietnamese invasion of Kampuchea in 1978, the Kampuchean question became the dominant issue in ASEAN diplomacy, which further hindered any aggregation.

Consistently high levels of aggregation over lengthy periods of time are relatively rare. High aggregation is likely to occur only where economic objectives are directly and closely connected to political interests and policy, as with Saudi Arabian bilateral relations with West European states after the 1973 Arab–Israeli War. Again, Kissinger's policy during the early 1970s of 'linkage' was based on the *realpolitik* concept of doing business with the Soviets on all possible fronts, in the hope of moderating Soviet behaviour and bringing about international and domestic change.[15] The Strategic Arms Limitation Treaty (SALT I) in 1972 was accompanied by a suite of cooperation agreements in trade, medicine and space. The first meeting of the Soviet–American trade commission took place six weeks after the signing of the SALT I agreement.[16] However, the original concept was increasingly revised to take on a more negative and then punitive meaning. The post-*détente* period from the early 1980s onwards was characterised by US attempts to 'disconnect' what remained of the formal functional economic–cultural-type links left over from the hey-day of *détente*.

LOW AGGREGATION

Low aggregation in bilateral relations can occur for a number of reasons. It is especially seen in small or micro-state external relations, which are very often typified by the dominance of a single economic issue. In general, micro-states would have limited international political interactions.[17] An extreme example is Papua New Guinea, whose external relations are to a large extent taken up with the mining and retailing of copper (the major export) from Bougainville, a substantial part of which goes to Japan. Another reason for low aggregation is minimal political attention or 'pick-up'. This itself may be a facet of limited foreign policy control.[18] Central decision-makers may be switching rapidly from domestic to international issues, machinery may be limited or there may be a high degree of individual departmental autonomy. Apart from these reasons, low aggregation can occur because of the dominance of one sector of a state's external relations, e.g. the Sabah territorial dispute in Malaysian–Philippine relations.[19]

SOME IMPLICATIONS

For most states aggregation in their external policy is normally relatively low since most governments tend to handle issues in a separate manner. When aggregation occurs it is likely to be between the political and economic levels of interaction. However, in general, the tendency for organisational autonomy limits the extent to which issues are related to one another. A further important aspect of the nature of the interactions between states is differential evaluation. An issue area may not only be perceived differently by another state but be given quite different degrees of importance. What may be high or central on one state's agenda in its bilateral relations, may be quite low for the other state. Thus, for example, in Malaysian–United States relations, an important bilateral issue, on the Malaysian side (Malaysia is a major tin producer) is the release of tin by the United States from the General Services Administration (GSA) stockpile, depressing tin prices. Whereas, for the United States the tin issue ranks low, and it is more likely to regard questions concerning Malaysia's security role in the South China Sea as more important.[20]

Finally, it is worth noting that by looking at disruptions or discontinuities in relations at various levels, questions can be raised about possible changes of direction. These might indicate that the state in question has acquired new political partners or is lessening its dependency either economically or politically, on one of the major powers. In addition, it is also possible to see whether a state's bilateral or multilateral relations recover quickly from a dispute or whether it has more lasting and widespread effects.

CHANGE AND REORIENTATION

States as a matter of course make routine and continuous adjustments to their external relations in order to improve political relations with another country, deal with particular trade problems, open up new contacts and a host of other matters. These readjustments are for the most part likely to be marginal. Fundamental shifts involving major changes in the pattern and extent of most sectors of external policy are relatively rare. Such a reorientation can take the form of the rejection of a long-standing ally, e.g. the break between the People's Republic of China and the Soviet Union from 1960; switching from one bloc or dependent relationship to another (e.g. Cuba, Ethiopia, Egypt) or diversification (e.g. Yugoslavia). Other fundamental reorientations can take the form of greater emphasis on self-reliance (e.g. Tanzania); internal socio-religious revolution (e.g. Iran) or isolation (e.g. Burma). Although a country may change its orientation in one of the ways outlined above fundamental shifts are not always permanent. Dissatisfaction with a revised orientation often leads to protracted and sometimes contradictory attempts to readjust.

The primary indicators of reorientation are substantial changes in patterns of trade, inward and outward visits, and agreements with other countries. In addition, for a developing country further indicators of potential or actual reorientation would be developments in civil–military relations, the performance of the core export earners, expropriation of foreign assets, foreign exchange liquidity or the collapse of an economic programme. Secondary indicators include: alterations in diplomatic representation, joining or leaving international or regional organisations; voting behaviour; trends in inward investment and joint venture agreements.

It is unlikely that reorientation would occur simultaneously or to the same extent in all the primary sectors. In fact, it may be some time before changes in the economic sector, for example trade patterns, become aligned with the new political orientation. The initial public indicators of fundamental reorientation include official statements, major ministerial changes, foreign visits or preferences shown in contracts. Reorientation itself may take anything between two and five years to complete. It may, as noted above, be subsequently short-lived and reversed, as in the case of the Cultural Revolution in China, or the Norwegian referendum which eventually kept Norway out of the European Community.[21]

MIXED ORIENTATION AND REORIENTATION

In general, states make adjustments to one or two sectors, or parts of those sectors, of their external relations, rather than try to carry out fundamental shifts. Such partial readjustments are likely sometimes to produce unusual configurations, as in the case of the 'mixed' profile of Mozambique, or Libya after 1969 which has highly antagonistic political relations with the United States, contrasting with continued oil and other economic links. These examples serve to underline the limited options, particularly at an economic level, but also in security terms, for many states. Examples of partial reorientation at a political level include the reduced international role of Yugoslavia after the death of Tito, Costa Rica's declaration of neutrality in 1983[22] and the several shifts in Malta's foreign policy orientation, including the development of political relations between Libya and Malta prior to the eventual declaration of neutrality in 1981.[23] Another indicator of partial readjustment of role is decline in participation in international conferences. For example, Indian involvement in international conferences has declined by two-thirds since the high point of non-alignment in 1970.[24] At a security level, for example, France and Greece have placed limitations on their participation in NATO, as part of a reorientation of their foreign policies.

Attempts to reorientate at an economic level have become increasingly frequent, especially by the larger developing countries and some of the newly industrialised countries. For example, Brazil as a leading newly industrialised country has been particularly concerned since 1984 to reduce its net imported oil account ($US4.6 billion at 1984 prices). As part of a policy of trade reorientation oil has been imported as far as possible from countries to which manufactured goods can be sold.[25] While oil links with Iraq (arms purchases) and Algeria (motor vehicles) have been retained, oil is no longer imported from Abu Dhabi, Libya or Kuwait. Of the other developing countries, Thailand, for example, began a major petroleum reorientation on economic grounds after 1982 away from Saudi Arabia, which accounted for 15 per cent of Thai imports.[26]

Thai foreign policy also placed importance on closer relations with the People's Republic of China, a new Asian petroleum exporter, as part of its policy of containing Vietnam after the Vietnamese invasion of Kampuchea. Trade redirection has also been used by other states such as Nigeria, following, for example, the military coup in 1983, which involved an attempt to shift to counter-trade policy.[27]

SUMMARY

Orientation and change are among the main areas of enquiry for longer-term assessments and reviews of a state's foreign policy. As such, assessments of this kind are concerned with the composition of the basic external policy profile of a country and any shifts which might indicate or suggest change in the fundamental pattern of relations with other members of the international community. The patterns of bilateral and multilateral relations may be conducted at different levels which may be 'aggregated' to a greater or lesser extent. As we have also argued, major shifts are relatively rare and in most cases tend to be reversed. Rather, longer-range assessments are likely to be concerned with identifying and explaining the significance of partial or limited reorientation which has to be distinguished from routine adjustment. In doing so, longer-range assessments need to strike a balance of interpretation between the short-run or operational problems and the more fundamental assumptions, whether public or secret, underlying policy.

REFERENCES AND NOTES

1. Attributed to Bismarck. Quoted by Livingston Merchant, 'New Techniques in Diplomacy', in E. A. J. Johnson (ed.) *The Dimensions of Diplomacy* (Johns Hopkins Press, Baltimore, 1964) p. 126.
2. Robert O. Keohane and Joseph S. Nye, *Transnational Relations and World Politics* (Harvard University Press, Cambridge, Mass., 1973) pp. x–xxv.
3. See H. S. Teitelbaum 'Immigration, Refugees and Foreign Policy', *International Organisation* (Summer 1984) esp. pp. 437–43; Edwin F. McWilliams, 'Hanoi's Course in Southeast Asia', *Asian Survey*, Vol. XXIV, No. 8 (Aug. 1984) pp. 878–85.
4 *Sunday Times*, 10 Aug. 1986.
5. For background on the civilian uses of satellites see, for example,

Conference on the Exploration and Peaceful Uses of Outer Space, Relevance of Space Activities to the Monitoring of Earth Resources, A/Conf. 101/BP/13, 28 April 1981; and on stratification, see Rita Cruise O'Brien (ed.) *Information, Economics and Power* (Hodder and Stoughton, London, 1983).

6. On Brazil's attempts to control its domestic market in mini and micro computers for Brazilian companies, through the October 1984 Informatics Law, see Anne Piorkowski, 'Brazilian Computer Import Restrictions. Technological Interdependence and Commercial Reality', *Law and Policy in International Business*, Vol. 17, No. 3 (1985) pp. 619–45.

7. S. Mendelson, *Money on the Move: The Modern International Capital Market* (McGraw-Hill, New York, 1980); Maxwell Watson, Russell Kincaid, Caroline Atkinson, Eliot Kalter, and David Folkerts-Landau, *International Capital Markets: Developments and Prospects* (IMF, Washington, DC, December 1986).

8. Peter Calvert overstates this in terms of the inadequacy of archives, in *The Foreign Policy of New States* (Wheatsheaf Books, Sussex, 1986) pp. 83–4, 95–6.

9. Robert Wendzel, *International Relations: A Policymaker Focus* (John Wiley, New York, 1980).

10. See K. J. Holsti, *Why Nations Realign* (George Allen and Unwin, London, 1982) Ch. 1.

11. See Fola Soremekun, 'Angola', in Timothy M. Shaw and Olajide Aluko (eds), *The Political Economy of African Foreign Policy* (Gower, Aldershot, 1984) pp. 36–7; Garrick Utley, 'Globalism or Regionalism? United States Policy Towards Southern Africa?', in Robert Jaster (ed.) *Southern Africa* (Gower, Aldershot, 1985) pp. 27–8.

12. Documents on the early post-independence period can be found in Peter Boyce, *Malaysia and Singapore in International Diplomacy* (Sydney University Press, 1968).

13. See *Far Eastern Economic Review*, 11 Aug. 1983, pp. 72–3.

14. See Alison Broinowski (ed.) *Understanding Asean* (Macmillan, London, 1982).

15. Henry Kissinger, *The White House Years* (Weidenfeld and Nicolson, London, 1979) pp. 127–30 for an explanation of the concept of linkage, and *Department of State Bulletin*, 14 Oct. 1974, p. 508.

16. The agreements included the Joint US–USSR Commercial Commission, 26 May 1972, *TIAS*, Vol. 26, Part 2 (1975) pp. 1335–39; commercial facilities agreement, 3 Oct. 1973, *TIAS*, Vol. 24, Part 2, 1973, p. 2223; long-term economic and industrial cooperation agreement, 29 June 1974, *TIAS*, Vol. 25, Part 2, 1974. The US–USSR commercial facilities agreement of 22 June 1973, lists the ten approved corporations allowed to operate in and with the USSR under the agreement, including Pullman, Occidental Petroleum, Chase Manhattan and the Caterpillar Tractor Company, can be found in *TIAS*, Vol. 24, Part 2 (1973) p. 1503.

17. See J. A. Ballard, *Policymaking in a New State. Papua New Guinea 1972–77* (University of Queensland Press, London, 1978).

18. For a discussion of the concept of foreign policy control in the context of French diplomacy and reorientation, see Edward L. Morse, *Foreign*

Policy and Interdependence in Gaullist France (Princeton University Press, NJ, 1973) pp. 24, 38–44.

19. See Lela Garner Noble, *Philippine Policy Toward Sabah* (University of Arizona Press, Tucson, 1977).

20. For the same kind of point illustrated over tariff barriers by Japan on Indonesian plywood exports see *Far Eastern Economic Review*, 14 Feb. 1985, p. 92.

21. One of the few accounts in English of the Norwegian attempts to join the EEC and the referendum is Hilary Allen, *Norway and Europe in the 1970s* (Universitetsforlaget, Oslo, 1979).

22. See *Financial Times*, 28 Feb. 1985.

23. *Italian Yearbook of International Law* (Napoli, Editorial Scientifica, 1983) pp. 352–3, on the exchange of notes between Italy and Malta, 15 Sept. 1981, on Malta's neutralised status.

24. See *Annual Report* (Government of India, Ministry of External Affairs, 1970–84).

25. Wayne A. Selcher, *Brazil's Multilateral Relations* (Westview Press, Boulder, Colo., 1978) pp. 221–2.

26. See *Monthly Review*, Bank of Thailand, Vol. 26, No. 2 (Feb. 1985) pp. 77–80 on Thai–Saudi trade relations.

27. See *Financial Times*, 26 Feb. 1985; *Sunday Times*, 5 May 1985.

CHAPTER FOUR
Diplomatic correspondence

In modern diplomatic practice states generally use four methods for communicating directly with one another and other international actors. These are notes, letters, memoranda and *aides-mémoire*. In addition political leaders and other national personalities communicate with one another directly or indirectly through speeches, statements, communiques and interviews with the press. Declarations, too, have become an important feature of modern international political life. We are, however, mainly concerned in this chapter with the four methods of diplomatic communication noted above. Examples are provided of some of the different usages of each of the forms of communication, although the variety of state practice makes it difficult to lay down hard-and-fast rules as to when one method should be used rather than another. The examples themselves have been chosen from a wide variety of international problems as a way also of introducing the reader to the documentation on some of the post-war issues. From this range of material it is hoped to convey some of the flavour and scope of diplomacy and diplomatic exchanges.

NOTES

Notes are the most widely used form of diplomatic correspondence. It is necessary to distinguish those notes which form a correspondence and may either be in the first or third person, from notes or letters which are used to bring an agreement into effect. The note is probably, despite the range of usage, the most formal of the four methods under discussion. When used in the third person the note generally commences with customary courtesies (the Embassy of -- presents its compliments to) and concludes in a similar manner (avails itself of the opportunity, etc.). In certain circumstances, for example protest notes or in third-person correspondence sometimes with an international organisation, customary formalities may be dispensed with. Paragraphs in the note are not normally numbered and the note is initialled but not signed. In some state practice, for example Japan, the third-person note is styled a *note verbale*. In these instances, the title *note verbale* is put at the head of the note, but there are no other significant differences.

Diplomatic notes are used for a variety of purposes ranging from routine matters of administration between an embassy and host foreign ministry, registration of treaties, granting or refusing overflight clearance, through to official protests at the actions of other states. An interesting illustration of an exchange of notes followed from the so-called Soviet 'peace note' of 10 March 1952 on German reunification. The Soviet note, proposing a peace treaty and the formation of an all-German government, was put forward at a time when cold war tension had heightened following the Berlin airlift crisis and the Bonn Basic Law establishing the Federal Republic. Negotiations were in progress between the Western powers to establish a European Defence Community (EDC) and ultimately incorporate a rearmed West Germany into NATO. The German problem was a central cold war issue and the Soviet proposal foundered among other things on the question of free elections and the unwillingness of the Western powers to let a four-power conference in Germany slow up progress on EDC. The following are extracts from the exchanges:[1]

Text of a Note to Her Majesty's Government in the United Kingdom Handed to Her Majesty's Ambassador at Moscow by the Deputy Minister of Foreign Affairs of the Union of Soviet Socialist Republics on the 10th March 1952.

The Soviet Government consider it necessary to call the attention of Her Majesty's Government in the United Kingdom to the fact that although seven years have passed since the war ended in Europe a peace treaty with Germany has still not been concluded . . . .

. . . Analogous notes have been sent by the Soviet Government to the Governments of the United States and France.

APPENDIX

Soviet government's draft of a peace treaty with Germany

Political provisions

1. Germany is restored as a united state. The partition of Germany is thereby ended and the united Germany obtains the possibility of developing as an independent, democratic peace-loving State.
2. All armed forces of the occupying Powers must be withdrawn from Germany not later than one year from the day the peace treaty goes into force. Simultaneously with this all foreign military bases on the territory of Germany will be liquidated.
3. Democratic rights must be guaranteed to the German people so that all persons under German jurisdiction, irrespective of race, sex, language or religion, may enjoy the rights of man and the fundamental freedoms including freedom of speech, press, religious cults, political convictions and assembly.
4. The free activity of democratic parties and organisations must be made secure in Germany, they being granted the right freely to decide their internal affairs, hold congresses and assemblies and enjoy freedom of press and publication.
5. The existence of organisations hostile to democracy and to the cause of maintaining peace must not be permitted on the territory of Germany.
6. All former servicemen of the German Army, including officers and generals, all former Nazis, save for those who are serving terms on conviction for crimes which they committed, must be granted civil and political rights on a par with all other German citizens for taking part in the building of a peace-loving democratic Germany.
7. Germany pledges not to take part in any coalitions or military alliances aimed against any Power which participated with its armed forces in the war against Germany.

Territory The territory of Germany is defined by the borders established by the decisions of the Potsdam Conference.

Economic provisions No restrictions are placed on Germany as to the development of her peaceful economy, which must serve the growth of the welfare of the German people. Nor will there be any restrictions on Germany in respect of trade with other countries, navigation and access to world markets.

Military provisions

1. Germany will be permitted to have its national armed forces (land, air and naval) necessary for defence of the country.
2. Germany is permitted to produce military materials and materiel, the quantity or types of which must not go beyond the confines of what is required for the armed forces established for Germany by the peace treaty.

Germany and the United Nations The States which have concluded the peace treaty with Germany will support Germany's application for admission to membership of the United Nations.

The British Government's reply was delivered to the Soviet Union by the Chargé d'Affaires in Moscow in a note of 25 March 1952. The note sets out the basic British position on the German question, including concern over the relationship between the formation of an all-German government and talks on a peace treaty, frontiers and German rearmament:[2]

> Text of a Note to the Soviet Government Delivered by Her Majesty's Chargé d'Affaires at Moscow on 25th March 1952.
>
> Her Majesty's Government in the United Kingdom in consultation with the Governments of France and the United States have given the most careful consideration of the Soviet Government's note of 10th March which proposed the conclusion of a peace treaty with Germany. They have also consulted the Government of the German Federal Republic and the representatives of Berlin.
> 2. The conclusion of a just and lasting peace treaty which would end the division of Germany has always been and remains an essential objective of Her Majesty's Government. As the Soviet Government themselves recognise, the conclusion of such a treaty requires the formation of an all-German Government, expressing the will of the German people. Such a Government can only be set up on the basis of free elections in the Federal Republic, the Soviet Zone of occupation and Berlin . . . .
> 3. The Soviet Government's proposals do not indicate what the international position of an all-German Government would be before the conclusion of a peace treaty. Her Majesty's Government consider that the all-German Government should be free, both before and after the conclusion of a peace treaty, to enter into associations compatible with the principles and purposes of the United Nations.
> 4. In putting forward their proposals for a German peace treaty, the Soviet Government expressed their readiness also to discuss other proposals. Her Majesty's Government have taken due note of this statement. In their view, it will not be possible to engage in detailed discussion of a peace treaty until conditions have been created for free elections and until a free all-German Government, which could participate in such discussion, has been formed. There are several fundamental questions which would also have to be resolved.
> 5. For example, Her Majesty's Government noted that the Soviet Government make the statement that the territory of Germany is determined by frontiers laid down by the decisions of the Potsdam Conference. Her Majesty's Government would recall that in fact no definitive German frontiers were laid down by the Potsdam decisions, which clearly provided that the final determination of territorial questions must await the peace settlement.
> 6. Her Majesty's Government also observe that the Soviet Government now consider that the peace treaty should provide for the formation of German national land, air and sea forces, while at the same time imposing limitations on Germany's freedom to enter into association

with other countries. Her Majesty's Government consider that
provisions of this kind would be a step backwards and might jeopardise
the emergence in Europe of a new era in which international relations
would be based on co-operation and not on rivalry and mistrust . . . .

The exchanges on the Soviet note, which became known as the
'battle of the notes' continued until September 1952. A four-power
conference was not convened until 1954 in Geneva. As Coral Bell
comments:[3] 'Since the Soviet negotiating position of March 1952 was
never really explored it is not of course possible to identify the note
with certainty as a "bargaining bid", rather than a delaying bid.'

PROTEST NOTES

When states find it necessary to protest at certain actions this may be
done verbally, by calling the ambassador or chargé to the foreign
ministry. Alternatively, depending on the context and type of protest,
a protest note may be issued. When put in the form of a note, the
purpose is usually to place on record for political or legal purposes
the state's position. This may form the basis for a claim or counter-
claim at a subsequent date, or be a means of seeking political support
in a wider forum.

A number of reasons for protests can be distinguished, such as
seeking to stop a policy developing (e.g. to contest a state's offshore
maritime legislation); secondly, to protect interests (e.g. to counter a
boundary claim by another state, or the occupation of territory);
thirdly, to affirm the right to do something (e.g. offshore
exploration); or fourthly condemn an action (e.g. repeated or serious
violation of air or sea space).

The following examples illustrate these and other uses. The first
illustration is taken from New Zealand's dispute with France over the
French decision in 1963 to alter the location of its long-term nuclear
test programme from the Sahara to the South Pacific. A number of
protests and other diplomatic efforts were made by New Zealand to try
and change the French decision. New Zealand subsequently took the
case to the International Court of Justice (ICJ) on 9 May 1973.[4] The
following are extracts from the second New Zealand note of protest,
the French reply of 25 June 1963[5] and the New Zealand position on
overflight.[6]

Note from New Zealand Embassy to French Ministry of Foreign Affairs,
22 May 1963

The French authorities have been aware for some time of the grave
concern felt by the New Zealand Government at various reports
concerning France's plans to conduct test explosions of nuclear devices
in the South Pacific region. The New Zealand Government has sought
clarification of the intentions of the French Government in this respect
through the New Zealand Embassy both in interviews with officials of
the Ministry of Foreign Affairs and in the Embassy's Note of March
1963. In that Note it was indicated that if reports concerning the French
Government's intention to test in the South Pacific were confirmed, the
New Zealand Government would wish to convey certain other views to
the French authorities. In spite of recurrent and increasingly detailed
reports, which have produced growing public anxiety in New Zealand,
it has continued to await official confirmation, in response to the
Embassy's Note, that a decision to proceed with the establishment of a
nuclear testing centre in the area has been taken.

On and about 2 May, reports of a press conference given in Papeete
by General Thiry, head of a French civil and military mission, appeared
both in the French metropolitan press and in New Zealand. It appeared
from the statements attributed to General Thiry that a decision to
establish a nuclear test zone in the area of Mururoa Atoll had been
taken. Oral confirmation that a nuclear test zone had been decided on
in the area described was subsequently given by the Ministry in
response to enquiries by the Embassy.

In these circumstances, and even though it is understood that a
period of some years may elapse before the first test can be held, the
New Zealand Government feels compelled without further delay to
present its views to the French authorities . . . .

The New Zealand Government must therefore protest strongly
against the intention of the French Government to establish a nuclear
testing centre in the South Pacific. It urges that the French Government
reconsider, in the light of the views advanced in this Note, any decisions
which may already have been taken.

Note from French Ministry of Foreign Affairs to New Zealand Embassy,
25 June 1963

Le Ministère des affaires étrangères présente ses compliments à
l'Ambassade de Nouvelle-Zélande et a l'honneur de lui faire part de ce
qui suit:

Le Ministère des affaires étrangères à pris connaissance avec attention
de la note 1963/10 du 22 mai par laquelle l'Ambassade de Nouvelle-
Zélande faisait connaître le point de vue de son gouvernement sur la
création d'un polygone de tir français pour des essais nucléaires en
Polynésie et au sujet de la cessation des essais nucléaires.

La position de la France à l'égard des expériences nucléaires est bien
connue et n'a pas varié. A de nombreuses reprises ses représentants ont
rappelé que l'immense pouvoir de destruction que représentent pour
l'humanité les armes nucléaires demeurerait intact si la suspension des

expériences n'était pas accompagnée de l'arrêt contrôlé des fabrications nouvelles et l'élimination progressive et vérifiée des stocks d'armes existants.

Le Gouvernement français demeure prêt à s'associer à tout moment à une politique de désarmement qui soit efficace et contrôlé. Mais en l'absence d'une telle politique et aussi longtemps que d'autres puissances possederont les armes modernes il estime de son devoir de conserver sa liberté dans ce domaine.

C'est dans cette perspective qu'une décision tendant a l'établissement d'un polygone de tir pour des essais nucléaires en Polynesie française a été prise. Un delai assez long s'écoulera encore avant que ce champ de tire soit équipé et que des expériences nucléaires puissent y être effectuées.

Au demeurant le Gouvernement français croit devoir rappeler qu'il ne sera pas le premier à effectuer de telles expériences dans le Pacifique. D'autres Etats l'ont fait avant lui ainsi que le sait le Gouvernement de la Nouvelle-Zélande et il pourrait en être encore de même à l'avenir.

Le Ministère des affaires étrangères croit devoir également souligner que les services français chargés de la realisation des essais nucléaires dans cette region veilleront tout particulièrement à assurer la protection des populations des pays riverains de l'océan Pacifique Sud. A cet égard le Gouvernement français se propose, ainsi qu'il en à déjà été fait part à l'Ambassade de Nouvelle-Zélande, de faire connaître aux autorités neo-zélandaises, au moment opportun, les conditions dans lesquelles se dérouleront ces expériences et les mesures prises pour éviter tout risque de retombées et éventuellement d'en discuter avec ces autorités.

Le Ministère des affaires étrangères saisit cette occasion pour renouveler à l'Ambassade de Nouvelle-Zélande les assurances de sa haute considération.

Note from New Zealand Ministry of External Affairs to French Embassy, 15 April 1966

The Ministry of External Affairs presents its compliments to the Embassy of France and has the honour to refer to the Embassy's Note No. 23 of 13 April 1966, which requested authorization for an aircraft of the French Air Force to overfly the islands of Niue and Aitutaki in the course of a flight from Noumea to Hao.

The Ministry desires to inform the Embassy that steps have been taken to advise the Ministry of Foreign Affairs in Paris that if the French Government proceeds with its intentions to conduct a series of nuclear weapons tests in the South Pacific Ocean, New Zealand, consistent with its obligation under the Partial Nuclear Test Ban Treaty of 1963, will be unable to grant authority for any visits to New Zealand territory by French military aircraft or ships or overflights of New Zealand by French military aircraft, unless assured that they are not carrying material intended for the test site, or for the monitoring of the tests, or for the support of forces and personnel engaged in the tests or in monitoring the tests, other than monitoring to detect possible health hazards . . . .

Note from New Zealand Ministry of External Affairs to French
Embassy, 19 April 1966

The Ministry of External Affairs presents its compliments to the
Embassy of France and has the honour to refer to the Embassy's Note
No. 23 of 13 April and the Ministry's Note No. PM 59/5/6 of 15 April
1966.

The Ministry has been in consultation with the Government of the
Cook Islands concerning the Embassy's request for authorization of the
DC8 of the French Air Force to overfly Aitutaki on 24 April in the
course of a flight from Noumea to Hao. The Government of the Cook
Islands has requested that the Embassy be informed that its position is
precisely the same as that of the New Zealand Government and that it
cannot grant permission for the overflight without a similar assurance
to that requested by the New Zealand Government.

The Ministry of External Affairs avails itself of this opportunity to
renew to the Embassy of France the assurances of its highest
consideration.

Note from French Embassy to the New Zealand Ministry of External
Affairs, 21 April 1966

L'Ambassade de France présente ses compliments au Ministère des
affaires extérieures, et a l'honneur de lui accuser réception de ses notes
en date des 15 et 18 avril derniers, qui contiennent la réponse du
Gouvernement neo-zélandais à la demande d'autorisation de survol de
l'île Niue et de l'archipel des Cook présentée au nom de son
gouvernement.

Les modalités de la réponse neo-zélandaise ont été communiquées au
Gouvernement français. Celui-çi a fait savoir a l'Ambassade qu'il
souhaitait annuler sa demande. De ce fait, au course de l'étape Nouméa-
Hao, qui avait fait l'object de cette demande, l'appareil militaire
français se tiendra à l'écart de tout territoire et eaux territoriales
néo-zélandais.

L'Ambassade de France saisit cette occasion pour renouveler au
Ministère des affaires extérieures les assurances de sa très haute
considération.

States in their conduct of international relations regard questions
to do with boundaries and territory, such as the publication of maps
by other states, claims and boundary adjustments, as sensitive
matters. In the second example, India found it necessary to protest to
the People's Republic of China about the map attached to the
Burmese–Chinese Boundary Treaty. India contested the map which
showed the western extremity of the Sino-Burmese boundary as
ending at the Diphu L'Ka Pass, whereas on Indian and other maps
the tri-junction was 5 miles north of the pass.[7]

Note from India to China, 30 December 1960

1. The Government of India present their compliments to the Government of the People's Republic of China, and with reference to the text and the maps attached to the Burmese–Chinese Boundary Treaty of 1 October 1960 which were recently presented to the Parliament of the Union of Burma, have the honour to bring to the attention of the Government of the People's Republic of China the following facts pertaining to the western extremity of the Burma–China boundary, where it meets the eastern extremity of the India–China boundary.

2. Although Article 5 of the Treaty does not specify the exact location of the western extremity of the Sino-Burmese boundary, in the map attached to the Treaty the boundary is shown as ending at the Diphu L'ka Pass. The traditional boundary of India west of the Sino-Burmese boundary follows the watershed between D-chu in India and Lat-te in the Tibet region of China; and the tri-junction of India, Burma and China is five miles north of the Diphu L'ka Pass, and not at the Diphu L'ka Pass itself. The coordinates of the tri-junction are approximately longitude 97° 23′ east and latitude 28° 13′ north. The fact that the traditional boundary running along the Himalayan watershed passes through this point has in the past been accepted by the Governments of Burma and China and it has for many years been shown correctly on official maps published in India.

3. The Government of India recognise that the text of the Treaty has left the exact location of this point unspecified. The Government of India are however obliged to point out that the extremity of the boundary between the two countries has been shown on the maps attached to the Treaty in an erroneous manner. As the location of the tri-junction at the Diphu L'ka Pass has an adverse implication on the territorial integrity of India, the Government of India wish to make clear to the Government of the People's Republic of China that they would be unable to recognise this map insofar as it prejudicially affects Indian territory.

    The Government of India take this opportunity to renew to the Government of the People's Republic of China the assurances of their highest consideration.

The third example of the use of protest notes is taken from the Libyan–Tunisian dispute over the delimitation of the continental shelf. During the course of the dispute the two sides signed a special agreement on 10 June 1977[8] to put the case before the ICJ. Prior to this Libya had granted oil concessions in the disputed sector of the Gulf of Gabes and undertaken exploratory drilling. Tunisia protested at the Libyan actions, but Libya rejected the Tunisian protests in a *note verbale* of 2 May 1976 and affirmed its right to carry out drilling on the disputed continental shelf.[9]

Note Verbale 1/7/76 Du 2 Mai 1976

Le ministère des affaires étrangères de la République arabe libyenne adresse ses compliments à la haute représentation de la République tunisienne et a l'honneur de la prier de transmettre ce qui suit au Gouvernement de la République tunisienne.

Se référant à la note du ministère des affaires étrangères tunisien no 1630 du 15 avril 1976 relative aux activitiés du bateau français *Maersk Tracker* lié par un contrat avec le Gouvernement de la République arabe libyenne pour effectuer des opérations d'exploration et de forage dans ses eaux territoriales et sur son plateau continental, le ministère des affaires étrangères de la République arabe libyenne désire affirmer ce qui suit:

1. Le Gouvernement de la République arabe libyenne rejette entièrement le contenu de la note du ministère des affaires étrangères tunisien no 1630 du 15 avril 1976.

En consequence, le Gouvernement de la République arabe libyenne attire l'attention du Gouvernement de la République tunisienne sur le fait qu'il va continuer à exercer ses droits légitimes sur son territoire et poursuivre l'exploration et l'exploitation de ses eaux territoriales et de son plateau continental.

Il prie donc le Gouvernement de la République tunisienne de reconsidérer sa note no 1630 du 15 avril 1976 et de ne pas faire obstacle aux opérations d'activité economique ou autres de la République arabe libyenne dans cette region.

A La Haute Représentation
De La République Tunisienne Sœur
Tripoli

The fourth illustration is taken from the famous U-2 incident of May 1960. On 1 May 1960, in a major incident on the eve of the Paris summit, the Soviet Union shot down a US U2 intelligence aircraft over Sverdlovsk. The United States issued the following note on 6 May 1960:[10]

As already announced on 3 May, a United States National Aeronautical Space Agency unarmed weather research plane based at Adana, Turkey, and piloted by a civilian American has been missing since 1 May. The name of the American civilian pilot is Francis Gary Powers, born on 17 August 1929, at Jenkins, Kentucky.

In the light of the above the United States Government requests the Soviet Government to provide it with full facts of the Soviet investigation of this incident and to inform it of the fate of the pilot ....

The Soviet Union issued a protest note on 10 May 1960.[11]

Soviet Note to the United States, 10 May 1960

The Government of the Union of Soviet Socialist Republics considers it necessary to communicate the following to the Government of the United States of America.

At 5.36 a.m. (Moscow time), on May 1, this year, a military plane violated the frontier of the USSR and invaded the air space of the Soviet Union to a distance of over 2,000 kilometres. The Government of the USSR, of course, could not leave unpunished such a gross violation of the Soviet state frontiers. When the deliberate nature of the flight of the intruding plane became obvious, it was brought down by Soviet rocket forces near Sverdlovsk . . . .

These and other data cited in the speeches by the head of the Soviet Government have utterly refuted the invented and hastily concocted story of the US State Department, set forth in an official press release on 5 May and alleging that the plane was conducting meteorological observations in the upper layers of the atmosphere along the Turkish–Soviet frontier.

It goes without saying that the Soviet Government has been compelled by the present circumstances to give strict orders to its armed forces to take all the necessary measures against the violation of Soviet frontiers by foreign aircraft . . . .

The Government of the Soviet Union strongly protests to the Government of the United States of America in connection with the aggressive acts by American aircraft and warns it that should such provocations be repeated, the Soviet Government will have to take retaliatory measures, the responsibility for whose consequences will rest with the governments of the states committing acts of aggression against other countries . . . .

The United States replied on 12 May to the Soviet protest note as follows:[12]

The Embassy of the United States of America refers to the Soviet Government's Note of 10 May concerning the shooting down of an American unarmed civilian aircraft on 1 May, and under instruction from its Government, has the honor to state the following.

The United States Government, in the statement issued by the Department of State on 9 May, has fully stated its position with respect to this incident.

In its Note the Soviet Government has stated that the collection of intelligence about the Soviet Union by American aircraft is a 'calculated policy' of the United States. The United States Government does not deny that it has pursued such a policy for purely defensive purposes. What it emphatically does deny is that this policy has any aggressive intent, or that the unarmed U-2 flight of 1 May was undertaken in an effort to prejudice the success of the forthcoming meeting of the Heads of Government in Paris or to 'return the state of American–Soviet relations to the worst times of the cold war'. Indeed, it is the Soviet Government's treatment of this case which if anything, may raise questions about its intention in respect to these matters.

For its part, the United States Government will participate in the Paris meeting on 16 May prepared to cooperate to the fullest extent in seeking agreements designed to reduce tensions, including effective safeguards against surprise attack which would make unnecessary issues of this kind.

In some circumstances states transmit protest notes through the United Nations in order to publicise their case by putting it on record, or have the matter discussed by the Security Council. Many aspects of the Cyprus problem have been disputed through the UN in this way, such as the lodging of a protest note by the Cyprus Government against Turkish incursions of its air space.[13] In the dispute between the United Kingdom and Guatemala over Belize, the Guatemalan Government lodged with the Secretary-General, on 17 September 1981, the text of a protest note sent to the United Kingdom, for circulation as a Security Council document:[14]

Letter dated 17 September 1981 from the representative of Guatemala to the Secretary-General

(Original: Spanish, 17 September 1981)

I have the honour to reproduce below the text of a note of protest against the United Kingdom dated 16 September 1981 and delivered yesterday to the Embassy of Switzerland, which is handling that country's affairs in Guatemala. The note reads as follows:
    'The Ministry of External Relations presents its compliments to the Honourable Embassy of Switzerland, as the Embassy handling the affairs of the United Kingdom of Great Britain and Northern Ireland, and wishes to inform it that on Thursday, 10 September 1981, at 2 p.m., a British reconnaissance aircraft entered Guatemalan airspace without proper authorization, flying over several departmental capitals as well as over the national capital, at an altitude of 35,000 feet.'
    'This unusual act constitutes a flagrant violation of the most elementary rules of international law and an abuse of territorial inviolability. Moreover, it demonstrates the aggressive attitude of the British Government in provoking a peaceful nation so insolently.'
    'The Ministry of Foreign Affairs request the Honourable Embassy of Switzerland to convey to the Government of the United Kingdom the most energetic protest of the Government of Guatemala against this act.'
    Please arrange for this communication to be circulated as a Security Council document, with reference to Guatemala's request drawing the Council's attention to the dispute with the United Kingdom concerning the Territory of Belize.

Signed Eduardo Castillo Arriola
Permanent Representative of Guatemala to the United Nations.

Again, the United States protest note to Libya following the clash in the Gulf of Sirte, was transmitted to the President of the Security

Council as a means *inter alia* of reaffirming US policy on freedom of navigation in international waters and the right of self-defence:[15]

Letter dated 19 August 1981 from the representative of the United States of America to the President of the Security Council
(Original: English, 19 August 1981)

In accordance with Article 51 of the Charter of the United Nations, I wish, on behalf of my Government, to report that United States aircraft participating in a routine peaceful naval exercise in international waters in the Mediterranean Sea were subject to an unprovoked attack by Libyan aircraft. The attack took place at 0520 hours GMT on 19 August 1981. Acting in self-defence, United States aircraft returned fire, and two Libyan aircraft were shot down.

The United States Government today transmitted the following protest to the Government of Libya:

'The United States Government protests to the Government of Libya the unprovoked attack against American naval aircraft operating in international airspace approximately 60 miles from the coast of Libya. The attack occurred at 0520 GMT on 19 August 1981. The American aircraft were participating in a routine naval exercise by United States Navy Forces in international waters. In accordance with standard international practice, this exercise had been announced on 12 and 14 August through notices to airmen and to mariners. Prior notification of air operations within the Tripoli FIR (flight information region) had also been given. In accordance with these notifications, the exercise which began on 18 August will conclude at 1700 GMT 19 August.'

'The Government of the United States views this unprovoked attack with grave concern. Any further attacks against United States Forces operating in international waters and airspace will also be resisted with force if necessary.'

In view of the gravity of Libya's action, and the threat it poses to the maintenance of international peace and security, I ask that you circulate the text of this letter as a document of the Security Council.

(Signed) Charles M Lichenstein
Acting Representative of the United States of America to the United Nations.

OTHER USES OF NOTES

A number of other uses of notes need to be distinguished. First of all a collective note is one which is presented by several parties to a government or international institution on a matter upon which they wish to make joint representation. In the case of a regional organisation (e.g. ASEAN, Caribbean Community (CARICOM)), the text may be delivered by the current chairman, secretary-general or individual ambassadors as appropriate. In a similar way letters may take a collective form.[16] An interesting example is provided by the collective letter to the UN Secretary-General signed by Fiji, Ireland and Senegal, representing the participating members of United Nations Interim Force in Lebanon (UNIFIL), on the serious difficulties encountered by UNIFIL in carrying out its mandate in the Lebanon. Another illustration can be seen in the collective letter of Argentina, Brazil, Chile and the United States to the President of the Security Council in their capacity as countries guaranteeing the 1942 Peruvian–Ecuadorian Protocol of Peace, Friendship and Frontiers.[17]

Apart from collective notes or letters, other uses take the form of identical and similar notes. The FRG, for example, sent identical notes to France, the United Kingdom, the United States and the USSR on the implications of the 1970 German–Polish normalisation treaty for other relevant treaties involving those powers:[18]

Note from the Federal Government to the Three Western Powers, 19 November 1970

The German Federal Foreign Office presents its compliments to Her Britannic Majesty's Embassy and has the honour to communicate to the Embassy the following text of a note of today's date of the Government of the Federal Republic of Germany to the Government of the United Kingdom of Great Britain and Northern Ireland.

In the course of the negotiations which took place between the Government of the Federal Republic of Germany and the Government of the People's Republic of Poland concerning this Treaty, it was made clear by the Federal Republic that the Treaty between the Federal Republic of Germany and the People's Republic of Poland does not and cannot affect the rights and responsibilities of the French Republic, the United Kingdom of Great Britain and Northern Ireland, the Union of Soviet Socialist Republics, and the United States of America as reflected in the known treaties and agreements. The Federal Government further pointed out that it can only act in the name of the Federal Republic of Germany.

The Government of the French Republic and the Government of the United States of America have received identical notes.

In the case of similar notes, states may agree after consultation to draft broadly similar though not identical language. This may occur when a number of states consult each other concerning the effect of reservations made by another state when acceding to an international treaty. Again, groups of states may agree to use similar language when reserving their positions on an issue.

A quite different usage of note is in the sense of 'speaking notes' or *bout de papier*, which may be left at the end of a call or a meeting to act as a form of *aide-mémoire* to reduce the likelihood of misunderstanding about the points made. An example of the use of speaking notes occurred during US–North Vietnamese talks[19]: 'The US delegation repeated its position at twelve different meetings and on at least one occasion US negotiator Cyrus Vance read from 'talking points', which he left on the table for his counterpart Colonel Han Van Lau to pick up.' In United Nations practice, finally, documents are issued by the Secretary-General with the title 'note'. These are not third- or first-person notes as such, have no formalities of introduction or conclusion but resemble rather memoranda. As such they tend to contain formal statements recording details of conference meetings or intersessional consultations.

LETTERS

Along with notes, letters are extensively used for diplomatic correspondence. Letters of correspondence should be distinguished, like notes from letters which bring agreements into effect, although the opening and closing formalities are generally the same. Of the several uses of letters a number are worth highlighting. In the first place, a personal letter from one head of government (or foreign minister) to another is often used after changes of government or if relations between the states have been 'frozen' for some time due to a dispute. The letter may be delivered by an ambassador, or, more often, by a special envoy. A personal letter from one head of state to another may be used to supplement a note,[20] as well as make a diplomatic initiative or appeal. For example, President Reagan in an attempt to break the deadlock in negotiations on the Cyprus problem, sent a personal letter of 22 November 1984 to the President of Turkey, General Kenan Evren, urging resumption of negotiations.[21]

In conflicts states warn enemies, and on occasion friends. The initial phase of the Cyprus problem provides a famous illustration of the latter. Against the background of growing Greek–Turkish Cypriot intercommunal violence and the possibility of military intervention by Turkey, President Johnson sent an extremely tough warning to Turkey on 5 June 1964. The so-called 'Johnson letter' has been described as the 'bluntest document ever sent to an ally'. In warning against intervention the letter to President Inonu continued[22]: 'I hope you will understand that your NATO allies have not had a chance to consider whether they have an obligation to protect Turkey against Soviet intervention, without the full consent and understanding of its NATO allies.'

The letter was also a model of Secretary of State, Dean Rusk, and Department of State drafting, in that it was sensitive to likely Turkish feelings and reaction. The tone of the letter was softened to appeal to Turkish national pride:[23]

> We have considered you as a great ally with fundamental common interests. Your security and prosperity have been the deep concern of the American people, and we have expressed that concern in the most practical terms. We and you fought together to resist the ambitions of the communist world revolution. This solidarity has meant a great deal to us, and I hope it means a great deal to your government and your people.

Letters are most commonly used to raise questions and explain policy, as well as set out intended lines of action. An example of the latter, which had a major impact on post-war Japanese orientation, is the so-called 'Yoshida letter'. The letter of 25 December 1951, from Prime Minister Shigeru Yoshida to John Foster Dulles, was the product of considerable pressure by Dulles, to persuade the Japanese Prime Minister to conclude a peace treaty with the Republic of China and not Peking. Yoshida was ambivalent as he sought to keep Japanese options open. However, he finally conceded shortly after the second meeting with Dulles on 18 December 1951 and accepted Dulles's draft memorandum. The Yoshida letter helped the peace treaty with Japan through the US Senate in March 1952. Japan continued to recognise the Nationalist regime in Taiwan until 1972, after which it changed its recognition policy, in the wake of revised policy of the United States (the so-called 'Nixon shock') to the People's Republic of China. The relevant section of the Yoshida letter sets out Japan's recognition policy as follows:[24]

> My government is prepared as soon as legally possible to conclude with the National Government of China, if that government so desires, a Treaty which will re-establish normal relations between our governments in conformity with the principles set out in the multilateral Treaty of Peace, the terms of such bilateral treaty to be applicable as regards the territories now or hereafter under the actual control of the Japanese and Chinese National Governments ... I can assure you that the Japanese Government has no intention to conclude a bilateral Treaty with the Communist regime of China.

In crisis diplomacy, states find it necessary sometimes to duplicate or reinforce the channels of communication. This might be a safeguard to ensure that their policy is actually getting through, or, alternatively an attempt to influence opinion in the other state by the use of a wide number of channels. The former was no doubt the reason why, in the Cuban missile crisis, the United States attempted to use the Secretary-General of the United Nations as one of the routes to communicate the US decision on a 500-mile quarantine around Cuba to the Soviet Union:[25]

> Letter of 27 October 1962, from Adlai E. Stevenson Defining Interception Area Around Cuba.
>
> Excellency:
>   My Government has instructed me to inform you that the 'interception area' referred to in your letter of 25 October to the President of the United States and in his reply of 26 October, comprises:
>   (a) the area included within a circle with its center at Havana and a radius of 500 nautical miles, and,
>   (b) the area included within a circle with its center at Cape Maysi (Maisi), located at the eastern tip of the island of Cuba, and a radius of 500 nautical miles.
>   You may wish to pass the above information to Chairman Khrushchev, so that he can proceed in accordance with his 26 October letter to you, in which he stated that he had ordered the masters of Soviet vessels bound for Cuba, but not yet within the interception area, to stay out of the area.
>   Accept, Excellency, the renewed assurances of my highest consideration.
>
> Adlai E. Stevenson

A further general category of correspondence worthy of comment is the many types of letters states address to the Secretary-General and other UN office-holders in the course of a dispute. These may serve one of a number of purposes such as putting a complaint, establishing a case, indicating that UN recommendations have been complied with, or, as in the following example, internationalising a dispute by seeking to put it before the Security Council:[26]

> Letter dated 16 September 1981 from the representative of the Sudan to the President of the Security Council
>
> (Original: English)
> 16 September 1981)
>
>   Upon instructions from my Government, I have the honour to inform you that in another wanton act of aggression aimed at destabilising the security and tranquillity of the Sudanese people, the occupying Libyan armed forces in Chad have once again committed a series of hostile acts of aggression against the sovereignty and territorial integrity of the Democratic Republic of the Sudan.
>   In gross violation of the principles of respect for sovereignty, territorial integrity and non-interference in the internal affairs of other

States, the Libyan forces have escalated their acts of aggression against the Democratic Republic of the Sudan as follows:

1. On 10 September 1981, a Libyan military plane violated Sudanese airspace and bombed a number of Sudanese villages in the vicinity of Eltina area in western Sudan. No casualties were reported.

2. On 15 September, at 0600 hours and 0930 hours a number of Libyan planes based in Chad have twice bombarded Kulbus area in western Sudan. Four persons, including two children, were seriously injured in the souk (market-place).

3. On the same day, 15 September, at 1100 hours, two Libyan aircraft overflew the Sudanese city of El Geneina in another provocative act.

The Democratic Republic of the Sudan strongly condemns these repeated acts of aggression by Libya against the sovereignty and territorial integrity of the Sudan in flagrant violation of the principles and objectives enshrined in the Charter of the United Nations.

The Democratic Republic of the Sudan would like to draw the attention of the Security Council to the dangerous situation arising from the repeated Libyan acts of aggression against the Democratic Republic of the Sudan which would undoubtedly lead to the destabilization of the region and threaten international peace and security. The Democratic Republic of the Sudan trusts that the Council will closely follow the situation and take all necessary and appropriate measures to ensure that such Libyan acts of aggression would immediately stop and not be repeated.

My Government reserves the right to seize the Security Council of the above-mentioned situation and requests that this letter be circulated as a document of the Council.

(signed) Abdel-Rahman Abdalla
Permanent Representative of the Sudan to the United Nations

The last usage of letters discussed in this section is that of the conduct of negotiations by correspondence. In exchanges of this type states might seek to obtain agreement about interpretations of a treaty or draft article, establish general principles or question certain interpretations. A clear example of this type of 'positional' negotiation can be found in the diplomatic correspondence of the opening sessions of the Preparatory Commission for the International Sea-bed Authority. The Preparatory Commission, or 'Prep. Comm.' as it became known, had been set up as part of the machinery envisaged under the Law of the Sea Convention, which was opened for signature on 10 December 1982. The purpose of the Commission was to establish rules and regulations for the international management of deep sea-bed resources in line with the provisions of the convention. Several states, including the Soviet Union and India, were anxious to register as so-called 'pioneer' investors, within the timetable laid down by the convention, and have their proposed areas of exploration registered with the Commission. Difficulties arose in that the convention envisaged exchanges of coordinates taking place, although at that point generally accepted procedures for this and other matters connected with the working of the Commission had not been agreed upon.

Some states, including France, generally sought to protect their position, while others criticised the Soviet and Indian interpretations. The exchange opens with the Soviet letter to the chairman of the Preparatory Commission on 6 April 1983:[27]

> The delegation of the USSR to the first session of the Preparatory Commission for the International Sea-bed Authority and for the International Tribunal for the Law of the Sea hereby transmits to the Commission the following information provided for in paragraph 5(a) of resolution II.
> ... the absence in resolution II of any provisions concerning reciprocal obligations of certifying States regarding the exchange of co-ordinates of areas for the purpose of determining the existence of conflicts has thus far precluded the possibility of initiating negotiations with other certifying States on the resolution of such conflicts ....
> The Soviet Union also assumes that all certifying States which by 1 May 1983 send such notifications to the Preparatory Commission, their enterprises or companies will, after the resolution of any conflicts that may arise, be registered as pioneer investors, that they will be allocated pioneer areas in pursuance of their applications and that these areas will in future be considered areas previously allocated as pioneer areas as specified in paragraph 5(a) of resolution II.
> The USSR delegation requests that this letter be circulated as an official document of the Preparatory Commission.
>
> (signed) I. K. Kolossovksy
> Chairman of the USSR delegation to the first session of the Preparatory Commission for the International Sea-bed Authority and for the International Tribunal for the Law of the Sea.

The Soviet position and that of India, was opposed by France in a letter of the 28 April:[28]

> Letter Dated 28 April 1983 from the Permanent Representative of France to the United Nations Addressed to the Chairman of the Preparatory Commission
>
> My Government has taken note of the letter dated 24 April 1983 addressed to you by the Permanent Representative of India to the United Nations (LOS/PCN/7).
>
> In that letter, the Government of India proposed that prospective certifying States should exchange by 1 May 1983 the co-ordinates of the areas in which pioneer investors would like to conduct pioneer activities within the meaning of resolution II governing preparatory investment and that negotiations should be initiated by that same date

with a view to resolving any possible disputes. In addition, the Government of India stated that, if it did not receive any response on that matter by 1 May, it would feel free to proceed with the procedure laid down in resolution II. The Government of India thus suggested that it could already be registered at the current stage as a pioneer investor.

The French Government cannot accept such a position, with respect to which it has the same objections as those set out in the letter dated 27 April 1983 which it had the honour to send to you in response to the letter of 6 April from the Chairman of the delegation of the Union of Soviet Socialist Republics (LOS/PCN/8). It holds that no right or pre-emption can be based on the letter from the Permanent Representative of India or on any steps taken subsequently by India, acting either alone or with the Soviet Union or any other country.

I should be grateful, Sir, if you would have this letter circulated before 1 May as an official document of the Preparatory Commission.

(signed) Luc de La Barre de Nanteuil
Permanent Representative of France to the United Nations.

The French position was supported by Canada. In particular Canada was concerned to see the talks, which it had initiated in July 1982, on procedures for dealing with disputes about overlapping mining site claims, to be concluded before a state could register with the Preparatory Commission as authorised to approve mining operations.[29] In reply the Soviet Union disputed the French interpretation and commented as follows on the significance of the Canadian-initiated talks:

Preparatory Committee for the International Sea-bed Authority and for the International Tribunal for the Law of the Sea

Letter dated 29 April 1983 from the Permanent Representative of the Union of Soviet Socialist Republics to the United Nations Addressed to the Chairman of the Preparatory Commission[30]

The Soviet Union has studied the letter dated 27 April 1983 from the Permanent Representative of France to the United Nations addressed to the Chairman of the Preparatory Commission for the International Sea-bed Authority.

... an attempt is made in this letter to place on the same footing States which have signed the Convention and States which have not signed it, and to confer on the latter rights granted only to signatory States ....

The Canadian initiative regarding consultations among interested countries for the purpose of drafting a 'Memorandum of understanding on the settlement of conflicting claims with respect to sea-bed areas', to which the Permanent Representative of France refers, does not and cannot impose any obligations on signatory States. The Soviet Union also appreciates the usefulness of achieving the relevant 'gentleman's agreement' concerning such an understanding; however, it does not consider this to be essential, since all questions concerning conflict resolution are settled by resolution II. The procedure for the resolution of possible conflicts of this kind has long been established by international practice, to which paragraph 5 of resolution II refers *inter alia . . . .*

During the exchange of letters, a number of states, including the United Kingdom,[31] Belgium and Indonesia formally reserved their position:[32]

Letter Dated 27 April 1983 from the Representative of the United Kingdom of Great Britain and Northern Ireland Addressed to the Chairman of the Preparatory Commission.

The delegation of the United Kingdom have noted the letter dated 6 April 1983 from the Chairman of the delegation of the Union of Soviet Socialist Republics addressed to the Preparatory Commission for the International Sea-bed Authority and for the International Tribunal for the Law of the Sea (LOS/PCN/4).

It is the view of the United Kingdom that it is in the interests of all States with deep sea mining interests that there should not be overlapping of exploration areas in the deep sea-bed. In the absence of generally agreed arrangements for eliminating any possible overlaps, and having regard to its contingent interest, the United Kingdom reserves its position on the matters contained in that letter.

I request that this letter be circulated as an official document of the Preparatory Commission.

(signed) Paul Fifoot
Leader of the United Kingdom delegation to the Preparatory Commission.

Following these exchanges the Indian note of 12 May indicated that coordinates had been exchanged with the Soviet Union, and both countries subsequently sought registration as pioneer investors:[33]

Note Verbale Dated 12 May 1983 from the Permanent Representative of India to the United Nations addressed to the Chairman of the Preparatory Commission

The Permanent Representative of India to the United Nations presents his compliments to the Chairman of the Preparatory Commission for the International Sea-bed Authority and for the International Tribunal for the Law of the Sea and, in continuation of his note of 24 April 1983 (LOS/PCN/7) and upon instructions received from the Government of India, has the honour to state as follows.

The representatives of the Union of Soviet Socialist Republics and India met in New Delhi on 29 and 30 April 1983 and ensured themselves that, since the USSR intends to apply to the Preparatory Commission for registration and allocation of a pioneer area in the

Pacific Ocean and India intends to apply to the Preparatory
Commission for registration and allocation of a pioneer area in the
central Indian Ocean, pursuant to the resolution governing preparatory
investment in pioneer activities relating to polymetallic nodules, the
areas in respect of which they intend to apply to the Preparatory
Commission do not overlap one another. There is thus no conflict or
controversy between the two countries in this regard . . . .

Letter dated 20 July 1983 from the Acting Permanent Representative of
the Union of Soviet Socialist Republics to the United Nations addressed
to the Chairman of the Preparatory Commission[34]

. . . the Union of Soviet Socialist Republics, in accordance with
resolution II of the United Nations Conference on the Law of the Sea,
and as a certifying State, hereby submits to the Preparatory Commission
on behalf of the Soviet enterprise Southern Production Association for
Marine Geological Operations ('Yuzhmorgeologiya'), which is located
in the town of Gelendzhik in the Krasnadorskiy district, and the
General Director of which is Mr I. F. Glumov, an application for
registration of the enterprise as a pioneer investor.

It is certified that this Soviet enterprise expended, before 1 January
1983, 40.9 million roubles on pioneer activities, as defined in resolution
II, including 16 million roubles in the location, survey and evaluation
of the area in respect of which this application is submitted. It is also
certified that the list of coordinates of the area was submitted before 10
December 1982 by the Soviet enterprise concerned to the USSR Ministry
of Geology as the State body with responsibility for issuing licences.

In accordance with paragraph 3(a) of resolution II, the application
covers an area of the sea-bed 300,000 sq km having sufficient estimated
commercial value to allow two mining operations. The area has been
divided into two parts of equal estimated commercial value.

The data and information referred to in paragraph 3(a) of resolution
II are being transmitted to the Preparatory Commission in a sealed
packet in order to preserve their confidentiality as annex 1 to this
application (5 maps)

The coordinates of the area, because of their strict confidentiality, are
being kept by the Permanent Representative of the USSR to the United
Nations in a sealed packet which will be transmitted immediately to the
Preparatory Commission at your request as annex 2 to the application.

MEMORANDUM

A memorandum is essentially a detailed statement of facts and related
arguments. It resembles a note, but is stylistically far freer, has no
opening or closing formalities and need not be signed. It may have a

security classification and for convenience is often delivered with a covering letter, as in the following example:[35]

Letter dated 13 July 1981 from the representative of China to the
Secretary-General
(Original: Chinese/English)
(14 July 1981)

I have the honour to transmit herewith the text of a memorandum of the Ministry of Foreign Affairs of the People's Republic of China on Sino-Vietnamese relations and request that this be circulated as an official document of the General Assembly and of the Security Council.

(signed) Ling Qing
Permanent Representative of the People's Republic of China to the United Nations

Annex

Memorandum of the Ministry of Foreign Affairs of the People's Republic of China of 13 July 1981 on Sino-Vietnamese Relations.

For some time the Vietnamese authorities have fabricated numerous lies and made unbridled slanderous attacks on China attributing to China the cause of the seriously deteriorated Sino-Vietnamese relations and of the turbulence in Indo-China and South-East Asia, in an attempt to confuse the right and wrong and cover up their acts of aggression and expansion so as to invent excuses for their intensified pursuance of the policy of regional hegemonism. Therefore, the Chinese side deems it necessary to state the truth of the matter in order to set the record straight.

I. Why Sino-Vietnamese Relations Continue to Deteriorate

Since the end of Viet Nam's war of resistance against United States aggression, the Vietnamese authorities have taken a whole series of measures to worsen Sino-Vietnamese relations. At present, they are stepping up these anti-China activities. Their professed willingness to improve Sino-Vietnamese relations is a sheer (sic.) gesture meant to deceive people . . . .

II. The Root Cause of Tension in Indo-China lies in the Vietnamese Authorities' Attempt to Seek Regional Hegemony

The Vietnamese authorities assert that the present tension in Indo-China is caused by the so-called 'Chinese ambitions' rather than the policies of aggression and expansion they have pursued with the support of the Soviet Union. They even try to make people believe that the invasion and occupation of Kampuchea by 200,000 Vietnamese troops is for the purpose of dealing with the 'China threat'. However, the deeds of the Vietnamese authorities have provided an explicit answer as to who has single-handedly created turbulence and disaster in this region.

After the unification of Viet Nam in 1976, the Vietnamese authorities went ahead with an ambitious plan in an attempt to establish their hegemonist rule in Indo-China. After it succeeded in gradually bringing Laos under its total control, Viet Nam launched a large-scale war of aggression at the end of 1978, and occupied large parts of the Kampuchean territory and its capital Phnom Penh. At present, there are 50,000–60,000 Vietnamese troops and nearly 10,000 Vietnamese experts, advisers and secret police in Laos, controlling Laos' military, political economic, cultural, propaganda and external affairs . . . .

Modern usage of memoranda is very wide. For example, during the Iranian hostage crisis, the response of the United States Government of 8 November 1980 to the Iranian conditions set for the release of the US diplomatic hostages was delivered to the Iranian authorities by Algeria under a memorandum of 12 November 1980.[36] In 1970, Chancellor Willy Brandt and the GDR's Chairman of the Council of Ministers, Willy Stoph, held two historic meetings, first at Erfurt in March and then in Kassel. Following the Kassel meeting, Chancellor Brandt's twenty-point programme on the normalisation of inter-German relations, was set out in a document which became known as the 'Kassel Memorandum'.[37]

The following illustrations indicate some further contexts within which memoranda have been used. In the first example, the Soviet Union delivered a memorandum to Japan on 27 January 1960, after the conclusion of the United States–Japanese Treaty of Mutual Co-operation and Security. The memorandum was a mixture of protest, warning and a statement of policy on the disputed northern islands:[38]

Memorandum from the Soviet Union to Japan, 27 January 1960

A so-called 'Treaty of Mutual Co-operation and Security' was signed between Japan and the United States on 19 January, this year. The contents of this treaty seriously affect the situation in the Far East and in the area of the Pacific, and therefore the interests of many states situated in that vast region, above all, of course, such direct neighbours of Japan as the Soviet Union and the Chinese People's Republic.

Under this treaty the stay of foreign troops and the presence of war bases on Japanese territory are again sanctioned for a long period with the voluntary consent of the Japanese Government. Article 6 of this treaty grants the United States 'use by its ground, air and naval forces of facilities and areas in Japan'. The treaty's reservations regarding consultations on its fulfilment cannot conceal the fact that Japan may be drawn into a military conflict against the will of the Japanese people.

The treaty perpetuates the actual occupation of Japan, places her territory at the disposal of a foreign power and alienates from Japan the islands of Okinawa and Bonin, and its provisions inevitably lead to the military, economic and political subordination of Japan . . . .

The Soviet Government has repeatedly drawn the Japanese Government's attention to the danger of every step in international policy that increases the threat of a new war. It is obvious that at present there are particularly weighty grounds for such a warning. The conclusion of the military treaty by no means adds to Japan's security. On the contrary, it increases the danger of a catastrophe which would be the inevitable result of Japan becoming involved in a new war.

Is it not clear to everyone today that in conditions of a modern rocket-nuclear war the whole of Japan, with her small and densely populated territory, dotted, moreover, with foreign war bases, risks sharing the tragic fate of Hiroshima and Nagasaki in the very first minutes of hostilities? ...

Considering, however, that the new military treaty signed by the Government of Japan is directed against the Soviet Union, and also against the Chinese People's Republic, the Soviet Government cannot allow itself to contribute to an extension of the territory used by foreign armed forces by handing the aforesaid islands over to Japan.

In view of this, the Soviet Government considers it necessary to state that the islands of Habomai and Shikotan will be turned over to Japan, as envisaged in the joint declaration of the USSR and Japan of 19 October 1956 only on condition that all foreign troops are withdrawn from the territory of Japan and that a peace treaty is concluded between the USSR and Japan.

A common use of memoranda is in disputes to support a claim,[39] or establish a case, as in the Sino-Vietnamese example cited earlier. A particular line of policy of interpretation can be similarly set out to another government or organisation in a memorandum. During the Congolese Civil War, for example, the UN Secretary-General Dag Hammarskjöld issued a unilateral declaration of interpretation, in the form of a memorandum, on the controversial question of the nature and scope of the role of the UN peacekeeping force in the Congo and its relations with the central and provincial governments:[40]

Statement by Mr Hammarskjöld on the interpretation of paragraph four of the Security Council resolution of 9 August, 12 August 1960

The Secretary-General, with reference to the Security Council resolution of 9 August 1960 (S/4426), has the honour to inform the Council of the interpretation which he has given to the Central Government of the Republic of the Congo, as well as to the provincial government of Katanga, of operative paragraph 4 of the resolution.

Memorandum on Implementation of the Security Council Resolution of 9 August 1960, Operative Paragraph 4

1. Operative paragraph 4 of the resolution of the Security Council of 9 August reads: '*Re-affirms* that the United Nations Force in the Congo

will not be a party to or in any way intervene in or be used to influence the outcome of any internal conflict, constitutional or otherwise'. The paragraph has to be read together with operative paragraph 3, which reads: '*Declares* that the entry of the United Nations Force into the Province of Katanga is necessary for the full implementation of this resolution'.

2. Guidance for the interpretation of operative paragraph 4 can be found in the attitudes upheld by the Security Council in previous cases where elements of an external nature and elements of an internal nature have been mixed. The stand of the Security Council in those cases has been consistent. It most clearly emerges from the policy maintained in the case of Lebanon which, therefore, will be analysed here in the first instance.

3. In the Lebanese question, as considered by the Security Council in the summer of 1958, there was a conflict between the constitutional President Mr. Chamoun, and a group of insurgents, among them Mr Karame, later Prime Minister of the Republic. The Government called for United Nations assistance, alleging that a rebellion was fomented from abroad and supported actively by the introduction of volunteers and arms across the border . . . .

8. Applying the line pursued by the Security Council in the Lebanese case to the interpretation of operative paragraph 4, it follows that the United Nations Force cannot be used on behalf of the Central Government to subdue or to force the Provincial government to a specific line of action. It further follows that United Nations facilities cannot be used, for example, to transport civilian or military representatives, under the authority of the Central Government, to Katanga against the decision of the Katanga provincial government. It further follows that the United Nations Force has no duty, or right, to protect civilian or military personnel representing the Central Government, arriving in Katanga, beyond what follows from its general duty to maintain law and order. It finally follows that the United Nations, naturally, on the other hand, has no right to forbid the Central Government to take any action which by its own means, in accordance with the purposes and principles of the Charter, it can carry through in relation to Katanga. All these conclusions necessarily apply, *mutatis mutandis*, as regards the provincial government in its relations with the Central Government.

9. The policy line stated here, in interpretation of operative paragraph 4, represents a unilateral declaration of interpretation by the Secretary-General. It can be contested before the Security Council. And it can be changed by the Security Council through an explanation of its intentions in the resolution of 9 August. The finding is not subject to agreement or negotiation . . . .

A further illustration of the use of a memorandum is the Finnish Government's proposal for the convening of a European security conference which was put to Western and other governments in its memorandum of 5 May 1969:[41] (extracts)

Memorandum from the Finnish Government on the Convening of a
European Security Conference, 5 May 1969

The Government of the Soviet Union approached recently the
governments of European countries in the matter of the arrangement of
a European security conference and of its preparations. This proposal
concerning a special preparatory meeting was extended to the
Government of Finland on 8 April 1969.

The Government of Finland has on several occasions stated that
Finland considers a well prepared conference on European security
problems useful. The Government of Finland considers well-founded
the view of the Soviet Union that such a conference should be convened
without any preliminary conditions. The participants should have the
right to present their views and to make their proposals on European
questions . . . .

At the Foreign Ministers' meeting of Finland, Denmark, Iceland,
Norway and Sweden, held in Copenhagen on 23 and 24 April 1969, a
joint position was defined according to which 'preconditions for
conferences on security problems are that they should be well prepared,
that they should be timed so as to offer prospects of positive results, and
that all States, whose participation is necessary for achieving a solution
to European security problems, should be given opportunities to take
part in the discussions . . . .'

This is why the Government of Finland considers that the
preparations for the conference should begin through consultations
between the governments concerned and, after the necessary conditions
exist, a preparatory meeting for consideration of the questions
connected with the arrangement of the conference could be
convened . . . .

The Government of Finland is willing to act as the host for the
security conference as well as for the preparatory meeting provided that
the governments concerned consider this as appropriate.

The Government of Finland will send this memorandum to the
Governments of all European States, to those of East and West
Germany and to the Governments of the United States of America and
Canada . . . .

Finally, memoranda are frequently used in connection with
treaties. In this usage the memorandum is to present to the other party
a particular interpretation or understanding of a clause or section of
the agreement. The memorandum may become the subject of a later
exchange of letters. An interesting illustration of memoranda used in
this way are the memoranda of the United Kingdom and the People's
Republic of China, contained in the Draft Agreement on the Future
of Hong Kong. The two memoranda set out the quite different
interpretation each of the parties gives to the definition and meaning
of Hong Kong citizenship contained in the agreement.[42]

AIDE-MÉMOIRE

The *aide-mémoire* is used widely and like a memorandum is extremely versatile in terms of the contexts within which it can be used. It is rather less formal, however, than a memorandum. In essence an *aide-mémoire* is drafted on the basis of discussions which have been held and is used to put forward new proposals such as a visit, conference, trade fair, an interpretation of policy or provide new information. Extracts from the following three examples taken from United States practice indicate the wide variety of contexts in which an *aide-mémoire* can be used. The first example is from the United States dispute with Algeria over diplomatic property. The United States had acquired the property in 1948 and after Algerian independence carried out development work in 1962 on the site in order to build a new embassy. However, United States Embassy staff were subsequently refused entry to the site by the Algerian authorities. Later negotiations for an exchange of property for the Villa Mustapha Rais were inconclusive. In an *aide-mémoire* of 13 April 1979, the Department of State referred to discussions with the Political Counsellor of the Algerian Embassy, the essence of which was to link progress on the Algerian request for new chancery space in the International Centre in Washington to the United States claim regarding the Villa Mustapha Rais. The *aide-mémoire* in part reads:[43] 'The Department of State wishes to be responsive to the desire of the Algerian Embassy to obtain a suitable site for a new Chancery. At the same time, settlement of the United States claim, which dates from November 1964, remains a pressing concern of the United States Government.'

In the second example, Venezuela delivered an *aide-mémoire* to the United States on the question of US sugar imports from the Dominican Republic:[44]

Venezuelan *aide-mémoire* to the United States, 26 September 1960

The Government of Venezuela has learned with surprise and great concern of the recent decision taken by the Government of the United States for acquiring 321,000 tons extra of sugar from the Dominican Republic.

The Embassy of Venezuela, in compliance with instructions from its Government, wishes to make known to the Department of State the unfavourable repercussions that this decision has caused in the political circles of the country, that is complicating its present political situation and that undoubtedly will extend to all the continent, in the moment in which there is required greater understanding and solidarity to defend the unity of the Americas.

The Government of Venezuela considers that this decision of the Government of the United States impairs that which was agreed in the Sixth Meeting of the American Foreign Ministers which recently took place in San José, Costa Rica, and disorients the continental public opinion with respect to the collective efforts that should be carried out in order to maintain the prestige and the solidarity of the inter-American system.

Upon expressing these sentiments of its Government, the Embassy of Venezuela would appreciate receiving the assurances of the Government of the United States to the effect that it will continue, within its constitutional and legal powers, its efforts toward modifying the present situation, thus also to achieve the collective application of effective economic sanctions for the objective of complying with that which was decided in the Foreign Ministers' meeting above referred to.

The United States replied in an *aide-mémoire* of 30 September:[45]

The Department of State refers to the Embassy's *Aide Mémoire* of 26 September 1960, expressing the concern of the Government of Venezuela on learning 'of the recent decision taken by the Government of the United States to acquire three hundred and twenty-one thousand extra tons of sugar from the Dominican Republic'.

It is believed that the concern of the Venezuelan Government derives from a misunderstanding of the nature of the action taken. When the Congress of the United States, in July 1960, modified the existing sugar legislation to authorize the President to reduce imports from Cuba it specifically provided that any resulting deficit in imports should be made up by authorization to purchase sugar from other producing countries including the Dominican Republic, in accordance with a detailed formula made obligatory by the law. The President allocated the required increase in quota to the Dominican Republic but delayed authorizing such purchases. In the light of the events which led up to the Sixth Meeting of Foreign Ministers at San José in August of this year and the results of that meeting the President asked the Congress to change the law and grant discretionary authority with respect to authorization for such purchases from the Dominican Republic. The Congress, however, adjourned without action on this request.

The debate in the Congress regarding the proposed revision of the legislation received widespread publicity and it was believed therefore that knowledge of the existing legislation was adequate throughout the American republics, when, following the failure of Congress to provide relief, the President was unable to delay further the implementation of the law as regards authorization for such purchases.

On taking this action, the President observed the spirit of the Sixth Meeting of Foreign Ministers within his existing authority, by imposing a fee of two cents per pound on purchases of sugar from the Dominican Republic, which purchases the law required to be authorized. ...

In 1976 Canada purchased eighteen long-range patrol aircraft from the Lockheed Corporation of the United States. Shortly before the purchase, the United States Government in an *aide-mémoire* to Canada of 29 April 1976, gave certain undertakings in the event of Lockheed insolvency, that Canada would receive advantage and considerations no less favourable than would the United States. The *aide-mémoire* also contained the US view regarding mutual security interests involved in Canadian acquisition of a modern long-range patrol capability:[46]

> With respect to Lockheed's overall financial viability, its ability to continue as a corporation and to fulfill the terms of its proposed contract with the Canadian Government, the United States Emergency Loan Guarantee Board (ELGB) and the United States Department of Defense have recently reviewed Lockheed's financial position and have expressed confidence in Lockheed's prospects . . . .
> The United States Government shares with the Canadian Government a strong interest in the successful completion of the proposed Canadian procurement of eighteen Lockheed LRPA aircraft. In the view of the United States Government, the acquisition of these aircraft will substantially enhance Canada's ASW patrol capability, improve North American defense arrangements, contribute to NATO's overall security and thus is in the best interest of the United States. The proposed Canadian purchase will complement the purchase of a large number of Lockheed maritime patrol aircraft planned by the United States Government and should work to the mutual advantage of the two Governments . . . .
> If a situation were to occur under US bankruptcy laws involving voluntary or involuntary reorganization or bankruptcy of Lockheed which might affect Lockheed's contract performance, the United States Government, recognizing that it is in its best interest to do so, will act with Canada in all matters relating to the Canadian LRPA contract to obtain for Canada advantages and considerations no less favorable than those that might be obtained by the United States with respect to performance of its own defense procurement contracts . . . .

SUMMARY

Of the main means of diplomatic correspondence – notes, letters, memoranda and *aides-mémoire* – the note (*note verbale*) is probably the most formal despite the range of subject-matter it is used for. Exchanges of letters between heads of government have become an important element in the conduct of personal diplomacy. Written communication, in fact, whatever its form, is, despite developments in other forms of communication, still central to diplomacy. It is the means by which states put their position on record, explain the details of their policies, record protests, support claims, seek collective approval and carry out many other actions which make up the business of international relations.

REFERENCES AND NOTES

1. Correspondence about the future of Germany, 10–25 March 1952, Cmd. 8501, March 1952. Reprinted by permission of the Controller of Her Majesty's Stationery Office.
2. Ibid., pp. 4–5.
3. Coral Bell, *Negotiations from Strength: A Study in the Politics of Power* (Chatto and Windus, London, 1962) p. 99.
4. Nuclear Test Cases, Vol. II, *New Zealand v. France*, ICJ, Pleadings, Oral Arguments, Documents, Annex III, p. 13, contains the list of notes exchanged. ·
5. Ibid., pp. 14–16.
6. Ibid., Annex IV, pp. 40–1.
7. *Documents on International Affairs 1960* (Oxford University Press, London, 1964) p. 492.
8. Case concerning the continental shelf, *Tunisia v. Libyan Arab Jamahiriya*, ICJ, Pleadings, Oral Arguments, Documents. Vol. 1, pp. 21–6.
9. Ibid., Annex 33, p. 260.
10. *Department of State Bulletin*, 23 May 1960, p. 818.
11. *Soviet News*, 11 May 1960.
12. *Department of State Bulletin*, 30 May 1960, p. 852.
13. See letter 13 Aug. 1981, from the representative of Cyprus to the Secretary-General, SCOR, 36th year, Supplement for July, Aug., Sept., S/14630, New York, 1983, pp. 40–1.
14. Ibid., S/14694, p. 76.
15. Ibid., S/14632, pp. 41–2.
16. This may take the form of an authorised statement. See for example Carlos Romulo's statement outlining the ASEAN position on Kampuchea, including the need for Vietnamese troop withdrawal and a UN-sponsored international conference, in SCOR, 36th year, S/14386, p. 51. The Vietnamese position, rejecting an international conference in favour of regional dialogue and consultation can be found in the collective letter of Laos, People's Republic of Kampuchea, and Vietnam, of 19 May 1981, in *Communist Affairs: Documents and Analysis*, No. 1 (Jan. 1982) pp. 134–5.
17. SCOR, 36th year, S/14384, pp. 49–50, and S/14362, pp. 35–6 for background information.
18. C. C. Schweitzer, D. Carsten, R. T. Cole, D. P. Kommers and A. J. Nicholls, *Politics and Government in the Federal Republic of Germany Basic Documents* (Berg Publishers, Leamington Spa, 1984) p. 305.

19. Gareth Porter, *A Peace Denied: The US, Vietnam and the Paris Agreement* (Indiana University Press, Bloomington, Ind., 1975) p. 74.
20. See for example Mr Macmillan's appeal for restraint to Mr Khrushchev in his letter of 19 July 1960, following East-West difficulties in the Committee of Ten on Disarmament, the second 'U-2' crisis and the Congo Civil War: 'I write to you now so plainly because I have the memory of our frank discussions with you in my mind. I simply do not understand what your purpose is today. If the present trend of events in the world continues, we may all of us one day, either by miscalculation or mischance, find ourselves caught up in a situation from which we cannot escape. I would ask you, therefore, to consider what I have said and to believe that I am writing to you like this because I feel it my duty to do so'. *Hansard,* Vol. 627, Col. 253-6.
21. *The Sunday Times,* 16 Dec. 1984.
22. Edward Weintal and Charles Bartlett, *Facing the Brink* (Charles Scribner's Sons, New York, 1967) pp. 23-4.
23. Ibid., p. 24.
24. See Chihiro Hosoya, 'Japan, China, the United States and United Kingdom, 1951-2, The Case of the "Yoshida Letter" ', *International Affairs,* Vol. 60, No. 2 (Spring 1984) pp. 256-7.
25. See U Thant, *View from the UN* (David and Charles, London, 1977) Appendix I, pp. 466-7.
26. SCOR, 36th year, S/14693, p. 76.
27. LOS/PCN/4, 8 April 1983.
28. LOS/PCN/12, 29 April 1983.
29. LOS/PCN/15, 29 April 1983.
30. LOS/PCN/17, 29 April 1983.
31. LOS/PCN/13, 29 April 1983.
32. LOS/PCN/20, 12 May 1983.
33. LOS/PCN/21, 13 May 1983.
34. LOS/PCN/30, 24 Oct. 1983.
35. SCOR, 36th year, Supplement for July, Aug., Sept. 1981, S/14589, pp. 14-17. The Vietnamese reply is at S/14610, 22 July 1981, p. 28.
36. Pars News Agency, Tehran, 21 Dec. 1980.
37. Schweitzer et. al., op. cit., p. 381.
38. *Soviet News,* 29 Jan. 1960.
39. For example paragraph 3 of the Additional Memorandum of Morocco to the Secretary-General, of 14 Sept. 1960, on the dispute with France over Mauritania, states: 'The Notes which the Government of Morocco has dispatched since then, whenever France unilaterally changed the status of Mauritania, are eloquent in this connexion. They place the Moroccan territorial claim in clear perspective and deny to the Government of France any exercise of competence in respect of Mauritanian territory.' GAOR, Fifteenth Session, Agenda item 79, Doc. A/4445/Add. 1.
40. SCOR, 15th year, Supplement for July, Aug., Sept. 1960, S/4417/Add. 6, pp. 64-5, 70-1.
41. Finnish Embassy, London.
42. *A Draft Agreement on the Future of Hong Kong,* Misc., No. 20 1984, Cmnd. 9352, pp. 28-9.
43. *Digest of United States Practice in International Law, 1979* (Department of State, Washington, 1983) pp. 576-7.

44. *Department of State Bulletin*, 24 Oct. 1960, p. 641.
45. *Department of State Bulletin*, 24 Oct. 1960, pp. 640-1.
46. *Digest of United States Practice in International Law, 1976* (Department of State, Washington, 1977) pp. 746-8.

CHAPTER FIVE
Negotiation

INTRODUCTION

The aim of this chapter is to discuss both the nature of negotiation and the main characteristics of the negotiating process.

Negotiation can be defined as an attempt to explore and reconcile conflicting positions in order to reach an acceptable outcome. Whatever the nature of the outcome, which may actually favour one party more than another, the purpose of negotiation is the identification of areas of common interest and conflict.[1] In this sense, depending on the intentions of the parties, the areas of common interest may be clarified, refined and given negotiated form and substance. Areas of difference can and do frequently remain, and will perhaps be the subject of future negotiations, or indeed remain irreconcilable. In those instances in which the parties have highly antagonistic or polarised relations,[2] the process is likely to be dominated by the exposition, very often in public, of the areas of conflict. In these and sometimes other forms of negotiation, negotiation serves functions other than reconciling conflicting interests. These will include delay, publicity, diverting attention, or seeking intelligence about the other party and its negotiating position.[3]

The process of negotiation itself is sometimes conceived of in an 'across the table' sense. While the proceedings may take this form at some stage, the overall process, especially in a multilateral context, is better understood as including more informal activities leading up to or during negotiation, such as lobbying, floating a proposal through a draft resolution and exchanges of proposals and other consultations.[4] Negotiation too, of course, can be carried out 'at a distance', through formal or informal diplomatic correspondence, telephone or telex.[5] The mode of negotiation itself may also change during negotiations from an 'across the table' working session, to correspondence between the parties about certain principles or detailed provisions of an agreement. Changes in the mode of this kind and other similar tactical demands for recess during negotiation can have either positive or negative effects on the process of reaching agreement. Change to negotiation by written means may serve to expedite the negotiating process, particularly if major principles and matters of substance have been resolved, reflecting substantial convergence over areas of common interest. If, however, unresolved issues remain from perhaps earlier rounds of exchanges, the possibilities for reopening these, uncertainty over the concession rate and the opponent's intentions, together with the effect of the delay, become important intervening considerations.[6]

Before we consider in detail particular definitions of negotiation, one further general observation is useful at this point. So far negotiation has been discussed in terms of the purpose and some features of the process; a third significant area relates to the changing forms of agreement which have been developed in more recent state practice. An important feature of modern practice, discussed at the end of the chapter, is the growth in 'unconventional' forms of agreement, in response to the complexity of issue areas and trend to multiparty agreements involving sovereign and non-sovereign actors.

Of the analytical literature,[7] Fred C. Iklé's book, *How Nations Negotiate* has had an important impact on the study of negotiation. Iklé has avoided a broad definitional approach which subsumes negotiation within the notion of bargaining or communication.[8] Such broader conceptions have tended to ignore or obscure features of the negotiating process, such as agenda setting, and the impact of the negotiating process on outcomes, in that they have focused on the wider context or setting of certain types of politico-strategic negotiation, involving warnings, threats and the use of coercive diplomacy.

In contrast, Iklé defines negotiations explicitly in terms of an exchange of proposals:[9]

> negotiation is a process in which explicit proposals are put forward ostensibly for the purpose of reaching agreement on an exchange or on the realisation of a common interest where conflicting interests are

present. It is the confrontation of explicit proposals that distinguishes negotiation from tacit bargaining and other forms of conflict behaviour.

CLASSIFICATION

A valuable aspect of *How Nations Negotiate* is the fivefold classification of international negotiation according to the purpose of the parties.[10] In the first of these, *extension* agreements (e.g. aviation landing rights, tariff agreements, renewal of a peacekeeping force mandate, renewal of leasing arrangements for an overseas military base), the purpose is to continue the existing state of affairs, and, as such, extension agreements are frequently, though not always, routine in nature. *Normalisation* agreements are intended to bring to an end conflict through, for example, cease-fire arrangements, a peace treaty or the re-establishment of diplomatic relations. Negotiations for the purpose of normalisation may involve a substantial degree of *redistribution* – the third category of negotiation. In a redistribution negotiation changes in the status quo or existing arrangements are sought in relation to, for example, territorial boundaries, voting powers in an international institution, budgetary contributions and similar matters. The fourth category is the *innovative* agreement. In negotiations on an innovative agreement the parties seek to establish different sets of obligations or relationships by transferring some degree of political and legal power to non-state institutions, as in the Treaty of Rome; devising new regulatory institutions such as the International Sea-bed Authority[11] or cooperative institutions as in the Mano River Declaration.[12] The Sino-British agreement of 1984 on the future of Hong Kong provides an interesting example of a normalisation and innovative agreement, setting out the status and powers of Hong Kong after it becomes a Special Administrative Region of the People's Republic of China in 1997.[13]

In the final category are negotiations for *side-effects*. In this type of negotiation one or more of the parties may seek objectives not directly related to reaching agreement. These can include putting on record statements of position, propaganda, gaining information about the negotiating position, strengths and weaknesses of the other party or undermining the resolve of an opponent.

The above categories provide a useful basic classification of negotiations, which can also be used to review changes in relations between states. The categories of course represent ideal types and in practice negotiations are often 'mixed' in character,[14] containing elements of pure bargaining,[15] normalisation and redistribution, because of factors such as the scope of the subject-matter or the extent of the differences between the parties. It is possible too for a party to misperceive or miscalculate the other's intention, regarding the negotiations, for example, as extension rather than redistribution.[16] Furthermore, in protracted and complex negotiations a party may change its strategy during the course of the negotiation from one of 'optimising' or seeking a high level of concessions to one of 'satisficing' in which more workable or less dramatic achievements are accepted, thus altering the form of the negotiation.[17]

While the basic fivefold classification scheme encompasses many types of negotiation, others are not so easily accommodated. These include: negotiations on communiques ('textual', interpretative, ideological); inward or outward ministerial visits (bidding on dates, venues, agenda and matters of protocol); and draft articles in a working group of a multilateral conference (interpretative, with negotiations focusing on particular meanings, formulae and concepts). In addition, 'linked' negotiations have become a feature of bilateral negotiations between industrialised and developing countries in which the successful conclusion of one issue may be related to an entirely different political or economic issue. For example the government purchase of an item such as a naval vessel may be linked to changes in an air service agreement.

The basic scheme of classification discussed above can be complemented by considering negotiation in terms of the subject-matter. The indicative categories illustrating the range of modern negotiation are given in Table 5.1.

INFLUENCES SHAPING NEGOTIATIONS

Broadly, three clusters of variables can be distinguished: the negotiating environment or setting, available assets and contingent variables. The first category – the setting – includes such factors as the location of the talks,[18] whether the negotiations are bilateral or multilateral; the extent to which the parties have regularised or

Table 5.1 Classification of subjects handled in international negotiations

Subject	Illustration
1 Political	Communiques; draft resolutions; extradition; cultural agreement; boundary changes; exchanges of POWs; air highjacking; establishment of diplomatic relations; mediation; improvement or normalisation of relations
2 Development	Loan; bilateral aid (personnel, equipment); project finance, international capital market borrowing; inward investment; capital transfer; debt rescheduling
3 Contractual	Offshore exploration rights; sale/purchase of oil, LNG; equipment purchases; hiring of foreign personnel
4 Economic	Trade agreement; balance of payments standby facility; tariff; anti-dumping; textile quota agreement; trade redistribution negotiation; sanctions
5 Security	Transit; overflight; establishment of border commission; arms purchase; bilateral security pact; joint development of weapons; mandate of peacekeeping force; base agreement; arms control
6 Regulatory	Convention against the use of mercenaries; law of the sea; flags of convenience; air services; fisheries; environmental; GATT; international commodity agreement; shipping; health; narcotics
7 Administrative	Inward/outward visit; acquisition of land or buildings for embassy; opening trade mission; visa abolition agreement; consular access to detained nationals; headquarters agreement; closure of international or regional organisation

friendly contact;[19] the amount of domestic support and the degree of directly or indirectly related international tension. The setting can influence:

1. The procedural conduct of negotiations as a result of the establishment of several working groups in a multilateral conference[20] or through institutional competence, such as the European Economic Community (EEC) Commission's responsibility for third-party fisheries agreements.[21]
2. The scope of negotiations (e.g. working out the terms of reference of a peacekeeping force).[22]
3. The content of a summit conference agenda.[23] Again, a mediator can attempt to structure a negotiation by putting forward

proposals for an agenda, interpreting or articulating differences, as well as attempting to alter the pace of negotiation.[24]

A further effect of setting can be seen in the long-running conferences of the United Nations Conference on Trade and Development (UNCTAD) in which decision-making became protracted because of extensive formal statements of position in plenaries and the procedure of agreeing bloc or regional positions during the substantive sessions of the conference, which then had to be tabled to opposing blocs or groups.[25]

Second, there are those variables associated with the capabilities of the negotiating parties, such as the number and skill of diplomatic personnel,[26] the range of specialist expertise, proximity of negotiators to central power and the capacity to control the communications process in conflict.[27] Of these, negotiating style – that is, the characteristic ways in which national and international decision-makers approach negotiation as a result of such influences as tradition, culture, bureaucratic organisation and perceptions of role – has received considerable attention. A number of studies have highlighted characteristics such as legalism,[28] attachment to declaration of principles, inflexibility[29] and crudeness.[30] In one case, the remarkable combination of meticulous deliberation and 'true grit' is seen as the hallmark of one particular national style.[31] A further, and indeed crucial component of negotiating capability is the range of deployable assets. These will include the extent of domestic approval, the nature and range of effective means, trade-off possibilities and the degree of external support.

The third category – contingent variables – consists first of all of such factors as the internal politics connected with the development and attainment of negotiating positions. Other contingent variables include the cohesion of a government or its delegation, how far 'opening' positions are re-evaluated, the concession rate, the impact of feedback and the influence of external events, such as a change of government, border clash or other incidents.[32]

THE PROCESS OF NEGOTIATION

Basic model

A basic model by which bilateral and some multilateral negotiation can be conceptualised is one in which the negotiations are seen as being a progression, in which the parties agree an agenda, outline and explore opening positions and seek compromises in order to narrow gaps between positions until a point of convergence is reached, which forms the basis for substantive agreement.[33] The model may be put schematically as follows:

1. Preparatory phase. (i) Preparation of national position; (ii) agree venue; (iii) outline agenda approved; (iv) level at which talks are to be conducted.
2. Opening phase (procedural). (i) Confirm credentials of the parties; (ii) re-establish purpose and status of the talks (e.g. whether they are informal or preliminary discussions, formal talks or whether any follow-up talks are envisaged and at what venue; (iii) working documentation; (iv) working procedures:
    (a) recess (if any);
    (b) language to be used.
    (c) rules of procedure;
    (d) agree which text or draft (if any) will be used as the basis for negotiation;
    (e) whether there is to be an agreed record.
3. Opening phase (substantive). (i) confirm or amend agenda; (ii) exposition of opening position.
4. Substantive negotiation. (i) Exploration of areas of difference; (ii) construction of areas of agreement.
5. Adjournment of the negotiation for further rounds of talks (if appropriate).
6. Framework agreement reached.
7. Legal clearance and residual drafting amendments.
8. Initialling or signature of final agreement.
9. Statement on proceedings or communique.

Process

The preparatory and initial phases of a negotiation can take some considerable time. Thus matters such as the choice of the parties to be invited, for example the participation of the Vietminh at the 1954 Geneva Conference,[34] the National Liberation Front (NLF) in the 1968 Vietnam talks[35] and the Palestine Liberation Organisation (PLO) in the proposed Geneva Middle East talks,[36] can be very contentious – so too can the content of the agenda[37] and even the shape of the negotiating table[38] become major obstacles to substantive progress in the initial phases of negotiation.

As far as procedural issues are concerned, the extent to which these may be dispensed with as routine or become contentious issues, depends very much on the closeness in the relations between the parties, the organisational setting and the kind of issues involved.[39] The early stages of the SALT I negotiations were taken up with the not uncommon problem of the ordering of items for discussion. In this case difficulties arose over whether to deal with an anti-ballistic missile (ABM) treaty first before moving on to offensive systems, or treat these in parallel.[40]

At the substantive phase, the negotiating process can take one of a number of forms. In 'polarised' negotiations, the process, as noted earlier, tends to be characterised by lengthy initial phases which involve exposition of positions and issues of principle.[41] In other forms of negotiation the progression can be conceptualised as one in which the parties move from opening positions, to seek compromises, narrow gaps between positions until a point of convergence is reached on an item or issue, which then forms the basis for the expansion of areas of agreement. This type of process might be incremental, or, less commonly, 'linear'. The latter form of progression is found for example in certain kinds of multilateral trade negotiations in which, ideally, a generally agreed 'across the board' tariff reduction is negotiated, so reducing the need for bilateral haggling. In practice, the 'linear' approach of the Kennedy Round was rapidly broken down as states attached lists of exceptions to their offers of tariff reduction.[42] A further illustration of the 'linear' approach can be found in the negotiating methods used by officials in the Committee on Trade and Tourism of ASEAN, which has progressively made percentage cuts or zero-rated categories of goods traded within ASEAN.[43]

Typically, the incremental process will involve attempts to narrow differences using one of a number of methods, such as establishing generally agreed principles; moving through an agenda by leaving areas which are sticking points on to other items upon which progress can be made; or trade-offs around blocs of concessions.[44]

A second element frequently involves the search for *referents*. These might include attempting to gain agreement for special rights such as access, transit or landing rights, compensation or a pricing and specification formula in an international weapons supply contract. Other forms of referents may be of a conceptual nature such as the search to establish an agreed strategic 'language' in an arms control negotiation or mutually agreed conceptions of 'cost'. The search for and construction of referents forms a central part in negotiations of an incremental type. Without these negotiations tend to become bogged down or protracted. This type of difficulty can be seen for example in a number of international civil aviation renegotiations in which one of the parties attempts to revise route structures and schedules, but fails in the negotiations to reach mutually agreed definitions of cost.

Apart from these types, the substantive phase of certain bilateral or multilateral negotiations might be quite informal. Not all the phases outlined above would be gone through. Negotiators might confine themselves to broad general issues and leave details to a later date for officials to bargain over and clarify. Informal negotiations may also occur at the margins of *other* negotiations, particularly in regional organisations, for example the European Community which perhaps may be addressing different issues. Furthermore, informal negotiations might lead to an agreement for example to adjust foreign or domestic policies (such as to intervene in currency markets or to apply drug laws more rigorously) in which nothing appears on paper. In these instances, the use of informal negotiations depends on the relations between the parties, the type of issue under discussion and other reasons such as the wish of the parties to retain some degree of flexibility and freedom of action.

COMPLEX MULTILATERAL DIPLOMACY

In a second type of negotiating process – complex multilateral diplomacy – the concepts outlined in the 'convergence' model of negotiations do not adequately explain contemporary multilateral negotiations such as UNCTAD or UNCLOS. In both cases the proceedings of the conferences are distinguished by the innovative objectives and considerable structural uncertainty over the form possible outcomes might take.[45] An important feature of multilateral diplomacy of this type is the effort to establish and construct a package from the 'bottom up'.[46] In addition, structural complexity tends to be handled in a number of different ways such as altering the level of responsibility in order to achieve a different perspective as well as flexibility (e.g., by changing the level of representative in a negotiation), frequent redefinition of the problem and the use of innovative negotiating structures.

Three further features of the process of building up acceptable packages in multilateral negotiations are worth commenting on. In the first place, the diffusion of political power means that a number of states are able to wield a greater amount of influence than they normally would outside the context of such conferences. For example at the Law of the Sea Conference, Malta, Fiji, Cameroon, Peru and Venezuela have, through the skill and expertise of their individual representatives, played highly active roles.

For some states that influence may last only as long as their special area of interest remains unresolved; others, perhaps because of the chairmanship of a committee, specialist knowledge or skill in breaking deadlock, manage to play a consistently more important role on major issues. Minor powers like these have the capacity to block, delay or facilitate compromise like others, yet they have the advantage of far fewer domestic constraints. For larger powers constraints could stem, for example, from a large and divided delegation, pressure from a domestic 'constituency' or the need to appear frequently constructive. The representatives of minor states frequently enjoy a great deal of delegated power; in contrast, for the major powers the intervention in negotiation of a minister or senior adviser is not always appreciated by the technical negotiator, since the balance of initiative and decision shifts to the political élite.

The second principal feature of the process of constructing consensus is that it is disjointed and fragmented. Substantial areas of disagreement remain as efforts are made to trade blocs of issues or construct packages. In practice, there is considerable uncertainty as to the degree of support such efforts enjoy, since they are often made by the few or on a delegated basis, which then have to be presented and 'negotiated' as acceptable. During the process of structuring packages, issues tend to be postponed to a later date or partially resolved, pending an overall settlement. The protracted nature of the negotiating process often means that issues which are only partially resolved can be reopened, thus temporarily halting or reversing the progress which has already been achieved. Examples of this occurred at the seventh session of UNCLOS when the United States reopened the question of the regime for marine scientific research, and, within UNCTAD, when the major industrialised states reopened the question of the articles of agreement for the Common Commodity Fund.[47]

A third feature of multilateral conference diplomacy is the 'issue learning curve'. In complex innovative negotiation, negotiators progressively increase their knowledge of the issues at stake during the exploration of opposing positions and so gradually come to understand the ramifications of the problems as well as recognising potentially new dimensions for conflict or consensus-building.[48] The continued discovery of new facets of an issue presents negotiators with the opportunity to delay the search for agreements or maximize negotiating demands. A clear example of this phenomenon is provided by the negotiations on the issue of the regime for the international sea-bed which was probably the most complex and protracted issue at the UN Law of the Sea Conference. The construction of a regime for managing deep sea-bed resources brought together in a unique and novel manner an immense range of problem areas straddling private and public international law, involving such questions as the legal status of mining consortia, taxation, the rights of pioneer mining investors, the powers of the Global Mining Enterprise and the constitution of the Sea-bed Mining Council. The process of reaching consensus on the regime was complicated further by the format of the regime. Unlike some international agreements establishing institutions which set out a general framework for the powers and functions of an organisation, the sea-bed regime has quite detailed provisions on production rates, taxation and so on. In the event, the overall regime which began to emerge gained the support of developing countries within the Group of 77 (G-77), but not the United States or a number of other sea-bed mining states.

THE DYNAMIC OF NEGOTIATION

The dynamic aspects of negotiation can usefully be understood through three concepts: focal points, the concession rate and momentum. Focal points may take a number of forms such as the British Government's demand for a policy of balance over the European Community budget and a specific reduction in contributions; blocs of policy issues, as in, for example, European Community membership negotiations with Spain and Portugal, or particular assurances might be sought, as over the issue of guarantees on the political structure of Hong Kong after 1997, in the Sino-British talks on the future of the colony. As Iklé suggests:[49] 'focal points are like a notch where a compromise might come to a halt, or a barrier over which an initial position cannot be budged'.

Focal points therefore serve not only to reduce the options negotiators have to work within, but also act as a means of evaluating compromise. Secondly, the flow of negotiation will be influenced by the concession rate. In effect, the perceived extent to which a party makes a unilateral or reciprocal modification to its position serves to demonstrate *engagement* in or *commitment* to the negotiations. Concessions as such may be made either informally or formally. The possibility of a change of position can be indicated informally by modifications in negotiating style. In other instances a willingness to reach agreement may be signalled by not actually raising a sensitive item or by omitting it from conditions attached to a negotiating bid.[50] Formally, a concession may be indicated in several ways such as tabling a draft proposal, suggested modifications to an article in an agreement or contract or withdrawal of a proposal.

The overall concession *rate* can be considered as consisting of sub-clusters of concessions, the pace of which will be influenced by several variables, including the degree of latitude in a decision-maker's instructions, whether parts of an issue remain 'closed' or non-negotiable and the extent to which decision-makers are operating under time constraints or deadlines. In bilateral negotiations, concessions tend to be more easily identified, unlike in complex multilateral diplomacy where the number of parties and scale of issues, some of which are quite often novel, make the construction of areas of agreement difficult. In multilateral negotiation, two elements in the concession rate need to be distinguished. First, there are those attempts at working group level to reach negotiated solutions. Second, there are the initiatives by the secretariat or specifically designated conference chairmen to construct so-called 'packages', which link together broad areas of agreement or postpone partly resolved or contentious items. Another form of 'package' might entail a straight trade-off of concessions. The interplay between the low-level (working group) concessions rate and the construction of overarching packages is one of the main distinguishing features of complex multilateral diplomacy.

The third concept in terms of the dynamic of negotiation is the idea of momentum. Loss of momentum in negotiations may occur for several reasons such as the absence of a key negotiator, lack of movement on an issue or talks becoming bogged down in detail. Conversely, momentum may be sustained by regular negotiating sessions, the use of contact groups or third parties, as well as the concession rate discussed above.[51] Negotiators more rarely may seek to increase the momentum of negotiations by an ultimatum or setting a deadline. In the Sino-British talks on the future of Hong Kong, for example, the People's Republic of China set a deadline of 1 September 1984 for the conclusion of a framework agreement.

CHARACTERISTICS OF CERTAIN NEGOTIATIONS

The preceding sections of this chapter have looked at the negotiating process in general and some of the concepts which can be used to understand the processes of bilateral and multilateral negotiation. In the section on classification (Table 5.1) seven indicative categories were put forward as a way of grouping and reflecting the range of modern negotiation. Analysis of a number of negotiations in the categories would suggest that certain of the negotiations in the particular classes do have some broadly similar characteristics. In the first category, for example, negotiations on communiques tend to be 'textual' in nature, with limited scope for trade-off, since the drafting is normally in the concluding phases of the proceedings.[52] As such communiques are invariably negotiated under extreme time constraints, preferred positions tend to be either accepted or not, differences glossed to minimise public divergence and silence the norm on areas of major disagreement.

The effect of time constraints can be also seen in many other negotiations such as *ad hoc* law-making conferences, ministerial meetings of international organisations and multilateral conferences (category six), which have to be concluded by a specific date.[53] The closer to the conclusion of the conference the pace of negotiating (unless heavily polarised) tends to increase, with lengthy sessions and a not uncommon feeling of having to produce something – a joint statement, agreed text or conclude the outstanding provisions of an agreement (despite differences) – all of which may have varying effects on the degree of generality or precision of the terms of the agreement.

In category six, negotiations over regulatory agreements tend to be highly complex and structurally distinguished from other categories by mixed delegations of government and commercial interests, high degrees of direct or indirect non-governmental group lobbying and the relatively small number of core issue areas. Civil aviation negotiations (or more strictly renegotiations) tend to focus on one or two issues such as passenger capacity or new services. Agreements of the regulatory category are the least stable. Negotiations to change existing arrangements are normally lengthy, spanning several years of often inconclusive talks, as illustrated by Japan's unsuccessful efforts to revise the 1952 US–Japan Civil Air Transport Agreement from 1976.[54]

The international debt crisis has given rise to a new and unusual genre of financial 'rescue package' negotiations.[55] Debt rescheduling negotiations (category two) are multiparty negotiations involving heads of government, foreign and finance ministers, banking consortia, international banking officials and domestic economic, labour and banking interests in the rescheduling state.[56] In these types of negotiations, political and economic élites in the rescheduling state are likely to be highly divided over strategies and policies, as the negotiations are conducted against a backdrop of shifting constraints in the form of deadlines, target dates and coercive pressures arising from the problems of meeting conditions attached to the rescue package. The pressures surrounding the rescheduling state were summed up by one director of a ministry of finance:[57] 'I go to New York and start ringing at one in the morning. The first hour to India and Singapore, the next hour I spend ringing the Middle East and then Germany, then Paris, then London and so it goes on'.

In category three, contractual negotiations tend to be handled at a specialist level. Contractual negotiations are also, unlike many other negotiations under discussion, distinct in that there is much less frequent ministerial or senior official involvement owing to the technical nature of the discussions, unless there is a major impasse. Negotiated agreements are frequently less stable, with renegotiation disputes arising out of the failure of a contracting party to purchase, for example, less oil or gas than was agreed in a supply contract, or because price fluctuations in a commodity contract make the agreed pricing formula unattractive. The overall process of renegotiation can be quite lengthy, with the likelihood of adverse repercussions on other bilateral relations.[58]

DEVELOPMENTS IN INTERNATIONAL AGREEMENTS

A number of important developments have taken place in the form and nature of modern international agreements. In the first place the increasing diversity of participants in the international system has led to the growth of agreements not just between sovereign states, but between states and a wide range of other actors ranging from international organisations, corporations, international credit banks, to shipping consortia. Secondly, these changes have been reflected in the growing informality of instruments which are negotiated and in particular the growth in usage of memoranda of understanding. The trend is in part influenced by national style, as well as convenience, since agreements and arrangements of this type avoid the requirement of constitutional approval. This usage, too, sometimes reflects the short-term intentions of the parties or incomplete nature of the agreement. Informal agreements have also been negotiated by states which do not have diplomatic relations to cover such matters as trade or fisheries regulation. In a third sense, the inability of states to finalise precise terms or reach definitive agreements has been reflected in the ways in which obligations are formulated. In this respect a number of novel forms of clauses giving effect to incompletely negotiated obligations have been developed such as the so-called 'gentleman's agreement', barter or counter-trade agreements and voluntary or self-limitation clauses covering ceilings on motor vehicle exports or steel production. These types of agreements or schedules in agreements have the advantage of flexibility and are intended to expedite the process of negotiation. On the other hand, the lack of durability of such arrangements and their potential for causing dispute has often offset the short-term advantages.

REFERENCES AND NOTES

1. Fred Charles Iklé, *How Nations Negotiate* (Harper and Row, New York, 1964).
2. See for example Robert L. Rothstein in *Global Bargaining* (Princeton University Press, Princeton, NJ) p. 150 *passim* on the polarised position during the integrated commodity negotiations at UNCTAD.
3. Iklé, op.cit., p. 31.
4. In a strict sense consultations are distinct from negotiation, although in practice the line between the two is blurred. Writing in the context of GATT, though applicable generally, Kenneth W. Dam notes: 'Although the carrying on of negotiations is to be distinguished from consultations, it is not clear to what extent the two exercises are to differ', in *The GATT* (University of Chicago Press, Chicago, 1970) p. 85.
5. Diplomacy by correspondence has been extensively used as a technique in conflicts by UN secretaries-general. The Secretary-General, perhaps rather more than national decision-makers, faces limitations on the amount of information he receives. In the 1968 El Al hijacking crisis for example the Secretary-General was not informed of the initiatives being made by the Italian Government. See U Thant, *View from the UN* (David and Charles, London, 1978) pp. 302–8.
6. In the Franco-American dispute on the removal of American military bases from France in 1966 the United States felt compelled eventually to end the exchange of diplomatic notes and move to direct discussion. As one American official put it: 'We don't advance anything by making

debating points in diplomatic notes'. Cited in Arie E. David, *The Strategy of Treaty Termination. Law Breaches and Retaliation* (Yale University Press, London, 1975) p. 121.

7. A review of this literature including labour and other economic relations can be found in Charles Lockhart, *Bargaining in International Conflicts* (Columbia University Press, New York, 1979) pp. 1–35.

8. For example, Lockhart, op.cit., and Thomas C. Schelling, *The Strategy of Conflict* (Oxford University Press, London, 1963), and *Arms and Influence* (Yale University Press, New Haven and London, 1966) pp. 131–41, for the concept of tacit bargaining.

9. Iklé, op.cit., p. 3, and Schelling's comment in *Arms and Influence*, p. 131.

10. Iklé, op.cit., pp. 26–58.

11. R. P. Barston, 'Law of the Sea Conference: Old and New Maritime Regimes', *International Relations* (David Davies Institute) Vol. VI, No. 1 (May 1978) pp. 306–10.

12. *UNTS*, Vol. 952, p. 264.

13. *A Draft Agreement between the United Kingdom and the People's Republic of China*, Misc. No. 20 (1984) Cmnd. 9352, especially Annex 1, pp. 14–23.

14. A similar difficulty arises over efforts to apply the distinction between the 'efficiency' aspects of negotiation (that is the search for mutually profitable adjustments) and the 'distributional' (the division of an object in favour of one rather than another party) to differentiate respectively innovative and redistributive negotiations. See Iklé's note on this, in Iklé, op.cit., p. 27.

15. 'Pure' bargaining is understood in terms of the relationship between demands and concession. Demands are made, which may or may not be backed by coercive threats, with the aim or expectation of extracting concessions. Negotiation, at least in a cooperative sense, is distinct in that although demands are made the process involves adjustments, compromises, 'bridging' formula and other 'integrative' behaviour. As Knut Midguard and Arild Underdal note, 'pure' bargaining 'consists of trying to get the other party or parties to make the largest number of concessions, while making the smallest possible concessions oneself', 'Multiparty Conferences', in Daniel Druckman (ed.) *Negotiations: Social Psychological Perspectives* (Sage Publications, Beverly Hills, Calif., 1977) p. 332.

16. This can happen at the outset of an air service negotiation in which one of the parties regards the issue as a routine extension, while the other uses the opening negotiations for redistribution.

17. See Lockhart, op.cit., p. 9, and Robert D. Tollison and Thomas D. Willett, 'Institutional Mechanisms for Dealing with International Externalities: A Public Choice Perspective', in Ryan C. Amacher and Richard James Sweeney (eds) *The Law of the Sea: US Interest and Alternatives* (American Enterprise Institute for Public Policy Research, Washington DC, 1976) esp. pp. 97–101 for a discussion of an optimal theory of negotiations.

18. Sofia, for example, was the venue chosen by the Soviet Union for the Soviet–Egyptian talks of November 1976, on the reappraisal of the

Egyptian–Soviet Treaty of Friendship. See Ismail Fahmy, *Negotiating for Peace in the Middle East* (Croom Helm, London, 1983) p. 177 *passim*.

19. The impact of setting on East–West commercial relations is discussed in *Soviet Negotiating Behaviour: Emerging New Context for US Diplomacy*, Committee on Foreign Relations, House Document No. 16–238, Vol. 1 (1979) Annex, which suggests that in US–Soviet economic relations 'the setting is a function of the familiarity and confidence in the US side', p. 565 *passim*.

20. See Volker Rittberger, 'Global Conference Diplomacy and International Policy Making', in *European Journal of Political Research* (Special issue: Negotiation), Vol. 70, No. 11(2) (1983) pp. 167–82.

21. Michael Leigh, *European Integration and the Common Fisheries Policy* (Croom Helm, London, 1983).

22. For the influence of setting on the formation of the UN peacekeeping force in Cyprus (UNFICYP) see R. P. Barston, 'Problems in International Peacekeeping: The Case of Cyprus', *International Relations* (David Davies Institute, London, Nov. 1974) pp. 559–84).

23. See for example Henry Kissinger, *The White House Years* (Weidenfeld and Nicolson, London, 1979) p. 1205.

24. For an analysis of Kissinger's role in the Arab–Israeli disengagement after the October 1973 War see William B. Quandt, 'Kissinger and the Arab–Israeli Disengagement Negotiations', *Journal of International Affairs*, Vol. 29, No. 1 (Spring 1975) pp. 33–48, and William R. Brown, *The Last Crusade : A Negotiator's Middle East Handbook* (Nelson-Hall, Chicago, 1980). On mediators in the Arab–Israeli conflict from 1948 to 1979, see Saadia Touval, *The Peace Brokers* (Princeton University Press, Princeton, NJ, 1982).

25. See comment by the Netherlands on the effect of the group system on UNCTAD negotiations, cited in B. Gosovic, *UNCTAD Conflict and Compromise* (A. W. Sijthoff, Leiden, 1972) p. 325: 'The group system in UNCTAD has played havoc with traditional negotiation, i.e. where the countries most directly concerned strove to work out a compromise and then tried to convince non-participants that the compromise was reasonable', TD/B/175/Add. 3 (3 Sept. 1968) p. 7.

26. See Arthur Lall, *Modern International Negotiation* (Columbia University Press, New York, 1966) pp. 323–44; Iklé, op.cit., Chs 6, 9 and 12; and P. J. Boyce, *Foreign Affairs for New States* (University of Queensland Press, St Lucia, Qld., 1977) esp. pp. 158–9, and 232–54.

27. The problem of establishing negotiating mechanisms to enable talks to be held with the Iranian authorities was perceived as a major constraint by United States decision-makers during the Iranian hostage crisis. See 'The Iran Hostage Crisis', *Report for the Committee on Foreign Affairs of the United States House of Representatives* (US Government Printing Office, Washington, DC 1981) pp. 382–3, for details of the mediatory role of Algeria, and more generally, for a collection of some of the major developments.

28. Harold Nicolson, *Diplomacy* (Oxford University Press, 1963) pp. 18, 30–8.

29. For example see Kissinger on Soviet negotiating style, op.cit., pp. 1131–2, 1148–53, 1241. In his discussion of the negotiations to end the Vietnam

War Kissinger provides an illuminating insight into the negotiating style of South Vietnam's President Thieu, which was strongly influenced by French diplomatic style: 'He (Thieu) fought with a characteristic Vietnamese opaqueness and with a cultural arrogance compounded by French Cartesianism that defined any deviation from abstract, unilaterally proclaimed principles as irreconcilable error', pp. 1322– 8.

30. An account of Egyptian negotiations with then Soviet Foreign Minister Andrei Gromyko can be found in Fahmy, op.cit., pp. 177–82. Fahmy notes the change in Soviet style from the tough formal approach session of the full delegation to that in the *tête-à-tête*.

31. Michael Blaker, *Japanese International Negotiating Style* (Columbia University Press, New York, 1977) pp. 54–8.

32. For example the grounding of the tanker *Amoco Cadiz* off Ushant, in 1976, causing major pollution damage, gave added weight to those seeking stronger anti-pollution measures at the Law of the Sea Conference. See R. P. Barston and Patricia Birnie (eds) *The Maritime Dimension* (George Allen and Unwin, London, 1980) p. 118.

33. See I. William Zartman, 'Negotiation: Theory and Reality', *Journal of International Affairs*, Vol. 29, No.1 (Spring 1975) pp. 71–2.

34. Sir Anthony Eden, *Full Circle* (Cassell, London, 1960) pp. 115–16.

35. Gareth Porter, *A Peace Denied: the US, Vietnam and the Paris Agreement* (Indiana University Press, Bloomington, Ind., 1975) p. 77.

36. I. William Zartman and Maureen R. Berman, *The Practical Negotiator* (Yale University Press, New Haven and London, 1982) p. 139 on the efforts to devise a procedural formula for PLO participation in the proposed Geneva conference.

37. The scope of negotiations in terms of what is included or excluded on the agenda can be contentious. In the Sino-Indian boundary negotiations dispute arose over determining which sectors of the boundary should be discussed. China regarded *inter alia* the boundaries of Sikkim and Bhutan as outside the scope of the Sino-Indian boundary question. See *Reports to the Government of India and China on the Boundary Question* (Ministry of Foreign Affairs, India, 1961) pp. 37–9.

38. The US spokesman Cyrus Vance initially proposed two long tables (a two-sided conference) for the Vietnamese peace talks. The Democratic Republic of Vietnam (DRV) insisted on a square table with one delegation seated on each of the four sides, thus showing the NLF as an equal partner. The US then proposed a round table, which the DRV accepted, but which was rejected by the South Vietnamese Government. A compromise eventually emerged through a slight alteration to the formula of a round table: two rectangular tables were placed at opposite ends of the table. See Porter, op.cit., p. 78.

39. Procedural differences over the order of questions or items on the agenda can lead to the opening up of wider substantive matters. The fifth restricted session of the Geneva Conference on Indo-China, 24 May 1954, was taken up with discussion of whether military problems (cessation of hostilities, measures concerning regular and irregular forces, prisoners of war) should take priority over political problems (international supervision of agreement, guarantees) as the basis for further meetings.

See secret telegram Secto 292, May 25, 1954, Smith (Head of Delegation) to State Department, in *Foreign Relations of the United States 1952-4: The Geneva Conference*, Vol. XVI (US Government Printing Office, Washington, DC, 1981) pp. 907-11.

40. Gerard Smith notes: 'Semenov claimed not to understand what I (Smith) meant by "in parallel"', *Double Talk: The Story of the First Strategic Arms Limitation Talks* (Doubleday, New York, 1980) p. 250.

41. Rothstein, op.cit., pp. 148-57.

42. Johan Kaufmann, *Conference Diplomacy* (Sijthoff, Leiden, 1968) p. 181.

43. Interview (personal source).

44. Another important method involves the construction of formulae to bring the positions of the parties together or break an impasse. See Zartman and Berman, op.cit., esp. pp. 109-46 and 166-79.

45. The concept of 'structural uncertainty' is discussed by John D. Steinbruner, *The Cybernetic Theory of Decision* (Princeton University Press, Princeton, NJ, 1974) p. 18 *passim*.

46. Gibert R. Winham, 'Negotiation as a Management Process', *World Politics*, Vol. 30 (1977-78) pp. 87-107.

47. R. P. Barston, 'The Law of the Sea Conference', in Barston and Birnie, op.cit., pp. 165-6.

48. See Steinbruner, op.cit., pp. 40-44, 136-9, for a discussion of causal and cognitive learning.

49. Iklé, op.cit., p. 213.

50. Fahmy notes, in discussing the Egyptian-Soviet negotiations to reappraise the Treaty of Friendship, that Foreign Minister Gromyko did not raise the debt issue either in the private meetings or full encounters, of the two delegations. 'In fact this was the first time in any negotiation that the debt was not mentioned', op.cit., pp. 181- 2.

51. See Kissinger, op.cit., p. 1137, and Zartman, op.cit., pp. 74-7.

52. See Fahmy, for an unusual example of communique negotiations held before a projected Egyptian summit conference, op.cit., p. 184.

53. An interesting account of the concluding phases of a GATT meeting is in 'Notebook: Behind the Scenes at the GATT Trade Talks', *New York Times*, 5 Dec. 1982.

54. Takayuki Hashizuma, 'US-Japan International Aviation Policies', in *Aerospace: Asia and the Pacific Basin* (Financial Times, London, 1984) pp. 18-22.

55. See Lars Kalderen and Qamar S. Siddiqi, *Sovereign Borrowers* (Butterworth, London 1984).

56. See Eugene L. Versluysen, *The Political Economy of International Finance* (Gower, Aldershot, 1981) pp. 178-84 for a case study of Peruvian debt renegotiations.

57. *The Observer*, 8 April 1984.

58. See for example J. Russell, *Geopolitics of Natural Gas* (Ballinger, Cambridge, Mass., 1983).

CHAPTER SIX

Diplomatic styles and methods

This chapter is concerned with the question of changes in diplomatic style and, secondly, discussing some of the main developments in diplomatic techniques. The concept of diplomatic style is a useful means of thinking about the characteristic ways in which states and other actors approach and handle their external policy. This is not of course to say that every decision will necessarily reflect features of the diplomatic style. Within diplomatic style are included negotiating behaviour, preference for open or secret diplomacy, the kinds of envoys used, diplomatic language, preferred institutions and types of treaty instruments such as memoranda or treaties of friendship.

Changes in diplomatic methods are looked at in five areas: (1) personal diplomacy; (2) East–West conferences; (3) bloc diplomacy; (4) associative diplomacy; (5) the use of consensus in multilateral diplomacy.

DIPLOMATIC STYLES

To what extent have styles changed? Without doubt the rapid expansion of the international system since the 1960s has affected styles in a number of ways. Probably the most important effect has been the growth of personal diplomacy at head of state or government level, and the corresponding rise in regional diplomacy, through meetings, conferences and less formal gatherings of political, diplomatic and technical experts. The expansion of the state community has also brought with it a greater richness and variety in diplomatic styles, particularly at head of state level. This trend has been reinforced by the instability of governments, especially in Africa. One effect of this, at the level of diplomatic officials, has been an increase in the number of military personnel holding diplomatic appointments.[1] Embassies themselves, as a result, can become places of exile and the classical functions impaired or not carried out at all. This, in fact, may reinforce a further noticeable development in diplomatic style, which is a tendency for newer actors to conduct their foreign policy from the centre rather than through their own foreign ministry and embassy channels, where these exist. This has important implications both for the process by which images and views about another party are formed, and, the execution of policy. Embassies may not in fact be providing information or feedback which the usual explanation or models of diplomatic and foreign policy organisations suggest. Rather, the interface between parties may be short-circuited, the decision process truncated and decision-making personalised around the office of head of state and key advisers or agencies. As noted in Chapter 2 the foreign ministry, in some states, may rank third or fourth in the list of top five ministries behind the prime minister's department, treasury, and the economic planning unit (see Ch. 2).

The general characteristics of the diplomatic style of some newer states, discussed above, contrast with more established regimes. The latter tend to have a plurality of bureaucratic interests, greater degrees of functional decentralisation and conventional feedback mechanisms. A further difference is that the main elements in the operating style of established states have become stabilised, and, to some extent, built in as standard operating procedures. Thus a number of features of the overall operating styles of the United States and Soviet Union, apart from variability in personal style at the executive level, have not greatly changed.

In United States diplomatic style, the presidential special envoy, has been used in a number of ways, as illustrated by General Marshall's mission to China or the roving envoy role of W. Averell Harriman, and is a distinctive feature of American style.[2] The special envoy becomes the additional 'eyes and ears' of the president, acting as a fact-finder or trouble-shooter, for example General Vernon Walters visited Colombo during the Sri Lankan Tamil separatist crisis in 1984 for talks with President Jayewardene.[3] Although the special envoy may provide the president with additional or competing assessments, as well as strengthen presidential control, the continued practice has been seen by some professional diplomatic service officers as an erosion of their areas of responsibility and influence. Other features of US style include the high use of memoranda of understanding and other informal instruments, endorsement by collective resolution and a preference for broad, package-type solutions in negotiations, the basis of which are not always conceptually clear. For example, the US notion of an 'umbrella' approach to the resumption of strategic areas control talks in 1984–5 gave Soviet officials the opportunity, publicly at least, to express puzzlement at the response of the United States, while extolling the merits of their seemingly narrowly defined approach.[4] In at least one important respect, US operating style would appear to be undergoing change towards multilateral institutional diplomacy.[5] Dissatisfaction with certain multilateral fora has resulted in increasing United States demands that international organisations get their houses in order and increase their political and economic efficiency. There has also been preference for bilateral or small group diplomacy, coupled with a general quest for workable, smaller-scale arrangements among like-minded parties such as the 1982 interim agreement with Britain, France and the FRG on arrangements on deep sea-bed mining.[6]

As far as the Soviet Union is concerned the dominant features of Soviet operating style remain the high level of inward visits (a characteristic also of United States diplomacy), the relatively few overseas visits by deputy foreign ministers, the use of party officials as ambassadors and the far greater targeting than the United States of non-governmental groups and individuals, as channels of communication and direct or indirect instruments of foreign policy.[7] Soviet decision-makers have traditionally shown an awareness of using and addressing foreign media and publics to transmit their intentions and policies. For example, Mikhail Gorbachev's initiatives setting out Soviet policy on resumed arms control talks, on satellite weapons in space and on reform were made public subsequently in eastern europe and Geneva for example after the Reykjavik summit. Other features of Soviet style are the distinctive methods of negotiating,[8] the preference for bilateral treaties of friendship[9] and the pervasive influence of the internal and external military security apparatus on the conduct of Soviet foreign policy.

Of the other developments which have affected diplomatic styles, frequent changes of regime through a *coup d'état* or re-establishment of civilian or mixed regimes have been major factors which have prevented the emergence, with one or two exceptions, of any clear

African styles.[10] Of note, however, is the re-emergence of Islamic or religious-based regimes. An immediate effect, in the case of Libya, was on the staffing and styling of Libyan embassies, which subsequently became retitled 'People's Bureaux'. In the case of Iran, the public presentational aspects of Iranian foreign policy changed dramatically after the fall of the Shah, especially in terms of language, the use of revolutionary communiques and frequent insistence on the use of reservations in international conferences dealing with the Palestine problem. A further change associated with the Khomeni regime is the dualist nature of Iranian foreign policy, comprising government-to-people diplomacy as well as traditional government-to-government diplomacy. 'People's diplomacy' has involved establishing direct links with Islamic groups in other Islamic and non-Islamic states, as vehicles for promoting Iranian interests.

Apart from questions concerning the style of old and new regimes, several changes have occurred in the representational aspects of diplomacy. The inseparability of political and economic issues in foreign policy has inevitably had repercussions on appointments at the highest, and indeed junior, levels of an embassy. The question for example of whether an ambassador to Washington, should come from the career diplomatic service, or be a non-career appointment from the commercial sector is not uncommon. A number of senior ambassadors in the diplomatic service of the city-state of Singapore,[11] are non-career officers from the business community. However, most established states continue to adopt a restrictive policy, relying on career officials. A change common to most states, nevertheless, is in the size and composition of delegations sent on missions overseas. It is now common practice for such delegations to be extremely large (forty and above) and be a mixture of business men, officials and political leaders, although the primary purpose for the delegation leader may be to resolve a political dispute. Even in such circumstances business coexists with politics.

The representational aspects of diplomacy have also been affected by the growth of multilateral diplomacy. Many newer actors find it impossible to cope with the plethora of committees, regional groups and coordinating meetings at large-scale conferences. Given the range and complexity of issues, not all foreign ministries are able to provide sufficient instructions to their representatives. As a result, abstention or non-participation in voting has become an everyday feature of the diplomatic styles of some new states under these conditions.

DIPLOMATIC METHODS

Personal diplomacy

Personal diplomacy has increased in importance as a feature of modern international relations. By using personal or direct diplomacy through visits, correspondence and telephone conversations, heads of government and other senior leaders establish contacts, promote their country's image or try and improve bilateral, official and other relations. Personal diplomacy through visits is also used frequently to put the seal of approval on a major project or agreement. Visits of this kind, whether they be ceremonial, psychological or have a substantive purpose, reflect the growing involvement in diplomacy of the head of state or government and a variety of key representatives of banks, corporations, regional institutions and other organisations.

In general, the growth of personal diplomacy has been brought about by changes in modern communications, and the spread of regional collaboration outside Europe, in Africa, Latin America, the Caribbean and Southeast Asia. Visits, too, have become synonymous with the presentational aspects of foreign policy – declarations, profile as well as problem-solving. In many instances visits, especially those to major powers, are undertaken with an eye on the domestic or electoral value in the home country. Another important reason for the continued use of personal diplomacy is that it may facilitate political transition. For example, in the Soviet Union, the setting of the state funerals of Soviet leaders has been used as an opportunity for brief but important contacts between the new leadership and foreign politicians. Similarly, a personal visit by one head of state or government to another, following a *coup d'état*, can be used to open up new relations.

Personal diplomacy plays an important part in alliance and other collaborative relations. In the European Community, twice-yearly summits have become the norm in Franco-German relations, symbolising the importance each accords the other, whereas annual summits are held by France with Britain and Italy. France extended the system of summits to Spain, following agreement on its accession into the Community, in a co-operation agreement signed during the official visit of King Juan Carlos in July 1985. The agreement provided for annual meetings of the French president and Spanish Prime Minister, the setting up of joint consultative committees on international and strategic issues and annual meetings of the defence ministers.[12] Regular, though far less formal meetings have long been a feature of Anglo-American relations.

French and British practice has differed in terms of the methods used to develop relations with their former colonies. In contrast to Britain, France in terms of its African diplomacy (as well as elsewhere) has relied heavily on presidential and foreign ministerial visits to both francophone and non-francophone states. A frequent purpose of such visits is to reassure allies of continued support. For example, the 1984 African–French summit in Burundi, attended by President Mitterand and the French Foreign Minister, was preoccupied with the question of Chad and French policy *vis-à-vis* Libya. The occasion also gave M. Mitterand an opportunity to engage in some pre-summit 'old'-style personal diplomacy, when he held private talks with President Mobutu aboard the latter's presidential yacht on the Congo.[13]

The projection of national images and export promotion are the other major purposes of personal diplomacy. For example, at the end of 1984, the British Prime Minister, Mrs Thatcher, travelled 250,000 miles in 130 hours, principally for the formal signing of the Hong Kong agreement in Peking with the People's Republic of China. The journey also took in meetings in Bahrain, Moscow, Delhi and Hong Kong, returning via Guam, Honolulu and Washington.[14] An economic mission was undertaken the following year to Southeast Asia. It is not surprising that the political geography of heads of government sometimes becomes confused in these circumstances. It is in fact worth while contrasting the *pace* of modern diplomacy with that shortly after the Second World War. For example, P. C. Spender (Australia) and British Foreign Secretary, Ernest Bevin, travelled to the United States aboard the liner *Queen Mary*, in September 1950. Bevin was travelling to the UN in New York, while Spender's mission was to gather support for a Pacific security pact. Spender sought to win the approval of the British Foreign Secretary, but at the end of a personal meeting recounts:[15] 'I felt that when I left Bevin's stateroom that despite the warm personal hearing, I had again failed to penetrate the United Kingdom indifference, if not opposition to the idea.' Within less than a decade shortly after that the first modern exponent of air travel in diplomacy, US Secretary of State John Foster Dulles, became one of the most travelled post-war secretaries of state covering some 560,000 miles and attending fifty conferences in little more than six years.[16] The tradition has been carried on, with the addition of 'shuttle' diplomacy, as used by Secretaries Vance in the

Cyprus crisis, Kissinger after the 1973 Arab–Israeli War and Haig in the Falklands conflict.

East–West summits and conferences

In the cold war period East–West relations have been handled through four-power conferences (United States, United Kingdom, France and the Soviet Union), limited membership conferences on specific issues, such as Indo-China in 1954, and bilateral personal visits or summits. The four-power summits at Geneva in 1954 and 1955 marked a return to something like the allied conference style of the Second World War, although the first Geneva conference was a departure, given the breakdown of the four-power conferences of foreign ministers by 1947. The 1954 Geneva summit on Berlin and that of the following year on disarmament and the reunification of Germany appeared to signal the prospect of a 'thaw' in East–West relations after the death of Stalin. The gap between the two sides on the German question, however, remained substantial.

From 1960 onwards questions to do with general disarmament and arms control moved outside the UN Disarmament Commission and four-power framework to the Ten Nation Disarmament Committee, an enlarged subcommittee of the UN Disarmament Commission, in Geneva. The move had the effect of distancing discussion of these issues from the general forum of the UN, although the General Assembly retained an interest. It also underlined the inner group of nuclear powers in which France and the People's Republic of China have insisted on remaining outside. In a procedural innovation the conference was subsequently enlarged to eighteen members (the Eighteen Nation Disarmament Committee or ENDC), with the inclusion of eight non-aligned or neutrals (Brazil, Burma, United Arab Republic, Ethiopia, India, Mexico, Nigeria and Sweden). A further departure was the broadening of the ENDC agenda to include test ban discussions, with which the 'neutrals' had previously not been directly involved. The ENDC was further enlarged in 1969 and renamed the Conference of the Committee on Disarmament (CCD). However, the 'neutrals' have consistently claimed that the enlargement merely created a parallel structure to the existing framework of private bilateral talks between the US and the Soviet Union, and that the conference lacked technical support to keep pace with the growing complexity of arms control.

For their part the United States and the Soviet Union have preferred to negotiate partial solutions either directly or in a limited group, as in the 1961 test ban negotiations and the 1963 Partial Test Ban Treaty, negotiated by the United States, the Soviet Union and the United Kingdom. The trend towards bilateralism was influenced by the Cuban missile crisis, which speeded up the conclusion of the Partial Test Ban Treaty and led to the establishment of the US–Soviet 'hot line' telegraph–teleprinter facilities agreement the following year.[17] During 1966-67 the main elements of the Non-Proliferation Treaty were negotiated in private by the US and Soviet co-chairmen of the ENDC and at meetings in 1967 in New York between Secretary Rusk and Foreign Minister Gromyko.[18]

United States–Soviet bilateralism was a dominant feature of the early part of the classical period of *détente* from 1971 to 1976. The Moscow summit of May 1972 was intended to be the centre-piece for a new phase of US–Soviet management, based on the framework laid down in the general principles for the conduct of US–Soviet relations. In effect, US–Soviet bilateralism was seen as replacing the four-power system of East–West management, which was left mainly with Germany and Berlin. Yet although formal and informal links were developed in trade, finance, science and technology and other areas, US–Soviet relations, at a political and security level, increasingly deteriorated from the middle 1970s.[19]

The classic period of *détente* was accompanied by three important developments in European diplomatic methods – *Ostpolitik*, the European Security Conference and the Mutual Balanced Force Reduction (MBFR) talks. The FRG's *Ostpolitik* relied heavily on bilateral negotiations and, above all, keeping the momentum of the almost blitzkreig-like pace going as a follow-up to the meetings of Brandt and Willy Stoph in Kassel and Erfurt in 1970.[20] The FRG was also concerned to control as much of the *Ostpolitik* as possible with European interests in mind, rather than the wider strategic considerations and trade-offs considered by the United States.[21] The overall result of West German diplomacy was a suite of bilateral agreements beginning with the FRG–Soviet Treaty (August 1970)[22] and other normalisation agreements in the following three years with Poland,[23] Czechoslovakia[24] and the GDR.[25] The Four-Power Agreement on Berlin was concluded in September 1971 and implemented on the basis of subsequent negotiations between the two Germanies.[26] Probably the most important outcome of *Ostpolitik* and the Berlin agreement was the legitimacy given to inter-German negotiations as an accepted bilateral method of dealing with the German problem and other aspects of East–West relations. The Soviet Union has viewed this development with some concern, so much so that it has found it necessary to intervene on occasion in order to put a 'brake' on the exchanges.[27]

As East–West relations deteriorated after the Helsinki agreement, the Conference on Security and Cooperation in Europe (CSCE) and MBFR lost the supportive diplomatic context provided by *Ostpolitik* and 'positive' superpower relations and have existed uneasily in the setting of the new cold war which developed from the late 1970s. Efforts to revive East–West superpower relations at a technical bureaucratic level have had only limited success.[28] Particularly, too, in a period of transition, East–West relations are sensitive to low-level incidents such as the Nicholson affair which can be used to promote or block negotiations.[29] Enhanced importance, moreover, is attached to regular superpower summits, such as between Gorbachev and Reagan in Geneva in 1985 as a means of giving impetus to negotiations apart from any symbolic value they might have.

The Soviet Union and Comecon

In the external relations of the Council for Mutual Economic Assistance (Comecon) three areas are of particular interest in terms of diplomatic methods. The first area concerns the methods used to deal with issues arising from questions to do with the membership, composition and expansion of the organisation. The other two areas concern Comecon's relations with Western institutions, such as the European Community, and the kind of response to demands emanating from multilateral redistributive conferences of the UNCTAD type.

Comecon was founded at the Moscow conference of January 1949, attended by the USSR, Bulgaria, Czechoslovakia, Hungary, Poland and Romania, who were subsequently joined by Albania and the GDR. Since then membership issues have become highly sensitive, reflecting the conflict between the 'northern' and 'southern' tier of the group. Subsequent questions of membership have tended to be dealt with on an *ad hoc* basis and a variety of formulae have been used to deal with different cases.[30] The process of resolving these questions has been complicated by political issues, such as those arising from Soviet–Yugoslav relations and the Sino-Soviet dispute, which have intruded into the management of Comecon intra-bloc economic relations. The organisation itself has also been used as a forum to conduct wider disputes between the members.

Since its inception Comecon has remained essentially European, but observer status has been granted to the People's Republic of

China (1956), North Korea (1957), Mongolia and North Vietnam (1958). The Sino-Soviet conflict led to the withdrawal of Albania from Comecon in 1962. In order to compensate for this and prevent the emergence of a rival grouping based on the People's Republic of China and North Korea, Mongolia was admitted to full Comecon membership in June 1962. Yugoslavia was also offered full membership at the December 1961 Comecon session, possibly as a counter to growing Chinese influence in the non-aligned movement. However, Yugoslavia rejected the offer, preferring to keep some measure of freedom of action, consistent with its non-aligned position and observer status at the Organisation for Economic Cooperation and Development (OECD). Yugoslavia was eventually readmitted to Comecon in 1964 as an associate member, attending seven of the twenty-two Comecon standing commissions (foreign trade, currency and finance, co-ordination of scientific and technical research, ferrous and non-ferrous metals, engineering and chemicals).[31]

The handling of Cuban admission to observer status in Comecon contrasts with that of Yugoslavia. Cuban admission was resisted by a number of the European members on the grounds that it would weaken Comecon by introducing additional economic demands, so diluting the core aims of the organisation. Similar concern was again expressed after 1978 with the heavy Soviet involvement in Vietnam. Cuba has in fact participated in only a limited number of Comecon commissions and was not admitted to full membership until 1972.[32] Although the Comecon Charter was amended in 1962 to allow non-European states to join, the only other non-European state admitted, apart from Mongolia, was Vietnam in 1978. Observer status has been given to Afghanistan, Angola, Ethiopia, Laos, Mozambique, the People's Democratic Republic of Yemen and Nicaragua.

Comecon and other institutions   In Comecon's external diplomacy, the North-South dialogue and the question of recognition of the European Community have raised difficult issues. The calls for a major new international economic order by developing countries after 1974 and corresponding attempts to establish new institutions within the framework of the North-South dialogue have met with a guarded response from the Soviet Union. While the general principles of the NIEO have been publicly supported, in practice the Soviet response to specific institutional proposals to deal with commodity problems, such as the Common Commodity Fund and financial contributions, has generally been cautious. The Soviet Union has not perceived itself in any sense as being part of the 'North'. Nor, in the Soviet view, can it be held responsible for the development problems of the South. Rather, the Soviet approach has preferred bilateral aid and security agreements with selected states, instead of undertaking commitments in a multilateral UN framework. While the North–South dialogue has been relatively unsuccessful as an experiment in multilateral 'bridging diplomacy', Soviet policy of distancing itself has put Comecon as a whole, with one or two exceptions such as Romania, at some disadvantage in terms of its public profile and political influence in the UNCTAD framework.[33]

With regard to the European Community, the Soviet Union has been concerned that the increasing integration and expansion of the Community might have wider spill-over effects on Comecon, making it a rival political and an economic centre.[34] The Soviet Union has formally pursued a policy of non-recognition since 1957, but has in practice been forced to grant *de facto* recognition to the Community. The absence though of formal recognition has had a number of effects on the mechanisms for conducting Comecon relations with the Community. In the trade field, Community exports to Comecon increased by 400 per cent between 1958 and 1970, but the lack of a formal trade framework has limited two-way trade, as reflected in the significantly lower Comecon trade figures into the Community. However, lack of recognition has not prevented meetings between Soviet and Community officials on specific trade problems, although these have been on an *ad hoc* basis and have not benefited from a formal framework.

Soviet recognition policy underwent revision in 1972 as a result of moves within the Community towards a common commercial policy. In October 1972 the Nine agreed to put into effect the first phase of the common commercial policy from the beginning of 1973, which limited the powers of member states to sign new bilateral trade agreements. In November 1974 the Community put forward for negotiation to Comecon a standard agreement between the Community and individual Comecon countries, which included a most favoured nation (MFN) clause.[35] This was followed in March 1975 with specific Community proposals for bilateral textile agreements under article 4 of the Multifibre Arrangement (MFA) of 20 December 1973.[36] Romania has been the only Comecon member to conclude such an agreement, which was signed on 10 November 1976.[37] Hungary and Poland have negotiated similar arrangements with the EEC through GATT, so as to avoid formally recognising the Community and breaching the non-recognition policy.[38]

After 1980, the issues of recognition and a trade framework became increasingly more important for Comecon, partly since the Polish debt crisis underlined the growing financial connections between Poland, as well as other Eastern European countries, with banking and trade institutions in Western Europe. Other financial links with the West have developed out of the major Comecon projects for developing energy resources, such as the Druzhba (Friendship) oil pipeline,[39] and the Orenburg gas pipeline which takes gas to the western parts of the Soviet Union.[40] Part of the Orenburg project, for example, was financed on the Euro-dollar market, illustrating a further structural aspect of the linkages with Western Europe.[41] Further talks were held in 1979–80 and 1985 on recognition but were inconclusive.[42] Although under review, Western policy has in the main preferred to rely on bilateral methods of cooperation with individual Eastern European states in view of the greater potential leverage these have over a collective recognition arrangement.

Western Economic Summits

An important innovation in Western diplomatic coordination is the creation of the Western economic summits. The summits began at Rambouillet in 1975 and have been held annually since. It was not until the London summit of 1977, however, that it was agreed that the summits should become regular features on the diplomatic calendar of the major industrialised countries – the United States, Britain, France, Italy, the FRG and Japan. Membership was subsequently extended to Canada and the European Community.

The Rambouillet summit was a product not only of United States political concerns about the cohesion of the Western alliance but also of a series of oil, monetary and trade crises. Two Western political leaders – Giscard and Schmidt – were important in bringing the summit about. Their cooperation also reflected a strong wish to create a more effective European voice both in alliance matters and more generally on wider international issues. As Cesare Merlini notes: 'The real innovation is that the leaders of the seven industrialised democracies now meet on a regular basis and with a consolidated membership, in a forum which has more or less direct and effective relationship with the existing institutions and alliances that link the participating countries among themselves and with others.'[43]

A striking feature of the summits is the attention given to economic questions. After Rambouillet an agenda was identified comprising six broad areas: the international economic situation; trade problems; East-West trade; relations with developing countries; energy and monetary problems. Of these, energy questions have not been greatly discussed. Although the focus of the summits has remained substantially economic, the agenda has been modified to include discussion of some political questions. The Bonn summit (1978) was the first to make non-economic decisions, with a special declaration on air piracy, committing the participant governments to halt flights to and from countries that refused to extradite or prosecute hijackers or return hijacked aircraft. Following the example of the Bonn summit, the communique after the Tokyo summit (1979), which agreed among other things oil import quotas, also included a statement on the plight of refugees from Kampuchea and Vietnam. The Venice summit in 1980, overshadowed by the Iranian hostage crisis, included discussion on the seizure of diplomatic personnel, hijacking, and the communique reiterated the participants' concern over the Vietnamese 'boat people'. The Williamsburg summit (1983) is unusual in that, in addition to decisions on monetary policy and East-West trade, security issues were included for the first time. Discussions were held on the implications of the transfer of SS20 missiles by the Soviet Union from Europe to the Soviet Far East, and the deployment of cruise missiles in Western Europe.

While there may be doubts about the substantive achievements of the summits, they nevertheless have served as a convenient framework in which the major Western leaders can establish personal contact, exchange views and take these into account when formulating their future policies. Apart from this, the summits have linked Japan institutionally with the Western powers. The summits thus provide an arena for initiation and endorsement of policies, criticism of other members and a stage from which to project national policies to the international press. In this connection the summits are also a forum for European-American exchanges, in which the Europeans have been careful to maintain their independence both individually and as a grouping. At the 1985 Bonn summit, for example, the final communique endorsed the positive response by the European Space Agency (ESA) to the American offer to co-operate in the United States Manned Space Station Programme, but continued: 'We also welcome the conclusions of the ESA Council on the need for Europe to maintain and expand its autonomous capability in space activity, and on the long-term European Space Plan and its objectives.'[44] In fact, an indirect benefit of the summits, particularly for Western Europe, is that they have encouraged the Western Europeans to improve the coordination of their policies in other organisations such as the EEC, OECD and the GATT. Apart from coordination, the summits have led to some increase in less obvious functional cooperation. For example the establishment of expert groups on agricultural research and food aid programmes for Africa, reporting to foreign ministers, and conferences sponsored by individual governments, e.g. on bioethics and neurobiology by the FRG, have created an additional functional level to the seven-nation diplomatic dialogue.[45]

The operation of the summits since Rambouillet suggests a number of limitations. Some loss of focus has occurred as a result of the extension of the agenda to include political and security questions. Related to this is the increasing tendency for the grouping to be seen as a general clearing-house for US policy on East–West security and arms control issues, supplementing NATO.[46] The inclusion of Japan, in this respect, has caused concern among the smaller NATO members, particularly Belgium and the Netherlands, which are excluded from the seven-nation framework.[47] The loss of focus coincided with a change of the style in US foreign policy from the 1981 Ottawa summit, away from a detailed agenda, specific agreements and lengthy communiques to stressing more personal contact and declarations of intent. Related to this is the impact of the external setting on the summit agenda, particularly the tendency for events immediately prior to or during the summit itself to intrude on the proceedings. For example the Bonn summit in 1985 was overshadowed by the US President's visit to the Bitburg war cemetery, and the timing of the announcement of US sanctions against Nicaragua, while collective action against Libya and the Chernobyl nuclear accident diverted the Tokyo summit from what Japan had hoped would be a summit devoted largely to economic matters.[48]

The emphasis given at the summits in fact to Western alliance issues, at the expense of North–South relations, has aroused a further concern, especially shared by France, about the appropriateness of the summits as a decision-making body. In the French view, there was doubt as to whether the summits should become involved with trade issues, which are more properly dealt with in GATT or a well-prepared international conference. Underlying this issue is the French concern that the seven-nation grouping is seen, and indeed projected, by some as a major vehicle for managing the international system. The summits are seen as being in danger of becoming an American-dominated club. Accordingly, France, at least publicly, has been a reluctant participant.[49]

ASSOCIATIVE DIPLOMACY

One of the more striking aspects of the evolution of modern diplomacy is the relations which regional organisations develop with *other* regional organisations, international institutions, groups of states and individual states. The attempts by individual states or groups to develop significant links within a treaty and institutional framework with other states or groupings beyond merely routine transactions can be described as 'associative diplomacy'. Associative diplomacy serves one or more of a number of purposes, including the creation of a larger grouping, the coordination of policies and mutual assistance within the grouping. Other purposes are maintenance of the political, economic or security influence of the 'primary' grouping, limiting the actual or potential coercive power of other groupings, ('damage limitation'), and enhancement of the identity of individual members in the grouping.

There are generally four main elements in associative diplomacy. These include the institutional and treaty framework, regular meetings of senior political leaders and officials, some measure of coordination of policies, and schemes to promote economic relations of the groups, such as trade credits, generalised scheme of preferences (GSP) project aid and financial loans. Associative diplomacy can involve one or more of the major sectors of public policy, including socio-cultural exchanges, economic (trade, technical and financial assistance) political and security relations. It is possible to distinguish, therefore, various types of associative diplomacy, such as for example aid-project dominated (e.g. EEC–African, Caribbean and Pacific countries (ACP)) or mixed economic–security (e.g. ASEAN dialogues).

In this section three examples – the ASEAN dialogues, the Euro-Arab dialogue and the Lomé Convention have been chosen, to illustrate the working of associative diplomacy, starting with the ASEAN dialogues.

ASEAN

The ASEAN case illustrates associative diplomacy in transition from one of initial concerns with development projects to international trade and security issues. ASEAN was established in 1967, although formal links with other states and international institutions did not develop significantly until after the Bali summit of ASEAN heads of government in 1976.[50] Prior to this, ASEAN had established formal dialogues, meeting regularly at official and ministerial level with Australia in 1974 and New Zealand the following year, to discuss trade and development projects. Relations with other groupings, such as the EEC were *ad hoc* up to the Bali summit and ASEAN did not follow up the European Commission's offer of a cooperation agreement, similar to that concluded with India in December 1973.[51] The 1976 Bali summit not only reformed the institutions of ASEAN, giving them greater economic emphasis but gave the impetus for enhanced ASEAN cooperation with third countries and international organisations. During 1976–77, in a period of intense diplomatic activity, ASEAN concluded a framework agreement on future project assistance with the United Nations Development Programme (UNDP) and formalised dialogue arrangements with Canada and Japan. The prime ministers of Japan, Australia and New Zealand met with ASEAN heads of government in August 1977 in Kuala Lumpur, which confirmed their position as core dialogue partners. The first formal meeting of the US–ASEAN dialogue was held in Manila in September 1977. These meetings were complemented by the discussions held between the ASEAN ambassadors to Brussels and the Committee of Permanent Representatives (COREPER), which led to the first ministerial meeting between the Community, including the Commission, and ASEAN in Brussels in November 1978. A cooperation agreement was signed with the European Community in March 1980.[52]

The associative diplomacy of ASEAN is conducted at four levels – the annual dialogue meeting, ministerial meetings with individual dialogue partners or international organisations, and at the level of officials dealing with particular projects, which are coordinated by the Joint Coordinating Committee (JCC) in each country. An unusual fourth level involves the encouragement of non-governmental contacts. Within ASEAN itself a noticeable feature is the effort to promote regional development through private sector cooperation. ASEAN private or non-governmental associations have been set up in traditional areas such as chambers of commerce, as well as others such as the ASEAN Bankers Association, Shippers' Council, jurists and journalists.[53] As part of ASEAN associative diplomacy at a non-governmental level, business councils have been established between ASEAN private sector groups and their counterparts in Japan,[54] the EEC and the United States.

The associative diplomacy of ASEAN has been concerned with both political and economic issues, though the latter have commanded the most attention. An important aspect of the economic dimensions is the development project assistance provided by individual dialogue countries. By 1981 some 150 projects were being jointly implemented in areas such as food production, nutrition, agricultural development, fisheries, forestry and communications. To coordinate cooperation with third countries ASEAN has devised a system of designated responsibility among its members: Indonesia speaks for ASEAN in its dialogue with Japan; Malaysia with Australia; the Philippines with the United States and Canada; Singapore with New Zealand; and Thailand with UNDP, Economic and Social Commission for Asia and the Pacific (ESCAP) and the EEC. This does not, however, limit or prevent individual ASEAN members from conducting bilateral relations outside the scope of the 'dialogue'. In addition ASEAN maintains a collective presence in each of the dialogue countries and other capitals. These are termed 'Asean committees in third countries', and include the committees in Brussels, Bonn, Geneva, London, Paris, Canberra, Tokyo and Wellington, made up of the chiefs of mission.

From an ASEAN perspective, the dialogues have contributed to the wider recognition of ASEAN's growing status and importance in international relations. The other direct benefit to ASEAN is the public support given through the dialogues for its position on the Kampuchean question. For the most part this has been consistent since the Vietnamese invasion of Kampuchea in 1978, although Australia and France have diverged somewhat from ASEAN's policy towards Vietnam.[55] For the dialogue partners, the importance attached to the dialogues varies according to the nature and degree of their regional involvement. Thus, unlike other dialogue partners except Japan, the primary interest of the European Community is economic, with ASEAN viewed in terms of the general Community policy of extending its formal links with other regional groupings for economic purposes. ASEAN, moreover, is institutionally 'recognisable' and familiar to the European Community, fitting in, if not mirroring, some of its own styles of decision-making. In contrast, the dialogues provide the United States with an opportunity to put across

US policies on regional security, and to a lesser extent economic policy, as well as seek ASEAN support on a wider range of international questions, such as North–South issues, GATT or the Iran–Iraq War.

During 1981–82 ASEAN began a review of the format and usefulness of the dialogues. Dissatisfaction within ASEAN was influenced by the growing number of trade disputes, particularly between ASEAN and the United States over the application of the US GSP,[56] as well as similar difficulties with the European Community GSP. The take-off of some of the ASEAN economies in the mid and late 1970s meant that increasingly ASEAN preoccupations were with trade access and less with conventional development assistance.[57] The ASEAN review of the dialogues in other words reflected the classical debate between trade-orientated development as against agricultural-based development assistance.[58] Ironically, ASEAN's appeal for greater trade access for its products had been enshrined some years earlier in ASEAN's major treaties, the Declaration of ASEAN Concord (section 3(iv)) and in article 6 of the Treaty of Amity and Cooperation in Southeast Asia, though these objectives had not been collectively pursued to any significant degree until the review of the dialogues.

Apart from trade access, dissatisfaction with the project aspect of the dialogues lay in two areas. First, over half of the 150 projects initiated since 1975 have been undertaken by international or regional institutions, rather than the dialogue partners, including those by UNDP (42), ESCAP (14) and IMO (5).[59] The take-up by individual dialogue countries has been low, with Japan setting up 9 projects, Canada 11 and the United States 13,[60] as against New Zealand 7, Australia 12 and the European Community 19.[61] Second, analysis of the projects indicates that more than half are low-level development schemes (e.g. livestock rearing, aquaculture).[62]

A third general area of dissatisfaction has been with the lack of focus or clear priorities in the dialogues.[63] As the dialogues progressed a number of member states began to feel that the content had become broad and the institutional procedures somewhat ritualised. There were doubts too on the part of some of the dialogue partners as to whether this form of associative diplomacy added anything over and above that which could be achieved through normal diplomatic and other channels. For example, there were no dialogue meetings at the level of officials between Canada and ASEAN between 1977 and 1981, although there were bilateral contacts outside the 'dialogue' framework.[64]

As a result of the review it was agreed that the dialogues with existing countries should be continued, but concentration should be on market access, international economic problems, commodity problems and socio-cultural cooperation. The review moreover revised the concept of dialogues by stipulating that any new dialogues would be implemented on a stage-by-stage basis and not with individual countries as in the past but with groups of countries for specific purposes, such as discussion on trade, industry or agriculture.

Euro-Arab dialogue

The Euro-Arab dialogue is the least 'institutionalised' of the forms of associative diplomacy under discussion. The dialogue was initiated after the European Community summit of December 1973 in Copenhagen and the exploratory meeting with Arab foreign ministers. In an *aide-mémoire* of 15 June 1974, the European Community subsequently proposed a dialogue with the Arab League. European Community interest in a dialogue had been initially influenced by the oil crisis and the need to secure stable oil supplies following the October 1973 Arab–Israeli War. Up to that point the different methods used to achieve that – bilateral deals with individual Arab states, a collective coordinated stance or the development of distinctive positions from the Americans, had achieved only limited results. For its part the Commission, too, was engaged in constructing links with Mediterranean and other states which led to agreements with Israel, the Maghreb and Mashreq states. On the Arab side, the dialogue offered the opportunity of changing European views on the PLO issue.

In June 1975 experts from the Arab League and the Community, including the Commission, met in Cairo and set up seven working committees including industrialisation, basic infrastructure, scientific and technical cooperation, culture and labour affairs. A general committee was established to oversee the dialogue.[65] There was, however, some doubt as to whether the Cairo meeting would go ahead in view of the conclusion of a trade and cooperation agreement by the Community with Israel the previous month.[66] More generally the issue underlined the conflicting interests and priorities of the Commission, and the differences between member states on Middle East questions.[67] For these and other reasons, including US sensitivity on oil and the primacy of its own political initiatives *via-à-vis* the Middle East, the Europeans preferred to keep the dialogue confined to low-level economic cooperation.[68]

Of the seven working groups at official level, the most active have been industrialisation, science and technology, and finance, in which investment protection of financial holdings in Europe was an issue of particular concern to some of the Arab countries. For the most part meetings at ambassadorial level have been ineffective, being confined to statements of known political positions. No meetings at foreign minister level were held prior to 1981.

In general the Euro-Arab dialogue has had only limited success as a form of associative diplomacy. That success has probably been more in the economic sphere than the political, particularly in linking Arab and European capital in co-financing development projects, especially infrastructure, such as the Douala port development in Cameroon or the bridge–barrage project for Mauritania, Senegal and Mali. Nevertheless, it is arguable that the amount of co-financing funds used would have been available anyway without the dialogue. Co-financing through Arab and European funds has though reduced the burden on the European Investment Bank (EIB) and European Development Fund (EDF) and possibly broadened the distribution of funds within the Lomé context.[69]

The limited scope of the Euro-Arab dialogue is partly due to the disparate nature of the grouping, bringing together representatives of some twenty-one Arab and the European states, together with the Commission and Secretariat of the League of Arab States. Support for the dialogue has been uneven on both sides. For example, Italy, France and Ireland have generally promoted the idea, whereas Britain and the FRG have shown varying support. On the Arab side, Tunisia, Algeria and the PLO have supported the dialogue from the outset, while Saudi Arabia, Egypt and several of the Gulf States, such as Oman, have preferred to rely on bilateral relations with European states.[70] As in the case of ASEAN associative diplomacy, reservations have been expressed, for example by France and Britain, about governmental involvement in large-scale development projects, which would be better left to the private sector.

The status of the talks has limited to some extent the progress of the dialogue. The Arab side's wish to raise the dialogue to foreign minister level and discuss Western policy on the PLO met with a lukewarm Western response. In 1978 the underlying political difficulties came to the fore when the Euro–Arab dialogue was suspended for twenty months, as a result of the signing of the Camp David agreement in September. Egypt was later suspended from the

League of Arab States which moved its headquarters from Cairo to Tunis.[71] The Euro-Arab dialogue was revived somewhat in 1980 against the background of the Iranian oil crisis and the European initiative on the Middle East, launched at the Venice seven-nation economic summit. However, the dialogue has remained low key,[72] in view of the expanding and obdurate nature of Middle East issues, the widening dimension of the Iran–Iraq War and the break-up of the Lebanon, all of which make the basis for continuing the dialogue even more fragile.

The EEC and Lomé

A notable feature of the expanding role[73] of the European Community is its associative diplomacy based on cooperation agreements. Many of the early agreements were little more than trade arrangements.[74] They were often limited in scope, for example to essentially French-speaking Africa, such as the Yaoundé agreement of 1963,[75] or were put together on an *ad hoc* basis after painstaking and arduous negotiations, as with the Maghreb and Mediterranean agreements between 1963 and 1980. The conclusion of the Lomé I Convention in February 1975 between the Community and 46 independent states in the ACP countries marked a major stage in the development of its associative diplomacy.[76] It has extended the political, economic and institutional links of the Community to the Caribbean, Pacific and eventually to most of Africa. Significantly, Asia and Latin America have been omitted from the Lomé framework. No doubt in the case of Asia, exclusion was based on a concern for the long-term challenge posed by textiles and other manufactured goods from the 'heartland' of the newly industrialised countries' revolution. In October 1979, Lomé II was signed with fifty-seven ACP countries and the convention further renewed in December 1984.[77]

During the Lomé I negotiations,[78] a number of ACP political leaders, along with others including Commonwealth Secretary-General Ramphal, felt that the South should develop their own institutions for coordinating their policies and promoting development. The Lomé framework offered some opportunity to develop South–South institutions. For the North (Western Europe), the convention was seen as one of the few successful parts of the generally weakened North–South dialogue. Subsequently the ACP states have developed a parallel institutional structure to the joint EEC-ACP institutions, which include the Council at Ministerial

Level, the ACP–EEC Committee of Ambassadors, the Joint (Parliamentary) Committee and Consultative Assembly.[79] At the Georgetown (Guyana) meeting in June 1975 the ACP states established an ACP council, the Committee of Ambassadors, and a secretariat was set up the following year in Brussels. The main work of the ACP Committee of Ambassadors is conducted through specialist subcommittees on, for example, commercial cooperation. Other joint subcommittees have been set up on sugar and banana exports, which are areas of particular concern in the diplomacy of a number of the Commonwealth Caribbean members of the ACP.

Within the ACP, the sugar producers have formed a subgroup of producing countries, which has met periodically to coordinate policies, for example, at the Georgetown conference in February 1985,[80] which was attended by fourteen of the eighteen signatories to the Sugar Protocol attached to the Lomé Convention.

Since Lomé II, the institutional machinery of EEC–ACP associative diplomacy has been strengthened through what has become known as the 'Article 108 Committee'. The committee, which meets at ministerial and technical working party level, is responsible for assessing the effectiveness of the financial and technical assistance provisions of the convention. In response to ACP criticism, the procedure of the 108 Committee, which is composed of equal numbers of representatives was further revised in Lomé III reducing the role of the European Commission and enhancing that of the ACP states in joint financial decision-making.[81] Prior to this the annual review and assessments of projects had in practice been mainly undertaken by the Commission. These changes have helped to reinforce the principle of joint administration on finance and improve the intergovernmental rather than technical aspects of EEC–ACP associative diplomacy.[82]

How far EEC–ACP associative diplomacy can develop through institutional and other changes seems broadly dependent on four sets of considerations. In the first place there is the problem of reconciling increasingly competing interests. As the membership has expanded, so the range of interests to be listened to, if not accommodated, has broadened. Should greater attention be given to the smaller Pacific states? Should the Community promote regional integration, or would particular national projects offer a more modest but arguably more effective route given resources? In this respect, the availability of EEC funds will be a major determinant of EEC–ACP orientation.[83] Export stabilisation schemes such as Stabex raise expectations, but clearly cannot cope with major crop failure.[84] Again, while many of the Caribbean and Pacific states have low populations their integrative project requirements, such as ports, security, fisheries and shipping services are capital intensive. In response to growing demands on EEC financial resources, the EIB has extended its operations so as to become an important instrument in EEC–ACP projects by providing risk capital.[85] However, continued shortage of development funds and disputes over distribution would have the effect of turning the Lomé Convention more into a conventional trade cooperation agreement. Related to this, the inability of the Community itself to provide sufficient project aid and other funds under Lomé has led to financial relations being developed between EEC–ACP institutions and other financial sources such as the World Bank, Arab funds and private capital. Although capital is sourced internationally, the growth of multi-source funding will make it more difficult for the Community to use the distribution of funds as a policy instrument, in that non-Community-sourced funds may favour regions of trade growth, particular countries or types of project (e.g. light engineering).

A further factor influencing the evolution of EEC–ACP diplomatic methods is the institutional arrangements linking the two groups. The establishment of parallel ACP institutions alongside the joint EEC–ACP institutions has caused considerable strain on ACP political and diplomatic resources. As might be expected the record of the joint committee is mixed. At the ACP level, the South–South diplomat still has to be persuaded about the career benefits of serving in an overseas secretariat. Another area of difficulty for ACP organisation concerns the powers of the office of secretary-general. Reaching agreement on an acceptable candidate has proved time-consuming and divisive. As in the OAU,[86] the inability of ACP members to agree a candidate has seriously impaired the office of secretary-general and led to calls for the revision of the election procedures.[87] In general, internal organisational problems within the ACP have acted as a limitation on the effectiveness of the ACP component of South–South diplomacy, as well as the joint EEC–ACP institutions.

MULTILATERAL DIPLOMACY

The growth of consensus decision-making is one of the developments in multilateral diplomatic methods worth particular comment. The post-war period saw the continued shift away from decision-making based on unanimity. However, more recently, there appears to be some return to the notion of unanimity with the growth in the practice of decision-making by consensus. Writing on unanimity, I. L. Claude notes:

> Traditional international law contributed the rule which served as the historic starting point for international voting and still serves as its basing point: the rule that every state has an equal voice in international proceedings and that no state can be bound without its consent. The ingredients of sovereign equality and sovereign immunity from externally imposed legislation were combined in the rule of unanimity.[88]

Nevertheless, the changing composition of the UN, including the emergence of the G-77 and the introduction of G-77 procedures into international institutions, has influenced the search for procedural solutions to avoid or at least lessen the confrontational aspects of majority–minority clashes. The rule of consensus is one such method. Others include weighted voting, as in the International Postal Union or the IMF, and the rule that governments may 'opt out' of participation as in the Council for Mutual Economic Assistance (CMEA) and Nordic Council of Ministers.[89] In the United Nations, other than strict abstention, the practice of non-participation in proceedings or voting is widely used.

The use of consensus decision-making in the UN dates particularly from the early 1970s. Consensus decision-making is distinct from unanimity in that unanimity implies that there is no opposition or request for a vote. Decision-making by consensus has come to mean the exhaustive search for widely acceptable solutions. In the UN system the consensus method has been widely used, e.g. at the UN Disarmament Commission[90] and the Law of the Sea Conference.[91] Elsewhere, consensus has been used in the CSCE and meetings of the G-77 non-aligned, although the practice of the G-77 also allows for opting out and reservations. In order to avoid undue delay and make decision-making more effective other variations have been developed, such as combinations of consensus, 'cooling-off' periods for consultation and voting, as in the 1975 and 1980 Non-Proliferation Treaty review conference.[92] In UNCTAD a combination of consensus and voting has been used. For example, the United States proposal for an International Resources Bank was voted on at UNCTAD IV at Nairobi and rejected.[93]

The practice of consensus would seem to have been widely adopted recently as a means of responding to the problem of dissatisfaction at majority voting and the difficulties created by the emergence of opposing blocs or groups in multilateral conferences.[94] Consensus decision-making clearly has advantages for the great powers in that lengthy decision-making, which is a feature of the consensus method, provides opportunities for advancing and protecting their policies through lobbying, supporting draft proposals and forming support groups, without the threat of being frequently voted down. Ultimately, however, the consensus method may break down and voting take place, as, for example, in the Law of the Sea Conference in 1982, when a majority of the participants felt that continued US opposition to the sea-bed mining provisions was holding up the finalisation of the overall convention.[95] But the advantages do not lie solely with the great powers. Minor powers and small states in some respects have enhanced opportunities for protecting their positions in the drafting process of a consensus system. Put differently, consensus may be a convenient political fiction which is maintained during a conference to prevent premature break-up or postpone a decision. States subsequently may choose to interpret the meaning of a text in different ways, and, indeed, implement it, if at all, in quite divergent ways.[96]

Other reasons for voting taking place include testing the legitimacy of a consensus, or pressure from dissatisfied states who wish to place on record their position, knowing that key states are unlikely to support the declaration or resolution. The latter was well illustrated in the debate in the International Maritime Organisation (IMO) in which a group of states led by Spain, and opposed by the United States, United Kingdom and Japan sought to obtain a majority vote prohibiting the dumping at sea of radioactive waste.[97]

One of the major disadvantages of consensus decison-making in international institutions and conferences is the protracted nature of the process. Decision-making is exhaustive and exhausting, as attempts are made to achieve compromise texts. At a procedural level, secretariats of international institutions and working group chairmen have, however, become important in research, and in developing and promoting their own and others' compromise formulae. The method has also led to the development of innovative negotiating techniques to overcome deadlock and maintain momentum. For example, at the seventh session of the Law of the Sea Conference the impasse in negotiations was broken by defining the remaining core issues (e.g. the system for the international administration of deep sea-bed mining) and setting up seven new negotiating groups on these issues. Again, at the eighth session in

1978, the establishment of a Working Group of 21 on deep sea-bed questions was a further procedural innovation. Unlike previous formal groups, membership was restricted and drawn from ten developed industrialised states, including the United States, United Kingdom, France, FRG, Canada, Australia and the Soviet Union and ten developing countries, represented *inter alia*, by Brazil, Peru, Mexico and the People's Republic of China.[98]

Apart from the length of the decision-making process, a further related criticism which has been made is on the kinds of agreements which result from consensus decision-making. Often the lowest common denominator dictates that the outcome may be a set of obligations with a very high degree of generality or one steeped in qualifications. The technique of putting square brackets round parts of the text where there is no consensus can sometimes produce a labyrinthine set of brackets, resembling more an algebraic equation than a draft treaty article.[99]

Finally, there is the question of whether decisions reached using consensus are likely to be more or less implemented, than those reached on the basis of majority voting or other methods. While it might be assumed that a consensus decision formally should command wide support, in practice the degree of support a set of proposals commands may be uncertain, as in other forms of negotiation. That uncertainty or ambiguity may never be tested by vote or ascertained until after the conference, when the state may feel it does not wish to be bound by the terms of the consensus reached. Writing in the context of UNCTAD, Krishnamurti, notes: 'many recommendations adopted by consensus in UNCTAD on trade, finance, least developed countries and other areas, remain only meagrely fulfilled'.[100] A frequently used term in discussion of the concept of consensus negotiation is the notion of a 'package deal'. In large-scale and complex multilateral diplomacy such a concept may not be a particularly exact means of understanding the negotiating processes. The 'package' may in fact be a political illusion.

CONCLUSION

Contemporary diplomacy has undergone several significant changes in methods in recent years. The growth and frequency of personal diplomacy by heads of state or government has confirmed a general shift in the involvement and responsibility of chief executives for external policy. In the main this has been at the expense of foreign ministers, who nowadays often tend to be overshadowed by their counterparts from finance and trade. A related development has been the undoubted spread of bilateral diplomacy. At a commercial level governments have become much more involved in the management of bilateral trade on an intergovernmental basis as well as with non-state entities. Politically, high-level visits serve a number of purposes, not least of which are the bypassing of conventional organisational channels and the establishment of personal contact. In multilateral diplomacy a number of different methods have been attempted, including associative diplomacy, North–South 'bridging' diplomacy and large Pan-European security conferences, with varying degrees of success. While large-scale multilateral conferences have continued to be successful at a sectoral level in establishing regulatory regimes such as law of the sea, world health or telecommunications, global-style conferences with vast, redistributive agendas have not. A common feature, especially with global negotiations, is not only with the range of the agenda but the size of the negotiating groups, which have necessitated extensive efforts at constructing representative negotiating groups which are politically acceptable. These and the other changes in diplomatic methods discussed in the chapter suggest that the international community is in a period of transition in terms of diplomatic methods as it seeks to find workable arrangements for its expanded membership.

REFERENCES AND NOTES

1. P. J. Boyce, *Foreign Affairs for New States* (University of Queensland Press, St Lucia, Qld, 1977) pp. 62–5.
2. Elmer Plischke (ed.) *Modern Diplomacy – The Art and The Artisans* (American Enterprise Institute for Public Policy Research, Washington, DC, 1979) p. 177.
3. *The Guardian*, 10 Dec. 1984.
4. In an effort to resume arms control negotiations the United States renewed its offer to hold 'umbrella talks' with the Soviet Union in October 1984. *The Guardian*, 16 Nov. 1984.
5. See John Gerrard Ruggie, 'The United States and the United Nations', *International Organisation*, Vol. 39, No. 2 (Spring 1985) pp. 343–56. On the US withdrawal from UNESCO, announced in Dec. 1983, see *Hearings*, Sub-committee on Human Rights and International Organisations of the Committee on Foreign Affairs, House of Representatives, 27 Sept. and 3 Oct. 1983; *US Withdrawal from*

UNESCO, Report of a Staff Study Mission, Committee on Foreign Affairs, US House of Representatives, April 1984; *Assessment of US-UNESCO Relations 1984*, Report of a Staff Study Mission to Paris-UNESCO, Committee on Foreign Affairs, House of Representatives, 1985; *Hearings*, Sub-committees on Human Rights and International Organisations and International Operations, Committee of Foreign Affairs, House of Representatives, 26 July, 13 Sept., 6 Dec. 1984.

6. *UKTS*, No. 46, 1982, Cmnd. 8685.
7. See Sir Curtis Keeble (ed.) *The Domestic Roots of Soviet Foreign Policy* (Gower, Aldershot, 1985).
8. *Sunday Times*, 18 Nov. 1984. See also Andrew Berding, 'Quiet Vs Unquiet Diplomacy', in Plishcke, op. cit., pp. 117-18 for further discussion of this, including the Soviet publication of the 1958 US-Soviet exchange of letters.
9. See Zafar Iman, 'Soviet Treaties with Third World Countries', *Soviet Studies*, Vol. XXXV, No. 1 (Jan. 1983) pp. 53-70.
10. Timothy M. Shaw and Solar Oja, *Africa and the International Political System* (University of America Press, New York, 1982) pp. 22-3. On the decline of personal diplomacy and the evolution of South African foreign policy style see Deon Geldenhuys, *The Diplomacy of Isolation: South African Foreign Policymaking* (Macmillan, Johannesburg, 1984) pp. 17-19, 241-3.
11. Interview. For an account of a Singapore diplomat-MP see Lee Khoon Choy, *An Ambassador's Journey* (Times Books International, Singapore, 1983).
12. *Financial Times*, 10 July 1985.
13. *The Guardian*, 10 Dec. 1984.
14. *Sunday Times*, 23 Dec. 1984.
15. Sir Percy Spender, *Exercises in Diplomacy: The Anzus Treaties and the Colombo Plan* (Sydney University Press, Sydney, 1969) p. 35.
16. See Elmer Plishke, 'The New Diplomacy', in Plishke, op. cit., p. 70.
17. 'Memorandum of Understanding Between the United States of America and the Union of Soviet Socialist Republics Regarding the Establishment of a Direct Communication Link, June 20, 1963 (with Annex) Updated 30 Sept. 1971, with the Provision for a Satellite Communications System', in John H. Barton, *International Arms Control* (Stanford University Press, Stanford, Calif., 1976) pp. 330-7.
18. Ibid., p. 298.
19. See R. P. Barston, 'Soviet Foreign Policy in the Brezhnev Years', *World Today*, Vol. 39, No. 3 (March 1983) pp. 81-90.
20. Terence Prittie, *Willy Brandt: Portrait of a Statesman* (Weidenfeld and Nicolson, London, 1974).
21. Hans W. Gatzke, *Germany and the United States* (Harvard University Press, London, 1980) pp. 222-3.
22. Lawrence L. Whetten, *Germany's Ostpolitik* (Oxford University Press, London, 1971) Appendix V, pp. 224-5.
23. C. C. Schweitzer, D. Carsten, R. Spencer, R. T. Cole, D. P. Kommers and A. J. Nicholls, *Politics and Government in the Federal Republic of Germany, Basic Documents* (Berg Publishers, Leamington Spa, 1984) pp. 303-4.

24. Ibid., p. 307.
25. Ibid., pp. 342–6.
26. Ibid., pp. 348–9.
27. See Vladimir V. Kusin, 'Gorbachev and Eastern Europe', *Problems of Communism*, Vol. XXXV (Jan.–Feb. 1986) pp. 47–8.
28. *The Times*, 1 and 2 June 1983 ('is there a way out of zero zero?').
29. Major Arthur Nicholson, a member of the United States military mission, was killed in an incident in East Germany in March 1985. Talks to resolve the issues surrounding the killing of Major Nicholson were confined to the respective commanders in Germany, while American essential interests were judged to be better served by continuing to press ahead with calls for a US–Soviet summit. *The Guardian*, 8 April 1985.
30. See Michael Kaser, *Comecon* (Oxford University Press, London, 1967) p. 100 *passim* for further discussion of the membership question. See also *The Times*, 2 July 1981, for details of the opposition of European members of Comecon to Vietnam, and aid for Cuba, Mongolia and Vietnam.
31. For details of the commissions see Kaser, op. cit., Appendix IV.
32. Kaser, op. cit., p. 104.
33. Robert M. Cutler, 'East–South Relations at UNCTAD: Global Political Economy and the CMEA', *International Organisation*, Vol. 37, No. 1 (Winter 1983) pp. 121–42.
34. On the internal debate to integrate the Comecon economies more closely see Kurt Weisskoff, 'Progress of the Comecon Integration Programme' in *Comecon Progress and Prospects* (NATO, Directorate of Economic Affairs, 1977) pp. 32–3.
35. European Communities, Information Directorate-General, Document 91/75, 'The European Communities and the Eastern European Countries'.
36. European Communities, Information Directorate-General, Document 13 Nov. 1976, 'European Community Textile Agreements Under the International Arrangements for the Trade in Textiles'.
37. *Financial Times*, 11 Nov. 1976.
38. *Comecon: Progress and Prospects* (NATO, Directorate of Economic Affairs, Brussels, 1977).
39. See Vladimir Sobell, *The Red Market: Industrial Cooperation and Specialisation in Comecon* (Gower, Aldershot, 1984) pp. 58–9.
40. Ibid., pp. 49–51.
41. For further details of the energy projects see J. Bethkenhagen, 'Joint Energy Projects', in *Comecon, Progress and Prospects*, p. 49 *passim*.
42. *Financial Times*, 28 June 1985.
43. Cesare Merlini (ed.) *Economic Summits and Western Decision-Making* (Croom Helm, London, 1984) p. 193.
44. Final Communique, Bonn summit, 2–4 May 1985, para. 17.
45. Final Communique, Bonn summit, 2–4 May 1985, para. 18.
46. *Financial Times*, 1 Oct. 1985.
47. An emergency NATO ministerial meeting was held on 15 Oct. at the request of Belgium and the Netherlands. *Financial Times*, 3 and 16 Oct. 1985. Italy and Canada were brought into the G-5 framework at Tokyo in

a compromise which allowed the G-5 to hold its own meetings. See *Financial Times*, 6 May 1986.

48. *Financial Times*, 3 May 1986.

49. *Financial Times*, 7 May 1985.

50. For the Declaration of ASEAN Concord, the Treaty of Amity and Co-operation in South East Asia, and other documents from the Bali summit, see *10 Years ASEAN* (ASEAN, Jakarta, 1978) pp. 111-25.

51. *Europe Information External Relations* (16 Feb. 1979) p. 5.

52. *Europe Information External Relations*, X/68/83-EN, (Feb. 1983) p. 4.

53. For a list of ASEAN non-governmental and private organisations see *10 Years ASEAN*, p. 239; ASEAN *Newsletter*, March–April 1984, pp. 2-4.

54. *Annual Report of the ASEAN Standing Committee 1982-3* (ASEAN Secretariat, Jakarta, 1983) p. 66.

55. For the Australian decision not to co-sponsor the ASEAN resolution of Kampuchea, see *Far Eastern Economic Review*, 24 Nov. 1983, p. 34, and 14 July 1983, pp. 10-11, on attitude to Vietnam.

56. See statement by Carlos P. Romulo at the 15th ASEAN Ministerial Meeting, 18 June 1982 (ASEAN Secretariat, Jakarta, 1982) p. 84.

57. See *Annual Report of the ASEAN Standing Committee 1982-3*, pp. 64 and 71.

58. See 15th ASEAN Ministerial Meeting, 14-16 June 1982, Joint Communique, p. 56, para. 54.

59. The project figures for dialogue partners have to be offset by financial contributions to the Asian Development Bank (ADB) made by dialogue partners.

60. For United States projects and objectives see *ASEAN Newsletter*, Jan./Feb. 1985, p. 9.

61. The Netherlands has two ASEAN projects, including setting up an ASEAN promotion centre in Rotterdam and on ASEAN export promotion. Details of other EEC projects with individual ASEAN members can be found in *Europe Information External Relations*, X/68/83-EN, Table IV, pp. 11-12.

62. Details of the projects can be found in ASEAN *Newsletter*, Vol. 2, No. 2 (July 1981) pp. 4-5, 10.

63. See remarks by Singapore's Foreign Minister, S. Dhanabalan, at the 15th ASEAN Ministerial Meeting, p. 62.

64. See remarks by Dr M. MacGuigan, Canadian Secretary of State for External Affairs, 15th ASEAN Ministerial Meeting, p. 69. An ASEAN–Canadian Cooperation Agreement was, however, signed on 25 Sept. 1981 in New York.

65. See *Joint Memorandum*, Cairo, 14 June 1975 (Commission of the European Communities, Brussels).

66. D. Allen, 'Euro-Arab Dialogue', *Journal of Common Market Studies*, Vol. XVI, No. 1 (1977-78) pp. 327-9.

67. The question of PLO participation in the Euro-Arab dialogue was resolved through the personal diplomacy of Irish Foreign Minister Garret Fitzgerald. Under the so-called 'Dublin formula', the two sides meet as delegations of the League of Arab States and the European Community. There are normally ten to fourteen experts in the delegations to the working committees.

68. See Allen, op. cit., p. 328, and Saleh Al-Manir, *The Euro-Arab Dialogue* (Frances Pinter, London, 1983) pp. 125–6.
69. Saleh Al-Manir suggests that co-financing between Arab and European funds may have had some redistributive effect (op. cit., p. 104) in moving the relative flow of Arab assistance commitments away from major Arab recipients and increasing the flow towards Africa.
70. Al-Manir, op. cit., p. 65.
71. In a curious compromise it was agreed that Egypt should be informed of the proceedings of EAD by the European Community but would not be allowed to participate.
72. See *Middle East* (March 1982) p. 16.
73. The Community has developed a number of working arrangements for Community participation in international organisations and agreements. In some instances Community participation is higher than observer status, as in the OECD, as provided for in the Supplementary Protocol. In others the working arrangements are structured, as with the joint working parties in UNESCO. Since many organisations deal with issues falling within the jurisdiction of member states, Community representation sometimes takes the form of 'dual representation'. Under this system the Community is represented by both the Commission and the member state holding the presidency, with the Commission normally, acting as spokesman on matters falling within Community jurisdiction, e.g. UN General Assembly, ECOSOC, UNCTAD. Other formulae include a single delegation of the Commission and member states, with the Commission acting as spokesman, as in the negotiation for the 1971 International Wheat Agreement, the 1973 International Sugar Agreement and the 1975 International Cocoa Agreement. The differences in the forms of representation reflect the evolution of Community competence, as well as its recognition in international fora. Efforts to change the status of the Community to accommodate it as a new legal entity have met with resistance. For details of the status of the Community in international institutions and regional intergovernmental organisations, see *The European Community, International Organisations and Multilateral Agreements*, 3rd rev. edn (Commission of the European Communities, Luxembourg, 1983) pp. 15–29. For the respective roles of the Commission and member governments in different negotiations, see Paul Taylor, *The Limits of European Integration* (Croom Helm, London, 1983) pp. 124 *passim* and p. 129.
74. On the arrangements with East Africa (Kenya, Tanzania and Uganda) see *Official Journal of the European Communities*, L282/55, 1970.
75. 2 ILM, 971.
76. *Official Journal of the European Communities*, L25/1, 1976; *UKTS*, No. 105, 1979, Cmnd. 7751.
77. The Third ACP–EEC Convention, signed at Lomé, 8 Dec. 1984, ACP–EEC Council of Ministers, BX-43-85-377-EN-C, 1985. See the special issue of *The Courier*, No. 89, Jan.–Feb. 1985, and *Lomé III, Analysis of the EEC–ACP Convention*, X/123/1985 (Commission of the European Communities, Brussels). The ACP include: Antigua and Barbuda, Bahamas, Barbados, Belize, Benin, Botswana, Burkina Faso, Burundi, Cameroon, Cape Verde Islands, Central African Republic, Chad,

Comoros, Congo, Djibouti, Dominica, Equatorial Guinea, Ethiopia, Fiji, Gabon, Ghana, Grenada, Guinea, Guinea-Bissau, Guyana, Ivory Coast, Jamaica, Kenya, Kiribati, Lesotho, Liberia, Madagascar, Malawi, Mali, Mauritania, Mauritius, Mozambique, Niger, Nigeria, Papua New Guinea, Rwanda, St Christopher and Nevis, St Lucia, St Vincent and the Grenadines, São Tomé and Principe, Senegal, Seychelles, Sierra Leone, Solomon Islands, Somalia, Sudan, Suriname, Swaziland, Tanzania, Togo, Tonga, Trinidad and Tobago, Tuvalu, Uganda, Western Samoa, Vanuatu, Zaïre, Zambia and Zimbabwe.

78. Carol Cosgrove Twitchett, *A Framework for Development: The EEC and the ACP* (George Allen and Unwin, London, 1981).

79. The Joint Committee and Consultative Assembly (256 parliamentary representatives) were merged under Lomé III because of the overlap between the two institutions. See *The Courier*, No. 88 (Nov.–Dec. 1984) p. 3.

80. *The Courier*, No. 90 (March–April 1985).

81. Although still referred to as the 'Article 108 Committee', the relevant article in Lomé III is 193.

82. Article 220(6) of Lomé III.

83. For the geographical distribution of EIB finance in ACP states, see *Annual Report of the ACP–EEC Council of Ministers, 1983*, Table 6, p. 79.

84. Stabex is a compensation scheme for loss of export earnings from agricultural products caused by falls in prices. Under Lomé II, minerals, which were excluded from Stabex, are covered by a scheme known as 'Sysmin'. This is designed to provide assistance to improve mining production. In contrast to Stabex which has been heavily used, Sysmin has not yet been drawn on much, except by Zaïre and Zambia. See Hamisi Kibola, 'Stabex and Lomé III', *Journal of World Trade Law*, Vol. 18 (1984) pp. 32–51.

85. On the EIB see Arnold Heertje (ed.) *Investing in Europe's Future* (Basil Blackwell, Oxford, 1983); *The Courier*, No. 83 (Jan.–Feb. 1984) pp. 7–14.

86. Election to the post of Secretary-General of the OAU has been a source of considerable controversy within the organisation. At the Mogadishu summit in 1974, twenty ballots were required before Eteki Mboumoua (Cameroon) was elected. The 1983 and 1984 summits were similarly deadlocked and an interim Secretary-General (Onu, Nigeria) was installed. See *West Africa*, 15 July 1985, p. 1409.

87. ACP Council, 37th meeting in Lomé, Dec. 1982.

88. Inis L. Claude Jr, *Swords into Plowshares* (University of London Press, London, 1964) p. 112.

89. See Klaus Tornudd, 'From unaminity to voting and consensus. Trends and Phenomena in Joint Decision Making by Governments', *Co-operation and Conflict*, Vol. 17 (1982) p. 165.

90. Rule 18, Rules of Procedure of the Committee on Disarmament, *The United Nations Yearbook* (United Nations, New York, 1979) Vol. 3, 1978, p. 487.

91. Appendix to 1974 Rules of Procedure, 27 June 1974. The agreement to use consensus was reached on 16 Nov. 1973.

92. See Tornudd, op. cit., pp. 170–1.

93. TD/2 136. See *UNCTAD IV*, Vol. 1, pp. 53-4. For other examples of voting in UNCTAD, see R. Krishnamurti, 'UNCTAD as a Negotiating Instrument', *Journal of World Trade Law*, Vol. 15, No. 1 (Jan.-Feb. 1981) pp. 14-18.
94. Ibid., pp. 18-29.
95. See R. P. Barston, 'The Law of the Sea. The Conference and After', *Journal of World Trade Law*, Vol. 17, No. 3, (May-June 1983) pp. 208-10.
96. See R. P. Barston, 'The Third UN Law of the Sea Conference', In G. R. Berridge and A. Jennings, *Diplomacy at the UN* (Macmillan, London, 1985) pp. 158 *passim*.
97. See IMO, LDC 9/12, 18 Oct. 1985, p. 37 *passim*.
98. See R. P. Barston and Patricia Birnie (eds) *The Maritime Dimension* (George Allen and Unwin, London, 1980) pp. 155-6.
99. As an example see the selected documents of the second Non Proliferation Treaty (NPT) review conference, in Stockholm International Peace Research Institute (SIPRI), *Yearbook, 1981*, pp. 346-65.
100. Krishnamurti, op. cit., p. 7.

CHAPTER SEVEN
International financial relations

Within the past decade questions to do with international financial relations have increasingly moved to the forefront of the international agenda. A noticeable feature of this development is the rise in importance of the International Monetary Fund (IMF) and the International Bank for Reconstruction and Development (IBRD) as international institutions responsible for the coordination and management of international liquidity and development finance. This chapter explores two areas: the main developments in the organisation and work of the Fund after 1973, and, the management of the international debt crisis, including the role of the Fund.[1]

HISTORICAL BACKGROUND

The IMF and the World Bank were formally set up on 27 December 1945, following the Bretton Woods conference, attended by forty-four countries.[2] Bretton Woods in fact was one of several major conferences held during the closing stages of the Second World War on the establishment of post-war institutions, including the United Nations conferences on food and agriculture at Hot Springs, Virginia, in May 1943, which culminated in the San Francisco conference of April 1945, setting up the United Nations. The Havana Charter, which was intended to establish an international trade organisation (ITO) to complement the IMF and the Bank, was, however, never ratified. It was not until 1947 that a much reduced version of an ITO in the form of the GATT was established at Geneva.

The framing and drafting of the Bretton Woods agreements was strongly influenced by the wartime setting and the need to prevent the recurrence of a collapse of the international monetary system similar to that of the 1930s.[3] The themes of reconstruction and the transition from a wartime to a peacetime international economy dominated the original conception of the Fund and the Bank. In this respect too the original conception of the Bank was weighted in favour of the reconstruction of the economies of the war-torn European states, rather than addressing the economic concerns of developing countries. It is interesting to note in this context that the Indian proposals at Bretton Woods to include specific reference to the need for assistance for developing countries in the articles of agreement made little headway.[4]

The Bretton Woods system

The Fund's main tasks, as set out in article 1, were the provision of international liquidity and assistance to members with balance of payments difficulties. Associated with these functions was the aim of promoting the orderly development of trade by discouraging direct controls, such as import quotas or discriminatory tariffs, to influence the balance of payments. Although, as noted above, the failure of states to ratify the Havana Charter, partly because of uncertainties caused by the scale of post-war reconstruction, meant that institutionally the IMF and the Bank were weakened since trade matters were not closely grouped with the work of the Fund or the Bank.

A key element of the Bretton Woods system was the maintenance of orderly exchange rates. An initial par value for the currencies of individual members was agreed, which could only be altered in the event of fundamental disequilibrium. The resoures which the Fund has at its disposal for extending balance of payments assistance to member countries are derived from subscriptions equal to their quotas (ordinary resources) and borrowings from official institutions. Subscriptions are paid partly in an acceptable reserve asset and partly in a member's own currency. Apart from their reserve position in the Fund, members have access to Fund credit in four tranches or segments of 25 per cent of their quota up to a limit of 100 per cent of quota. This is not necessarily an absolute limit and may be exceeded depending on the type of programme, assessed needs and the current guidelines on access.[5] Drawings (purchases) above 25 per cent of quota are subject to increasing *conditionality*. This involves Fund consultations with the member on performance criteria and reviews of its macro-economic policies.

The functions of the Fund can be summarized as: regulatory (exchange rates), financial (providing additional liquidity) and consultative (providing a forum for the collective management of monetary and financial relations). As Cohen notes: 'For the first time ever, governments were formally committing themselves to the principle of collective responsibility for the management of the international monetary order.'[6]

The institutional arrangements were based on the clear distinction in principle that the IMF was to be a revolving fund lending surpluses to deficit countries on a temporary basis. The IBRD, on the other hand, was to be responsible for long-term lending. In more recent times, however, the blurring of this distinction is especially noteworthy.

Institutional arrangements

Under the articles of agreement, the principal decision-making body in the Fund is the Board of Governors (article XII). It consists of one governor and one alternate governor appointed by each member of the Fund, who is usually the minister of finance or governor of the central bank and who serves for five years, subject to the approval of the appointing member. The Executive Board, which conducts the day-to-day business of the Fund, consists of both appointed and elected members. The members with the five largest quotas are each empowered to appoint an executive director, while the remainder are elected on a group basis. Elections are normally held every two years. In addition, the two members with the largest reserve positions in the Fund over the preceding two years may also each appoint an executive director, unless they are already entitled to do so by virtue of the size of their quotas. The Executive Board is chaired by the managing director, an office which has increasingly acquired significant, if discreet, political importance.[7] The Board of Governors have a number of powers not shared by the Executive Board, including the admission of new members, the determination of quotas and the distribution of the net income of the Fund. Since 1953 the governing bodies of both the Fund and the World Bank have held consecutive meetings in Washington, DC, and every third annual meeting is in a member country other than the United States.

The World Bank

In many respects the original aims and purposes of the Bank were not dissimilar from those of the Fund. As originally conceived (article 1), the Bank's purposes were to facilitate the investment of capital for productive purposes, including the restoration of economies destroyed by war, the conversion of productive facilities to peacetime needs and, only thirdly, encouraging the development of productive facilities in less developed countries. These aims were to be achieved through Bank guarantees and loans, although in practice the greater contributions to capital flows have not been through guarantees but direct lending. The Bank was established as a joint-stock bank, initially capitalized at $US10 billion. Under article 5 (section 3) each member has 250 votes plus one additional vote for each share of the stock held. Whereas in the Fund quotas were the bench-mark for drawing rights, in the Bank, the ability to borrow was independent of capital contributions.

The institutional arrangements of the Bank closely follow those of the Fund. These provide for a board of governors, executive directors and president, supported, like the Fund, by an international staff. Some twenty-three countries have traditionally provided ten or more staff to the Bank, with the largest concentration being made up of nationals from the United States, United Kingdom, FRG, Japan, Australia, Canada, Pakistan and India.[8] There are three main institutional differences between the Bank and the Fund. In the first place the Bank's articles of agreement provide for an advisory council, although in practice this rapidly fell into disuse. Unlike the Fund, the Bank, secondly and most importantly, contains no jurisdictional provisions which limit the sovereignty of its members in the financial field. As such the Bank's power of supervision, formally at least, is related to control over its own loan operations. The other difference relates to requirements for information. The Fund contains provisions on a wide range of information which members are obliged to provide on their payments, reserves and import–export positions. These have no counterpart in the Bank's articles of agreement, except for information required about projects financed by the Bank.

A special organisational feature of the Bank is the strong position of its president, who, as the chief executive, is responsible for recommending the terms and conditions of loans to the governing directors, as well as organisational questions relating to the staffing and running of the Bank. In practice the office of president has acquired importance, from the latter period of Eugene Black's presidency through that of Wood and particularly Robert McNamara, when the Bank's role changed from being a bank *per se* to become the central international development agency with a philosophy geared to project lending rather than more general programme aid.

Apart from operating as a development finance agency, the Bank has also acted in a dispute settlement role as well as providing financial and other consultancy services to members. For example President Wood acted as a mediator in the negotiations after the Suez crisis which led to the financial settlement between the United Arab Republic and the Suez Canal Company shareholders.[9] The Bank subsequently acted as fiscal agent for funds contributed by various governments towards the cost of clearance of the canal. A further example of the successful mediatory role of the Bank can be seen in the long-running negotiations involving the Bank, India and Pakistan over the development of the Indus waters, which culminated eventually in the Indus Waters Treaty of 1960.[10] With the creation of the International Finance Corporation (IFC) in 1956 and the International Development Association (IDA) in 1960, the three institutions became known as the 'World Bank Group'.

THE EVOLUTION OF THE FUND

The impact of the Fund and the Bank during the late 1940s and early 1950s was limited in view of the scale of post-war reconstruction. For the most part reconstruction finance was channelled from 1947 through the Marshall Aid Programme. Apart from the loans of 1947, the IMF made no further major loans until 1956. The shortage of Fund liquidity in effect meant that the United States became the residual source of international liquidity through the dollar, with the dollar acting as the major vehicle for international trade and investment and a reserve asset for central banks. However, a number of developments in the late 1950s and early 1960s served to alter the focus of operations of both the Fund and the Bank, as well as lessen the influence of the United States. In particular, from 1961 to 1963, there was an unprecedented increase in the accession of new members to the Fund, largely because of the rapid decolonisation in Africa, which raised the membership to 102.[11] The expansion in membership inevitably brought an extended range of interests into the Fund, and radically altered the scale of potential demands on Fund resources. Apart from this, the period from the late 1950s, saw the major Western European powers emerge as a leading decision-making group on international financial and monetary matters. By this stage European and Japanese recovery had moved out of the post-war reconstruction phase. Above all, the convertibility of Western European currencies (Japan followed in 1961) symbolised this transition, which was accompanied by a rapid development of the European capital markets. In contrast, serious balance of payments deficits after 1958 led not only to concern in the United States about international confidence in the dollar, but the overall role of the United States in the Bretton Woods system, as the leading banker and aid donor. Commenting on the changed monetary relationships, Solomon, for example, contrasts the visit of Treasury Secretary Robert B. Anderson and Under-Secretary of State Dillon, to Europe in 1960, to discuss with European officials ways of reducing the strain on the American balance of payments, especially the relief of US troop costs in Germany, with the visit eleven years earlier of Treasury Secretary John W. Snyder bringing with him in almost imperial style US proposals for a devaluation of sterling and other European currencies.[12]

Against this context, the Group of 10 (G-10) made up of Belgium, Canada, France, FRG, Italy, Japan, the Netherlands, Sweden, United Kingdom and the United States began to play an increasingly central role in negotiations on financial and monetary matters. The importance of the G-10, as the leading group within the Fund, can be seen institutionally in the borrowing arrangements, exclusive to G-10 members, known as the General Arrangements to Borrow (GAB).[13] The GAB, which was agreed by the G-10 after the Paris negotiations in December 1961 and approved by the Fund's Executive Board in January 1962, commenced with a US$6 billion credit line. Although this was a valuable source of supplementary finance for the Fund, the GAB could only be called upon to finance drawings from the Fund by the participants. Unlike other Fund arrangements, major amendments to the GAB, require the approval not only of the Executive Board but the agreement of all ten original participants.[14] The arrangements for the GAB remained essentially unaltered until 1982. The exclusivity to the G-10 of the GAB, coupled with the undermining of collective decision-making, led to criticism by industrialised countries outside the arrangements, as well as less developed countries.

SDRs

The influence of the G-10 was particularly illustrated during the negotiations to create a new reserve asset (later termed 'special drawing rights' or SDRs) from 1966 to 1968.[15] Much of the preparatory work was conducted within the G-10 framework. However, the position of the Fund was asserted by the then Managing Director, Pierre-Paul Schweitzer, who sought to broaden the framework of discussions beyond the G-10. In this Schweitzer was supported by the United States, which preferred the discussions to be held within the framework of the IMF, rather than face the possible concerted position of the EEC. Four meetings of the deputies of the G-10 and the executive directors of the IMF, ten of whom represented groups other than the G-10, were subsequently held during 1966–67. A further feature of the SDR negotiations was the close Franco-German collaboration, which has become a feature of the conduct of diplomacy on major international financial questions. Although the Fund itself did not in this instance take a leading role, the SDR negotiations did contribute to its technical status, through the secretariat work carried out by Fund staff. The SDR facility came into existence in July 1969, when sufficient approval was received (three-fifths of the members of the Fund having four-fifths of the total voting power) for the amendment to the Fund Articles of Agreement to come into force. The Fund made an initial allocation of SDRs the following year.

Other facilities

Two further facilities in the period under review, the establishment of the compensatory financing facility (CFF)[16] and the buffer stock financing facility, illustrate new areas of operations reflecting the Fund's expanded membership. The CFF, which was set up in 1963, was established to provide assistance mainly for the exporters of primary products who were experiencing payments difficulties due to fluctuations in export earnings. The CFF was complemented in June 1969 by the buffer stock facility, through which funds are made available to assist members in meeting their contributions under approved international buffer stock agreements, such as the international sugar, tin, cocoa and natural rubber agreements.[17] Unlike the CFF, this latter facility has not been greatly used owing to the problems of setting up and managing buffer stocks.

END OF BRETTON WOODS

The Bretton Woods system of par values and convertibility of the dollar was in effect brought to an end in August 1971, by the package of measures taken by the United States, which included the temporary suspension of dollar convertibility and a 10 per cent additional import tax, in response to the exchange rate crisis.[18] The dollar was further devalued in February 1973 and shortly afterwards most major currencies were allowed to float.

What form a future international monetary system might take was entrusted in July 1972 to the IMF's Committee of the Board of Governors on Reform of the International Monetary System and Related Issues (known as the 'Committee of 20'). In the event the Committee of 20 achieved few of its long-range tasks, being overtaken by the events of the Arab–Israeli War and the subsequent oil crisis, which narrowed the committee's focus of negotiation to more immediate concerns. The problems of conducting complex multilateral negotiation on monetary reform are summed up by Fleming in this observation on the Committee of 20:[19]

> Very few of the major countries established coherent national positions over the whole range of these issues, and only the United States brought out a fairly comprehensive statement of its position . . . . The Europeans handicapped themselves by trying to agree issue by issue on a joint EEC position. The less developed countries made great efforts to agree a common programme of reform through the Group of Twenty-Four, but this agreement was inevitably confined to a few isolated matters of common interest such as the nature of the link between SDR creation and development finance.

A number of immediate measures, however, set out in the second part of the committee's report, *Outline for Reform*, were later adopted by the Fund. These included the setting up of an oil facility and extended borrowing arrangements which are discussed separately below. The need for a broad-based advisory committee was also recognised and the Committee of 20 was continued as a committee of the Fund, under the title 'Interim Committee'.

POST-BRETTON WOODS

Following the exchange rate crisis of 1971–73 a number of broad changes took place over the next decade in the structure and role of the

Fund. With exchange rates for major currencies floating, the Fund's regulatory functions received less emphasis. The second of the Fund's functions, the provision of international liquidity, began to assume greater importance, particularly through the provision of standby arrangements. However, as the scale of lending operations increased in the 1970s, the Fund found it could no longer rely on the resources derived from members' subscriptions and subsequently had to negotiate additional bilateral arrangements ('borrowed resources') with individual states, notably oil producers and large industrial countries. Borrowed resources have been used to establish temporary facilities for members with large balance of payments imbalances in relation to their quota and requiring large resources for long periods over and above the normal limits of borrowing. The supplementary financing facility (SFF) was set up in 1979 and broadly similar arrangements continued under the enlarged access policy from 1981 after the funds had been committed under the SFF. Following the second oil crisis of 1979, the Fund became an important financial intermediary *vis-à-vis* central banks, developments agencies, the Bank for International Settlements (BIS) and creditor governments, as multi-funding operations were developed to meet enhanced payments difficulties. With this development, the Fund's third function, as a coordination and decision-making centre, came to assume more importance, especially after the onset of the debt crisis in 1982, although the Fund did not become the principal source of balance of payments support, since multilateral restructuring of debt and other financial support increasingly involved the central and commercial banks and other development institutions.

INSTITUTIONAL DEVELOPMENTS

In the main the formal and informal structural changes in the Fund's central institutions have had the effect of broadening the participation in decision-making by introducing a wider range of states into the processes of dialogue and negotiation. Some of these changes, however, have been pragmatic appreciations of alterations in the political or economic importance of states. Thus Saudi Arabia and the People's Republic of China have been added as single constituency members of the Executive Board. Saudi Arabia has appointed an executive director since 1978, which raised the executive directors to twenty-one.[20] In September 1980 the Board of Governors approved the increase in the number of elected members from fifteen to sixteen, which enabled China to elect a director with only that country as the constituency, bringing the total number of executive directors to twenty-two.

Interim Committee

The establishment of the Interim Committee as the successor to the Committee of 20 in October 1974 was an important addition to the formal decision-making machinery of the Fund. The committee brings together at the level of Fund governor, ministers or equivalent rank twenty-two representatives, each of whom may appoint seven associates, plus the Fund managing director, and observers from international and regional organisations. Switzerland also has observer status.

The Interim Committee, which meets usually twice a year, normally in conjunction with the IMF's annual meeting, and again in the spring, is responsible for the provision of advice and recommendations to the Board of Governors and Executive Board in three broad areas. These are: (i) the proposals of the Executive Board to amend the articles of agreement; (ii) measures to deal with sudden disturbances that pose a threat to the international monetary system; (iii) supervising the management and adaptation of the international monetary system. Between 1974 and 1976, for example, the Interim Committee has under its first and second areas of responsibility been concerned with the amendments to the Fund's articles to permit floating and the setting up and operation of the oil facility. Under the third area, the Interim Committee has examined the issue of SDR allocation, the Fund's enlarged access policy, and made recommendations on quota limits.[21] The Interim Committee continues to operate under its anomalous title since its intended successor, the council, envisaged as having decision-making powers rather than advisory ones like the committee, has never commanded sufficient political support to enable it to be set up.[22]

Development Committee

The Development Committee, the second of the two committees established as part of the recommendations of the Committee of 20, was intended to carry on its work on the transfer of real resources to developing countries. Unlike the Interim Committee it is a joint committee of the Fund and Bank. The committee consists of twenty-two members, generally ministers of finance, appointed in turn for successive periods of two years by each of the countries or groups of countries that nominates or appoints a member of the Bank's or IMF's Board of Executive Directors. In the main the Development Committee has lacked a clear set of tasks given its very broad mandate. Its large size, with anything up to 150 participants, has also contributed to the committee having little impact. The Development Committee conceivably could have occupied a more central role, other than as a discussion forum, as a link between the Fund and the Bank. However, in practice it has tended to occupy an area covered by other international institutions such as UNCTAD, and straddled the borderlines between orthodox IMF funtions, trade and development finance.

In recognition of the need to clarify the mandate and improve the effectiveness of the committee, a number of changes to its procedures were made in April 1979.[23] A more novel approach was taken in September 1984 in response to initiatives from the June 1984 London seven-nation economic summit, the Cartagena group of foreign and finance ministers and the September 1984 meeting of the Commonwealth finance ministers, which called for a special extended meeting of the Development Committee on specifically defined finance, trade and debt issues. A number of changes subsequently were made for the informal session of the Development Committee held in April 1985, including the curtailment of the heavily attended plenary sessions, which had tended in the past to be largely taken up with prepared statements. The agenda of the informal session was also coordinated with the parallel Interim Committee meeting. These and other changes have had the effect of moving the Development Committee somewhat more in the direction of the second of the two types of roles noted above, that is, as a vehicle for facilitating links between the Fund and the Bank.[24]

Group of 24

Apart from the Interim and Development Committee, the establishment of the Group of 24 in November 1971, known officially as the Intergovernmental Group of 24 on International Monetary Affairs (G-24), should be noted. The stimulus for the creation of the group, which is a ministerial committee of the G-77 and not an official committee of the Fund, came from the virtual exclusion of developing countries from the main negotiations conducted by the G-10 on the creation of the SDR and the 1971–73 exchange rate crisis.

The G-24 comprises eight members each drawn from Africa, Asia and Latin America. The People's Republic of China also attends as an invitee. The group has steadily increased its effectiveness, especially from the late 1970s, but it has not yet been able to develop the level of contact and coordination of the G-10. In fact since 1973 the G-10 has intensified its extensive network of ministerial and official contacts, through regular meetings of its finance ministers, the subdivision into the G-5 and meetings of the G-10 deputies, normally in Paris in conjunction with officials from OECD's Working Party 3. The G-24, however, has gradually developed from being simply a coordinating body to a forum for the preparation and presentation to the Fund and other institutions of its own concerted programmes, such as the 1979 Plan of Immediate Action. Meetings of the G-24 at deputy and ministerial[25] level usually take place prior to those of the Interim Committee.[26] The Fund provides secretariat support. Although the size and disparate range of interests has limited the degree of coordination, a core group has emerged, made up of Argentina, Mexico, Brazil, India, Pakistan and Yugoslavia, whose ministers and officials individually play important roles intergovernmentally and as staff in international financial institutions.

DEVELOPMENT OF FUND FACILITIES

The Fund has been concerned with five broad issues since 1973:

1. The problems generated by fluctuations in commodity prices, such as petroleum, or shortfalls in commodity export earnings from, for example, cereals, sugar, tin, rubber and other commodities;
2. Long-term arrangements to assist structural adjustment;
3. The enlargement of the resources of the Fund;
4. Increases in quotas;
5. The extended payments crisis.

In the main the Fund's approach, particularly on the first of these issues, has been based on augmenting the existing facilities, that is, standby arrangements, with a number of temporary facilities including those for oil, as well as the supplementary financing facility and enlarged access policy (see Table 7.1). To a large extent the use of short-term facilities has been influenced by the third of the issues, that is, the problem of enhancing the Fund's resources over and above that derived from members' subscriptions.

Table 7.1 Balance of payments assistance by and reserve tranche drawings on the IMF, 1948–86*

	Annual averages				Annual amounts													
	1948–49	1950–59	1960–69	1970–79	1973	1974	1975	1976	1977	1978	1979	1980	1981	1982	1983	1984	1985	1986
Fund policies and facilities (drawings)	389	263	1,632	3,049	733	4,053	4,658	7,010	3,425	3,744	1,843	3,753	7,082	8,784	14,133	8,105	4,199	4,202
Reserve tranche	286	104	608	888	391	966	723	991	80	2,536	147	359	310	1,336	1,514	814	185	382
Credit tranche (ordinary)†	103	159	985	916	228	1,265	641	1,478	2,895	421	648	855	1,662	1,064	1,925	1,351	1,402	2,136
Compensatory financing (export shortfalls)	—	—	39	453	113	107	239	2,308	241	578	572	980	1,231	2,333	2,827	807	740	568
Compensatory financing (cereal import excesses)	—	—	—	—	—	—	—	—	—	—	—	—	12	295	12	9	189	—
Buffer stock financing	—	—	—	10	—	—	5	90	—	36	38	—	—	144	308	2	—	—
Extended fund facility: (ordinary)†	—	—	—	61	—	—	8	—	209	174	132	339	1,041	1,057	2,214	1,660	83	125
Oil facility	—	—	—	690	—	1,716	3,043	2,143	—	—	—	—	—	—	—	—	—	—
Supplementary financing	—	—	—	31	—	—	—	—	—	—	306	1,218	2,040	1,711	1,678	200	—	—
Credit tranche	—	—	—	21	—	—	—	—	—	—	305	943	1,469	982	844	—	—	—
Extended facility	—	—	—	10	—	—	—	—	—	—	101	275	571	728	834	200	—	—
Enlarged access policy	—	—	—	—	—	—	—	—	—	—	—	—	787	846	3,655	3,262	1,600	991
Credit tranche	—	—	—	—	—	—	—	—	—	—	—	—	306	491	2,100	1,798	1,238	866
Extended facility	—	—	—	—	—	—	—	—	—	—	—	—	481	354	1,556	1,464	361	125
Fund-administered facilities	—	—	—	145	—	—	—	14	181	713	546	1,284	441	54	82	85	86	56
Oil facility subsidy account (grants)	—	—	—	9	—	—	—	14	28	25	19	28	50	9	14	—	—	—
Trust fund (loans)	—	—	—	136	—	—	—	—	153	688	527	1,256	368	—	—	—	—	—
Supplementary financing facility subsidy account (grants)	—	—	—	—	—	—	—	—	—	—	—	—	23	44	68	85	86	56

Source: International Monetary Fund, Bureau of Statistics.
†Drawings financed from the Fund's ordinary (i.e., nonborrowed) resources.
Components may not add to totals owing to rounding.
*In millions of US dollars 1948–69; in millions of SDRs, 1970–86.

Underlying the debate about enlarging the access to Fund resources are a number of different issues. As regards *borrowed* resources, some of the larger Western industrialised countries felt that the Fund might become unduly dependent on OPEC, although this view has to some extent been modified out of reluctant necessity. A separate issue has been whether there is actually a need for larger access on a continuing basis. Lack of agreement on this within the Fund has in turn prevented wider agreement on quotas versus borrowed resources to finance access. The issues of quota increases and other aspects of enlarged access, including SDR allocation are returned to at the end of the chapter.

As regards structural adjustment facilities, the Fund has implemented a number of the ideas discussed in the Committee of 20 including an additional permanent facility known as the extended fund facility (EFF), which was set up in September 1974. The EFF is intended to provide support for member countries willing to undertake medium-term structural adjustment programmes which are experiencing payments difficulties for structural reasons such as production difficulties, changing patterns of trade, or weakness in their payments position because of development-related imports. The EFF facilities normally run for three years for amounts greater than the members' quota.

Modifications have also been made to other permanent facilities. For example, the CFF was extended in August 1979 to include fluctuations in receipts from travel and workers' remittances in the calculation of the export shortfall. A further modification was made to the CFF in May 1981, partly on the initiative of the UN Food and Agricultural Organisation (FAO), to extend the CFF to provide coverage for cereal crop failure or a sharp increase in the cost of cereal imports. Purchases under the CFF between 1979 and 1981 amounted to nearly SDR 1 billion, almost one-third of total purchases from the Fund.[27]

Short-term facilities

Between 1974 and 1981 three short-term Fund facilities were set up using *borrowed* resources. These were the oil facilities (1974 and 1975) and the SFF. Both schemes were later augmented by special low-interest subsidy accounts for countries, defined by the UN Secretary-General and Fund staff, which were worst affected by oil price increases or other special factors.[28] The Fund's experience in establishing these facilities suggests a number of general difficulties with regard to the negotiation of borrowed resources. In the first place, the schemes have encountered political opposition. The first oil facility was opposed by the United States in response to OPEC policies, which after the outbreak of the October 1973 War classified countries for the purposes of the oil embargo on the basis of whether they were friendly to Arab interests (e.g. Britain, France and Spain), 'neutral' (e.g. Japan and West Germany) or hostile (e.g. United States and the Netherlands). Although the embargo ended in March 1974, oil price rises (the marker for Gulf crude rose to $11.65 after January 1974) had long-reaching effects on the economies of non-oil exporting developing countries, IMF facilities and the source of IMF funds.[29] United States opposition in the Interim Committee was later withdrawn through a compromise that modifications to the Fund's articles would make it possible for the Fund to use a wider range of member-country currencies, in conformity with Fund policies, so increasing the liquidity of the Fund.[30] A second general problem arises from the need to secure a pool of contributions. The first oil facility was extended in 1975 when the Interim Committee recommended borrowing up to SDR 5 billion. To reach the target the Fund had to conclude agreements with fourteen countries, seven of whom (mainly oil exporters) had contributed to the 1974 facility.[31] The United States was noticeably absent from the list of contributors.[32] Borrowing under the oil facilities was confined to 1974 and 1975. The oil facility was dissolved after 1983, which coincided with the softening of petroleum prices, by which stage outstanding repayments had been cleared.[33]

Not dissimilar difficulties were encountered over the establishment of the SFF (1977), although in this case the United States contributed to the financing of the facility. The scheme called for borrowing up to SDR 7.8 billion to provide additional support to countries with standby or extended arrangements, for adjustment programmes of up to three years. The facility took a considerable time to enter into operation (February 1979), a point criticised by the Interim Committee at its meeting in April 1978 in Mexico City.[34] To raise the required SDR 7.8 billion the Fund had to negotiate contributions, and later terms, with fourteen countries, plus the Swiss National Bank. Not only was the group amorphous, but it included a significant number of small contributions including those made by Qatar, Abu Dhabi, Kuwait, Belgium and somewhat curiously, Guatemala. The major contribution came from the FRG, Saudi Arabia and the United States. The contributions were on an 'on-call' basis and as part of the liquid reserve assets of the donor could be called or expire before being drawn down. Furthermore, as part of the terms and conditions, purchases were at US commercial rates at OPEC insistence which, with conditionality, made the facility less attractive.[35] Yet, the SFF was virtually fully drawn and no new commitments were permitted after February 1982.

Enlarged access policy

The unsatisfactory nature of the borrowing arrangements for the oil facilities and the SFF has influenced a move away from individual OPEC countries to a more stable and cohesive donor group. From 1981 the Fund has relied heavily for borrowed resources on a group made up of the central banks, the BIS,[36] the Saudi Arabian Monetary Agency (SAMA) and Japan. Saudi Arabia's enhanced role in the Fund (analogous to that of Japan in the World Bank), as a major contributor of borrowed resources, is perhaps one of the most marked recent features in the development of the Fund. In May 1981 an agreement was concluded by the Fund with SAMA to borrow up to SDR 8 billion over six years. This enabled the Fund to continue lending operations using a mixture of ordinary and borrowed resources after the phasing out of the SFF in 1982. In order to provide continued funding for the enlarged access policy, four new borrowing arrangements for SDR 6.8 billion were concluded with SAMA, the BIS, Japan and the National Bank of Belgium in April 1984. Although the enlarged access policy is properly regarded as a short-term arrangement, it has been extended *ad hoc* on an annual basis since 1984,[37] using short- and medium-term borrowed resources.

Quotas and Fund resources

While the short-term arrangements discussed above carried the Fund through the immediate period after 1982–83, the onset of the debt crisis raised major issues for the Fund concerning the adequacy of its ordinary resources. While previous quota increases in 1977 (32.5 per cent) and 1980 (50 per cent) had raised total quotas to SDR 61 billion, these had not kept pace with the growth in world trade and capital flows. The serious pressure which the Fund came under from a queue of debtor countries including Mexico, Brazil and Yugoslavia with major deficit problems, gave rise to a major and continuing debate, which coincided with the general debate on quota increases. The debate centred on the scale of lendable resources, the nature and efficiency of short-term solutions and the form longer-term arrangements might take.

What form the solutions should take has produced sharp differences within and between industrialised and developing countries. The position of the United States set out at the annual IMF meeting in Toronto in September 1982, envisaged an 'adequate' quota rise of 25 per cent and an additional permanent borrowing arrangement which would be available to the IMF on a contingency basis for use in extraordinary circumstances.[38] Underlying the United States position was the view that the Fund's lendable resources were adequate and a large quota increase was neither necessary nor appropriate. The United States also preferred, if possible, longer-term arrangements, rather than *ad hoc* rescue packages.[39] The Toronto proposals formed the basis of the agenda at the Group of 5 (G-5) meeting in Frankfurt on 9 December 1982.[40] The idea of a special crisis fund, based on modifications to the GAB, however, initially met some opposition, with the FRG and Japan expressing reservations on the feasibility of the scheme and the political cost of failure. Japan especially favoured a solution based on large quota increases. For the United States, however, modifications to the GAB would provide the Fund with more effective and usable resources for use in emergencies. A proposal based partly on an expansion of the GAB was also considered more politically acceptable by the United States in view of Congressional opposition to large quota increases. In contrast, the G-24 position called for a doubling of quotas, an SDR issue and a separate contingency fund.[41]

Although the Toronto meeting had set the date of the next Interim Committee meeting as April for the resolution of the quota issue, the widespread sense of urgency and mounting crisis was reflected in the advancement of the meeting to February and the quickening in the pace of negotiation.[42] The G-10 met in Paris on 17 January 1983 and formally approved a number of proposals which substantially modified the GAB.[43] These entailed increasing the credit lines from SDR 6.4 billion to SDR 17 billion and opening the GAB, under well-defined circumstances to non-participants.[44] As was noted earlier, the GAB had until that point been a facility for exclusive use by G-10 members consisting of credit lines between G-10 members and central banks on the one side, and the Fund on the other. A third element of the revised GAB proposals involved the participation of Switzerland through the Swiss National Bank, and an associated borrowing arrangement with Saudi Arabia on 8 January.[45] In addition, prior to the Interim Committee meeting on 10–11 February, the United States modified its position on quotas, moving to acceptance of a quota increase of between 40 and 50 per cent.[46] The level of quotas and revisions to the GAB were further discussed in an attempted compromise session between the Interim Committee chairman and members of the G-24, including Brazil, India and Mexico on 9 February.[47]

Quotas and access

The Interim Committee at its February 1983 meeting approved a quota rise of 47.5 per cent and the proposals to enlarge the GAB, which were subsequently endorsed by the Executive Board.

Nevertheless, substantial differences have continued both within and between industrialised and developing countries over the amount of lendable resources both the Fund and the Bank require. The enlarged GAB is not seen by most members of the G-24 as meeting the full requirement of a doubling in quotas.[48] Further uncertainty about resources has been caused by a number of other factors. In the short term, the US quota contribution of $US 8.4 billion met substantial Congressional opposition[49] before the IMF bill was approved by both Houses in November 1983.[50] In the second place, the United States has continued to adopt a restrictive attitude to the funding of both the IMF and the World Bank, including its IDA affiliate.[51] Furthermore, the US–Japanese bilateral negotiations in 1983–84 on the selective capital increase for the World Bank ran into difficulties as a result of the linkage by the United States of those negotiations with its dispute with Japan over access to Japanese capital markets, adding a further dimension of complexity to the discussions on the level and adequacy of IMF/World Bank resources.[52] Thirdly, the issue of quota increases became linked with that of the level of access to IMF resources. At the Interim Committee meeting in September 1983 a limited compromise, based on a United Kingdom proposal for split levels of quota access, determined by the severity of payment difficulties, which had been discussed earlier at the Commonwealth finance ministers' meeting, was agreed.[53] The level nevertheless remains below that sought by the G-24 in the 1984 Revised Programme. The Interim Committee itself has been unable to reach consensus on a further issue of SDRs. Taken together these factors have complicated and added a level of complexity and uncertainty to the resolution of the central issues concerning the level of Fund resources.

MULTILATERAL DEBT RESTRUCTURING

The international debt crisis which developed in mid 1982 posed major problems of management for the international community. Not only were there no established institutional arrangements to cope with the scale of debt restructuring or renegotiations, no single institution or state grouping was capable of providing unaided the necessary financial resources to meet the needs of deficit countries. Prior to 1982, restructuring of official and commercial debt was generally on a small scale. Banks, too, preferred to avoid formal renegotiations. Such restructuring as took place was generally of a conventional refinancing kind. Between 1975 and 1982, only a minority of negotiations (7 out of 28) rescheduled over $US300 million.[54] However, 5 official debt reschedulings from 1982 to 1985 were for more than $US1 billion (Mexico, Morocco, Brazil, Zaïre, Argentina) and over half of the 36 cases involved more than $US300 million.[55]

Another distinctive feature of the debt crisis was the suddenness with which the position of the major borrowers such as Mexico, Brazil, Venezuela, Chile and Yugoslavia, (see Table 7.2) deteriorated. The near-simultaneous loss of credit-worthiness by several large borrowers as a result affected perceptions of regional risk. For example the development of the Polish debt crises in 1981[56] created uncertainty about financial and commercial relations with other parts of Eastern Europe, especially Hungary and Romania. With the onset of the Mexican crisis in mid 1982, a similar regionalisation of risk took place. By the time the IMF met at Toronto, it seemed that the international community was faced with 'rolling over' one massive debt crisis after another.

Paris Club

Prior to 1982, multilateral official debt renegotiations were conducted mainly though by no means exclusively within the framework of the Paris Club. Other fora which have been used include aid consortia (e.g. for India and Pakistan) or special creditor groups, as in the cases of Mexico and Yugoslavia. States have also approached major creditor 'sources' on a bilateral basis to restructure some parts of their official debt.

The Paris Club, which mainly consists of OECD creditors,[57] is a forum within which countries negotiate restructuring of official debt, that is, loans from creditor governments and private export credits

Table 7.2 Countries reviewed, ranked by debt to banks at the end of December, 1982 (in millions of US dollars)*

1.	Mexico	62,888		15.	Sudan	1,119
2.	Brazil	60,453		16.	Bolivia	940
3.	Venezuela	27,474		17.	Zaïre	873
4.	Argentina	25,681		18.	Dominican Republic	866
5.	Chile	11,610		19.	Nicaragua	814
6.	Yugoslavia	9,821		20.	Zambia	590
7.	Nigeria	8,527		21.	Jamaica	521
8.	Peru	5,353		22.	Honduras	469
9.	Ecuador	4,488		23.	Senegal	410
10.	Romania	4,243		24.	Madagascar	299
11.	Turkey	3,971		25.	Togo	253
12.	Morocco	3,882		26.	Malawi	202
13.	Uruguay	1,531		27.	Guyana	129
14.	Costa Rica	1,261				

Source: Bank for International Settlements. *The Maturity Distribution of International Bank Lending.*

*Included in this table are Fund member countries that are currently in the process of formal multilateral debt restructuring (i.e. rescheduling or refinancing) with commercial banks or have completed such a process since 1978. Liberia also completed such a renegotiation in 1982; however, it is not included in this table because of its status as an offshore financial centre.

guaranteed or insured by export credit agencies in the creditor countries. The origins of the Paris Club date to 1956, when several European countries met in Paris to discuss rescheduling Argentina's foreign debt, and similarly in 1961 and 1962, when certain Brazilian debts were rescheduled. The Paris Club meets at the French conference centre. Meetings of the club are requested by the debtor country and normally involve ten to fifteen creditor countries, but sometimes as few as four. Meetings are often attended by representatives of the Fund, UNCTAD or OECD with the agreement of the debtor country. Normally, the Paris Club require the applicant country, if it is a Fund member, to have in place or under discussion an economic adjustment programme supported by Fund resources subject to upper credit tranche conditionality. The terms and conditions of the rescheduling agreement take the form of an agreed minute, although this does not have effect until bilateral agreements have subsequently been negotiated between the debtor country and each of its creditors. Since 1982 the majority of *official* debt restructurings have taken place within the framework of the Paris Club. The acute nature and frequency of many reschedulings (twenty-three debtor countries that are Fund members obtained twenty-nine official debt reschedulings in 1983 and 1984) has almost inevitably meant some relaxation of the Paris Club principle of limiting rescheduling to medium- and long-term debt by the inclusion of some short-term debt in the overall agreement.

BANK DEBT RESTRUCTURING

Prior to 1982 there was no formal or established framework for conducting commercial bank debt negotiations. Earlier renegotiations between commercial lenders and sovereign state borrowers had been both sporadic and generally involved relatively low amounts. Renegotiations tended to be treated as routine 'extension' negotiations. Since 1981 there has been a sharp increase in the number of countries seeking either debt restructuring through refinancing or rescheduling. The amount of commercial debt restructured rose substantially from an annual average of $US1.5 billion (1978–81), to $US5 billion in 1982, and dramatically to over $US60 billion by late 1983.[58]

A particular problem which has emerged in official and especially commercial debt restructuring for creditor and Fund analysts is establishing accurate assessments of the scale of debt. Two aspects should be distinguished. First is the accretion of substantial debt by state and parastatal agencies and government ministries, the volume of which may not always be fully known or centrally controlled.[59] This may include, for example, previously undisclosed credit lines for defence purchases or liabilities incurred by a state airline or shipping corporation.[60] This aspect of the debt crisis has underlined the tendency for the modern state to fragment through subunits carrying out independent or semi-autonomous political and economic external policies such as arms purchases, currency transactions, the acquisition of shipping and other assets.[61] A second and related difficulty stems from what might be termed the extraterritorial reach or 'offshore' presence of some modern states. In the context of the debt crisis, this has involved the problem of substantial extraterritorial borrowing by foreign branches and subsidiaries of developing country banks in major banking centres. For example, by 1982, Brazil had as part of its development strategy, 16 Brazilian banks abroad, with a total of 104 branches and outstanding deposits of $US10 billion.[62]

Restructuring negotiations

In general, restructuring negotiations have been conducted on a case-by-case basis between creditors and individual debtor countries, rather than with groups of countries. During 1983–84, for example, some thirty-two bank restructuring agreements were reached in principle with twenty-six countries.[63] From these and subsequent negotiations four main features are worth commenting on. The complexity of the negotiations arises from the extended range of parties, their conflicting interests and the need to orchestrate several sets of negotiations. In an extreme case such as Mexico, over 1,000 banks (apart from governments and other institutions) had some degree of involvement. Commercial bank steering or liaison committees emerged as powerful new actors, in a coordinating role between governments, central banks and international institutions.[64] The element of linkage, secondly, between various sets of negotiations, for example between the debtor country and the IMF, the BIS, creditor group and central bank is a further distinctive feature of the restructuring negotiations in the period after 1982. In this interlocking context, thirdly, deadlines have figured prominently for example for mobilising funds, setting economic adjustment target dates and over alterations to repayment schedules.[65] The Fund itself has assumed a new role in terms of the coordination and mobilisation of Fund and commercial bank resources. In a change of policy, the Fund has set deadlines for the mobilisation of a 'critical mass' of commercial bank funds *before* Fund resources themselves are committed.[66] In the Mexican restructuring negotiations, for example, a deadline of 15 December 1982 was set to commercial banks by which to raise the $US5 billion 'critical mass' of commercial bank finance.[67] The Fund's managing director also made individual approaches to a number of banks and the Italian authorities among others.[68] The other notable feature of the post-1982 restructuring negotiations is the extent to which they are extremely sensitive to a very wide range of domestic and external and transnational influences. In the Brazilian negotiations, for example, Brazil encountered difficulties in rescheduling $US11 billion because the negotiations became linked with the passage of the IMF quota bill before the US Congress, which had met substantial opposition.[69] At the same time the domestic steel lobby in the United States was also dissatisfied with the import concessions agreed by President Reagan during his visit to Brazil in December 1982.[70]

FURTHER DEVELOPMENTS

Since the initial Brazil and Mexican crises, governments, international institutions and banks have been concerned with the problem of finding longer-term arrangements to replace annual rescheduling or restructuring. In some instances, e.g. Mexico, Venezuela and Ecuador, multi-year rescheduling agreements (MYRAS) have been concluded which involve the rescheduling of bank or official debt maturities falling due in more than one year. In other arrangements the stretching of repayment has been achieved by provisions on trade credits, the phasing of repayments and goodwill clauses on economic performance.[71] The Fund has been associated with MYRAS and other similar agreements through standby arrangements, or, twice-yearly article 4 consultations, as in Ecuador's agreement of 24 April 1985 with the Paris Club.[72] In other instances, quite different approaches have been adopted by states such as periodic moratoriums (e.g. Bolivia) or unilateral limits on the percentage of total debt repayment (e.g. Nigeria). These latter developments, coupled with the possibility of a debtor 'cartel', have contributed to the continued international uncertainty surrounding the debt crisis. A further development of note is the formation of the Latin American 'Cartagena Group'. The Cartagena Group, which comprises Mexico, Brazil, Bolivia, Chile, Columbia, the Dominican Republic, Ecuador, Peru, Uruguay and Venezuela, has met regularly since 1984 at foreign and finance minister level.[73]

There are doubts too concerning the likelihood of continued bank and official funding to cover not only existing obligations but also new finance, i.e. finance not merely for rolling over payments of interest or principal on the scale required. For many of the banks the 1970s are viewed, as far as lending policies are concerned, as a period of overstretched resources. In the more restrictive trade and financial setting after 1982 banks are seeking accordingly to limit their exposure.[74] In view of this rescheduling decisions may prove increasingly difficult and particularly sensitive to international trade deterioration.[75]

A related set of concerns stem from differences of view over the strategies and policies which are or should be adopted. The range of views can be grouped according to: (i) those which are basically in agreement with the IMF philosophy and strategy but seek particular alterations; (ii) other conventional short- or medium-term solutions;

(iii) radical options; (iv) proposals that are marginal to the management of the debt crisis.[76] Underlying the IMF structural adjustment programmes, which tend to have some common features such as public expenditure reductions, exchange-rate modification, removal of subsidies, enhancement of exports and administrative reform, are three general assumptions. These are that the costs associated with adjustment programmes should be evaluated in the medium term and not by short-run effects; secondly, that export improvement policies should not be at the price of protectionist measures; and thirdly continued availability of capital on terms that are compatible with the country's ability to service its debt. A fourth and separate premiss is that the Fund is not, nor should it become, a development finance agency.[77] Of the other proposals for dealing with the debt crisis which were grouped above, there are those that can be considered at the margin such as changes in the institutional relations between the Fund and the Bank.[78]

These and other proposals to increase Bank lending and access to capital markets, while they may contribute to capital availability and capability to design macro-economic and sectoral programmes, do not in themselves address the central problems connected with the scale of debt and debt rescheduling.[79] Second are those proposals which basically accept the IMF approach, but within it seek to develop somewhat different sectoral approaches to the debt-servicing aspect to the debt crisis such as MYRAS or relating repayment schemes to export earnings.[80] Third, alternative short- and medium-term solutions have tended to be based on criticism of the effects of IMF adjustment on domestic economies, the need to end the reverse transfer of resources and calls for packages of measures including SDR issues. A further argument put by Lever and Huhne in contrast to the orthodox IMF position, is based on doubts as to the likelihood of continued funding being made available on a voluntary basis. Instead, in order to relieve debtors of negative transfers and keep bank debts 'performing', the proposals argued for government guarantees by advanced countries. The aim in Lever and Huhne's view would be that interest payments would no longer be dangerously or undesirably dependent on the debtor countries' continuous achievement of an export surplus.[81] In the fourth category, many of the more radical proposals for managing the debt crisis concentrate on measures to deal with the debt overhang. These include proposals for a debt moratorium and the ideas for some form of new international debt-discounting agency trading in debt, which would acquire developing country debt held by banks at a discount, paying the banks in long-term bonds against itself and become the creditor of the developing countries.[82]

While many of more radical solutions have made little headway, the various categories give some indication of the range of thinking, a context within which to put proposals such as the Baker plan,[83] and some idea of the experimental nature of both orthodox and radical 'solutions'. In this context the position of the Fund has altered *vis-à-vis* the banks and its role enhanced in terms of overseeing domestic policies at bank insistence. Yet although the Fund's role as a financial catalyst has become more central, the Fund itself does not provide guarantees to the banks on their loans to indebted countries.

The management of the debt crisis so far has seen the development of complex and at times innovative multilateral diplomacy. However, although the patching-up or rescue-operation element of that diplomacy has diminished, the uncertainty is underlined by the frequency of reschedulings and the acute vulnerability of the economies of petroleum-based major debtors to shifts in commodity prices, in effect making medium-term assessments hazardous and unprofitable.

SUMMARY

Since 1973 the role of the Fund has changed in a number of important ways. In particular, its second function as a source of international liquidity has increased in importance. Yet in establishing new facilities the Fund has, because of the limitations on its ordinary resources, had to negotiate borrowed resources with different sets of donor groups. However, more recently the Fund has been able to develop a more stable basis for its borrowed resources through formal links with the BIS, central banks, Japan and Saudi Arabia. Saudi Arabia itself has emerged as a major financial actor within the Fund, formally through association with the GAB and via other support operations carried out by SAMA.

The onset of the debt crisis coincided with the revised arrangements noted above. While these provided a medium-term basis of borrowed resources, the scale of the debt crisis put the Fund's overall resources under severe strain. Since 1982 the Fund has been involved in perhaps its most intensive period of post-war financial diplomacy. The management of the debt crisis has involved highly complex multilateral diplomacy, in which a new type of debt negotiations has emerged, involving creditor groups, bank liaison committees, central financial institutions, the BIS, governments and large numbers of non-governmental groups. The process of internationally mobilising large volumes of financial resources has led also to increased institutional linkage, in which the Fund has played an important part. An underlying assumption behind this process has been the common concern to reduce the risk of default. In this sense financial risk has been shared through aggregation.[84] This can be seen particularly in the use of cross-default clauses and the extensive growth of bridging and syndicated loans. The Fund itself has assumed a significant role in terms of the coordination of rescue packages, the mobilisation of resources and, through both formal and *de facto* certification, of the economies of Fund members. The Fund's role is changing too, not least in respect to its closer relationship with the World Bank.[85] Demands for an enhanced role for the World Bank in a way mirror the blurring of concepts associated with orthodox balance of payments support operations and development finance, which has occurred because of the very high levels of debt faced by some countries. Whatever changes take place, it is clear that the three issues of quotas, access to Fund resources and the availability of borrowed resources will continue at the centre of the Fund's international financial relations. The Fund's multifaceted role has been aptly summed up by de Larosière as 'part credit union, part referee and part economic advisor'.[86]

REFERENCES AND NOTES

1. For a selected bibliography on the Fund, see various IMF Staff Papers, e.g. Anne C. M. Salda, *The International Monetary Fund*, IMF Staff Papers, Vol. 31, Supplement (Dec. 1984).
2. Of these twenty-nine countries signed the agreement, which rose to thirty-five at the inaugural meeting of the Board of Governors at Savannah on 8 March 1946. The Soviet Union, which was present at Bretton Woods subsequently did not join the Fund. Three countries have subsequently left the Fund: Poland on 14 March 1950; Czechoslovakia on 31 December 1954; and Cuba on 2 April 1964. Of the countries outside the United Nations, Italy became a member in 1947, and the FRG and Japan followed in 1952. On the Bretton Woods conference, see, for example, J. Keith Horsefield, *The International Monetary Fund 1945–65, Volume 1: Chronicle* (IMF, Washington, DC, 1969) Ch. 5.
3. For the role of Keynes in the negotiations see John Morton Blum, *From*

the Morgenthau Diaries: Years of War, 1941-4 (Houghton Mifflin, Boston, 1967) p. 273 *passim*.

4. Horsefield, op. cit., p. 93.
5. For example the Fund concluded a standby arrangement in April 1985 with the Dominican Republic over twelve months, for purchases of up to the equivalent of SDR 78.5 million, which is equivalent to 70 per cent of the Dominican Republic's quota of SDR 112.1 million in the Fund. The standby arrangement is financed from the Fund's ordinary (subscription) resources. See IMF, *Survey*, 29 April 1985, p. 140.
6. Benjamin J. Cohen, *Organising the World's Money* (Macmillan, London, 1978) p. 93.
7. Managing Directors have been: Camille Gutt (Belgium) 1946-51; Ivor Rooth (Sweden) 1951-56; Per Jacobsson (Sweden) 1956-63; Pierre-Paul Schweitzer (France) 1963-73; H. Johannes Witteveen (Netherlands) 1973-78; Jacques de Larosière (France) 1978-86. See Margaret Garritsen de Vries, *The International Monetary Fund 1972-78*, Vol. 2 (IMF, Washington, DC, 1985) Ch. 52 for portraits of Fund staff.
8. See for example staff distribution of IBRD/IDA, Table H-7, Appendix H, in Edward S. Mason and Robert E. Asher, *The World Bank Since Bretton Woods* (The Brookings Institution, Washington, DC, 1973) pp. 879-80.
9. Ibid., p. 566.
10. In the nine years of negotiations the Bank played a prominent role in putting forward a number of proposals to bridge the gap between the two sides. For Black's personal correspondence with Nehru, see Mason and Asher, op. cit., p. 625.
11. Horsefield, op. cit., p. 496.
12. Robert Solomon, *The International Monetary System 1945-81* (Harper and Row, New York, 1982) p. 33.
13. See Michael Ainley, *The General Arrangements to Borrow*, Pamphlet Series No. 41 (IMF, Washington, DC, 1984).
14. Switzerland, which is not a member of the Fund, became associated with the GAB in June 1964. See exchange of letters between the Ambassador of Switzerland to the United States and the managing director of the Fund, 11 June 1964, in *Selected Decisions*, 10 (1983) pp. 148-52.
15. The currency value of the SDR is determined daily by the Fund by summing the values of a basket of five currencies, based on market exchange rates in US dollars according to the following amounts: US dollar (0.54); Deutsch mark (0.46); French franc (0.74); Japanese yen (34.0); pound sterling (0.071).
16. See Louis M. Goreux, *Compensatory Financing Facility* (IMF, Washington, DC, 1980) esp. pp. 25-50.
17. See A. I. MacBean and P. N. Snowden, *International Institutions in Trade and Finance* (George Allen and Unwin, London, 1983) Ch. 6.
18. For an evaluation of the Bretton Woods system, see W. M. Scammel, *International Monetary Policy: Bretton Woods and After* (Macmillan, London, 1975) Ch. 7.
19. Marcus Fleming, cited in Solomon, op. cit., p. 237.
20. The five other appointed executive directors were from the United States, the United Kingdom, FRG, France and Japan.

21. Interim Committee communique, IMF, *Survey*, 15 Oct. 1984, pp. 292–4.
22. A possible reason for this is that less developed countries feel that they have greater influence through the executive directors of the Fund, and that a council would weaken the Executive Board. See Solomon, op. cit., p. 628.
23. *Select Decisions of the IMF*, 11 (30 April 1985) pp. 367–8.
24. See Fritz Fischer, 'The Spring 1985 Meeting of the Development Committee', *Finance and Development*, June 1985, pp. 8–9.
25. The membership of the G-24 in 1985 comprised Algeria, Argentina, Brazil, Colombia, Egypt, Ethiopia, Gabon, Ghana, Guatemala, India, Islamic Republic of Iran, Ivory Coast, Lebanon, Mexico, Nigeria, Pakistan, Peru, Philippines, Sri Lanka, Syrian Arab Republic, Trinidad and Tobago, Venezuela, Yugoslavia, Zaïre.
26. See *The Times*, 18 Jan. 1983.
27. IMF, *Annual Report, 1981*, p. 84.
28. The eighteen identified were: Bangladesh, Cameroon, Central African Republic, Egypt, Haiti, India, Ivory Coast, Kenya, Mali, Mauritania, Pakistan, Senegal, Sierra Leone, Sri Lanka, Somalia, Tanzania, Western Samoa, Democratic People's Republic of the Yemen. IMF, *Annual Report, 1977*, p. 65.
29. Solomon, op. cit., p. 281. OPEC met in Kuwait on 16 Oct. 1973 and decided the following day to cut oil supplies by 5 per cent each month and to impose a total ban on certain countries supporting Israel. It was also agreed to raise posted prices from $US3 to $US5.12 per barrel. An extremely good analysis of OPEC including the embargo can be found in Albert L. Danielson, *The Evolution of OPEC* (Harcourt Brace Jovanovich, New York, 1982) pp. 159–99.
30. The entry into force of the second amendment to the Fund's articles made it possible to add to the total of usable currencies about SDR 1 billion in currencies that had previously not been used or sold only on an irregular basis. The Fund's holding of eleven currencies totalled about 85 per cent of all usable currencies at the end of April 1978, with the US dollar accounting for 50 per cent of the total. See IMF, *Annual Reports, 1975*, p. 55 and *1978*, p. 65. In practice, however, the bulk of the Fund's usable currency holdings is represented by a small number of currencies. At the end of 1980–81 the Fund's holding of five currencies accounted for a little over 70 per cent of its total usable resources, IMF, *Annual Report, 1981*, p. 88.
31. See IMF, *Annual Report, 1976*, p. 54.
32. See IMF, *Annual Report, 1975*, pp. 54–6.
33. See IMF, *Annual Report, 1981*, p. 90.
34. For the communique see IMF *Annual Report, 1978*, Appendix IV.
35. See Solomon, op. cit., pp. 280–1 and MacBean and Snowden, op. cit., p. 54.
36. *The Times*, 12 Dec. 1983.
37. IMF, *Annual Report, 1985*, p. 69.
38. IMF, *Summary Proceedings*, 1982, p. 51.
39. *The Times*, 7 Dec. 1982; *New York Times*, 3 Dec. 1982.
40. *The Times*, 11 and 13 Dec. 1982.
41. *The Times*, 10 Feb. 1983.

42. *New York Times*, 9 Dec. 1982.
43. *The Times*, 18 Jan. 1983.
44. Michael Ainley, *The General Arrangements to Borrow* (IMF, Washington, DC, 1984), pp. 49–51.
45. *Daily Telegraph*, 30 Dec. 1982; *The Times*, 10 Jan. 1983.
46. *The Times*, 18 Jan. 1983.
47. *The Times*, 10 Feb. 1983.
48. See Report by the Deputies of the G-24, 23 Aug. 1985, IMF, *Survey*, Sept. 1985, p. 13.
49. *The Times*, 19 Oct. 1983.
50. *The Times*, 19 Nov. 1983.
51. *The Times*, 27 Sept. 1983.
52. *The Times*, 14 April 1984.
53. *The Times*, 27 Sept. 1984.
54. See K. Burke Dillon et al., *Recent Developments in External Debt Restructuring*, IMF Occasional Paper 40 (Oct. 1985) p. 20.
55. 'Multilateral Official Debt Reschedulings 1975–1985', in Dillon et al., op. cit., Table 4, p. 8.
56. See William R. Cline, *International Debt: Systemic Risk and Policy Response* (Institute for International Economics, Washington, DC, 1984) pp. 273–81; *Hearings*, US Senate, Committee on Banking, Housing and Urban Affairs, second session, 22 Feb. 1982, esp. pp. 77–80; *Hearings*, US Senate, Committee on Foreign Relations, Sub-Committee on European Affairs, second session, 27 Jan. 1982, pp. 8–12.
57. Members of the OECD Development Assistance Committee (DAC) include, Australia, Austria, Belgium, Canada, Denmark, Finland, France, FRG, Italy, Japan, the Netherlands, New Zealand, Norway, Sweden, Switzerland, United Kingdom, United States and the Commission of the EEC.
58. E. M. Brau and R. C. Williams, *Recent Multilateral Debt Restructurings with Official and Bank Creditors*, IMF Occasional Paper 25 (Dec. 1983) p. 22. This excludes Polish reschedulings of $US4.6 billion in 1982. Poland at that stage was not a member of the Fund but filed an application for Fund membership of 10 November 1981 and eventually re-entered the Fund in 1986. See also, ibid., Table 11, p. 34.
59. For example Sri Lanka in Jan. 1986 ceased to allow state corporations and government-supported enterprises, such as Air Lanka, and the steel, shipping and cement corporations, to raise commercial loans from foreign sources. See *Financial Times*, 24 Jan. 1986. For further discussion see *World Development Report* (World Bank, Washington, DC, 1985) Chs. 4 and 5.
60. The debt accumulated by Pemex, the Mexican state oil company, including shipping purchases was a significant component of total Mexico debt amounting to some $US20 billion. See Joseph Kraft, *The Mexican Rescue* (Group of Thirty, New York, 1984) pp. 27–8.
61. On the problem for the Fund of the impact of undisclosed arms purchases on their assessments see *The Times*, 4 Feb. 1983; the relationship between Third World debt and arms purchases is discussed in M. Brzoska, 'The Military Related Debt of Third World Countries', *Journal of Peace Research*, Vol. 20, No. 3 (1983) pp. 271–7. See also

various issues of SIPRI *Yearbook* for arms purchase data, e.g. 1984, Appendix 7A, pp. 211–89.

62. See Carlos G. Langoni, 'The Rescheduling Experience of Brazil', in Khadiga Haq (ed.), *The Lingering Debt Crisis* (North–South Round Table, Islamabad, Pakistan, 1985) p. 113.

63. Dillon et al., op. cit., p. 14.

64. See William R. Rhodes, 'The Role of the Steering Committee: How it can be Improved', in *Re-scheduling Techniques: An International Conference on Sovereign Debt* (The Group of Thirty, London 3–4 Nov. 1983) p. 26 *passim*.

65. For example in the Brazilian restructuring negotiations, the BIS, in a move in support of the IMF following Brazil's failure to meet the May 1983 IMF target, informed the Brazilian authorities that it would not renew on 15 July the $US400 million bridging loan, which had already been extended twice. See *The Guardian*, 12 July 1983; *New York Times*, 15 July 1983.

66. Azizali F. Mohammed, 'The Case by Case Approach to Debt Problems', *Finance and Development*, March 1985, pp. 27–30.

67. Joseph Kraft, op. cit., pp. 47–9.

68. M. de Larosière intervened with the Italian bank Instituto Mobilare Italiano and sent a personal telegram to the Minister of Commerce seeking 'fullest cooperation', ibid., p. 53.

69. The IMF quota increase was criticised strongly on a number of grounds including the argument that it was bailing out US banks. The defence of the increase in the IMF quota relied *inter alia* on trade and international order arguments, see the statement by the Hon. D. T. Regan, Senate Committee on Banking, Housing and Urban Affairs, *Hearings*, 14 Feb. 1983, pp. 40–100, and particularly p. 69 *passim*. On US–Brazilian trade see *Hearings*, Sub-committee on International Economics of the Committee on Foreign Relations, Senate, 28 Sept. 1983, p. 41. The Brazilian debt crisis affected US exports to Brazil, which fell steeply in the first half of 1983 to $US1.2 billion, 30 per cent lower than the level of $US1.76 billion for the first half of 1982.

70. During President Reagan's visit to Brazil at the beginning of December 1982 a trade package was agreed which involved relaxation on imports of Brazilian sugar and US agreement to the continuation of Brazilian subsidies on exports including steel, for a further two years. A US Treasury loan of $US1.23 billion was also announced during the visit, though this was being disbursed as early as October 1982. See *New York Times*, 3 Dec. 1982; *The Times* 4 Dec. 1982; *New York Times* 8 Dec. 1982.

71. For details on the terms and conditions of bank debt restructuring from 1978 to 1985, see Dillon et al., op. cit., Table 17, Appendix IV, pp. 48–62.

72. Ibid., p. 24.

73. The text of the Cartagena Consensus, 22 June 1984, can be found in *Hearings*, Committee on Foreign Affairs, House of Representatives, second session, 1 and 8 Aug. 1984, pp. 62–72.

74. See P. N. Snowden, *Emerging Risk in International Banking* (George Allen and Unwin, London, 1985) pp. 85–6 and 134; Harold Lever and Christopher Huhne, *Debt and Danger* (Penguin Books, London, 1985) pp. 77–8. See also J. de Larosière's remarks at the Overseas Bankers Club,

London, 3 Feb. 1986, reprinted in IMF, *Survey*, 17 Feb. 1986, para. 1(2) on the decline in new net lending and the difficulties in assembling financing packages for certain indebted countries even though strong adjustment programmes had been started.

75. Charles Lipson, 'Bankers' Dilemmas: Private Cooperation in Rescheduling Sovereign Debts', *World Politics*, Vol. XXXVIII, No. 1 (Oct. 1985) pp. 224–5.
76. See Lever and Huhne, op. cit., Ch. 9; Cline, op. cit., Snowden, op. cit., pp. 126–37.
77. See remarks by J. de Larosière at Los Angeles World Affairs Council, 19 March 1986, para. 1(1).
78. See address of J. de Larosière on 22 Jan. 1986 to Bretton Woods Committee in IMF, *Survey*, 3 Feb. 1986, pp. 33, 43.
79. For Bacha's argument in favour of enhancing the World Bank, see Edmar L. Bacha and Richard E. Feinberg, 'The World Bank and Structural Adjustment in Latin America', *World Development*, Vol. 14, No. 3 (March 1986) pp. 342–5.
80. Dillon et al., op. cit., pp. 10–17.
81. Lever and Huhne op. cit., p. 139.
82. See Cline, op. cit., and Lever and Huhne, op. cit., pp. 137–8.
83. The proposals by US Secretary of the Treasury, James A. Baker III, were made at the Oct. 1985 meeting of the IMF and World Bank Boards of Governors in Seoul and called for new lending by the banks of $US20 billion over the next three years to the entire group of heavily indebted middle-income developing countries. See IMF/IBRD Press Release No. 13, 8 Oct. 1985; statement by James A. Baker III, 22 Jan. 1986 before the Bretton Woods Committee, *Treasury News* (Department of the Treasury, Washington, DC), in IMF, *Survey*, 3 Feb. 1986, p. 44. The group of fifteen countries comprised Argentina, Bolivia, Brazil, Chile, Colombia, Ivory Coast, Ecuador, Mexico, Morocco, Nigeria, Peru, Philippines, Uruguay, Venezuela and Yugoslavia.
84. David Folkerts-Landau, 'The Changing Role of International Bank Lending in Development Finance', IMF, *Staff Papers*, Vol. 32, No. 2 (June 1985) pp. 326–30.
85. See Christine A. Bogdanowicz-Bindert, 'World Debt: The United States Reconsiders', *Foreign Affairs*, Vol. 64, No. 2 (Winter 1985–86) pp. 259–73.
86. Remarks by J. de Larosière to the Los Angeles World Affairs Council, 19 March 1986. Cf. comments of Michel Camdessus, de Larosière's successor as managing director, in IMF, *Survey*, 20 April, 1987, p. 114.

CHAPTER EIGHT

Diplomacy and trade

TRADE AND FOREIGN POLICY

Trade has traditionally been a concern of diplomacy. Trade interests and trade policies are generally part of the central preoccupations of most states. Ideally, trade policy and foreign policy should support each other, in the same way that defence and foreign policy have a mutually supportive relationship. Yet trade policy, rather more than defence has tended to pull in divergent directions from foreign policy, unless, as is sometimes the case, economic issues dominate external policy. As a result an additional task for diplomacy is dealing with external problems arising from the *consequences* of differing lines of external policy. Divergency between trade and foreign policy can sometimes arise from the practice of having separate diplomatic and trade missions, reflecting the tendency to treat the political and economic aspects of foreign policy separately. Trade and foreign policy may also diverge because of demands made by established trade interests within states.[1] Trade interests may of course be acquired for a number of reasons such as long-standing commercial links, entrepreneurial exploitation of overseas markets or successful domestic lobbying as in the case of European, Japanese[2] or US farming interests. Such interests which either tacitly or formally become part of trade policy may create strains or ambiguity in foreign policy, for example the Taiwan lobby in the US, or demand changes in foreign policy, such as calls for the ending of sanctions against the Soviet Union by US grain farmers. Put differently, foreign policy decision-makers may consider that particular trade interests are incompatible with foreign policy, for example the US Government's attitude to oil operations by Chevron in Angola.[3] Under these circumstances, the task of diplomacy is to reconcile or explain divergent interests to appropriate external actors, or, bring the trade policy into line with foreign policy. The process of bringing trade and foreign policy into alignment can be difficult if trade interests, broadly defined, secure either sufficient economic importance, or official support to conduct trade separately or even at the expense of foreign policy. The latter is well illustrated by the long-running diplomatic dispute between the EEC and the US over the protective aspects of the EEC's Common Agricultural Policy (CAP).

Apart from the questions of divergence and primacy, trade policy may become a direct instrument of foreign policy. In this sense trade is used to support or further objectives which are not exclusively economic but political or military. The political uses of trade involve diplomacy in initiatives to develop goodwill, promote regional cooperation, gain political influence or strategic assets (e.g. bases) within another state, through to coercive sanctions and other forms of punitive behaviour.

THE INTERNATIONAL TRADE SETTING

In international trade, the classical functions of diplomacy, other than strict commercial promotion are evident in four areas. These are: (i) multilateral rule-making or rule-changing; (ii) the creation of a favourable political setting or legal framework at a bilateral or regional level; (iii) resolution of disputes; (iv) the creation of innovatory agreements. To these a fifth area, 'coercive' diplomacy, should be added.

The setting itself for international trade diplomacy has been distinguished by the post-war growth in the number of multilateral institutions with direct or indirect responsibility for trade (e.g. GATT, UNCTAD, ECOSOC, UNIDO, IFC, ILO). This institutional pluralism reflects the growth in the membership of the international community, as well as other factors such as developing country dissatisfaction with seemingly Western-dominated institutions, continued North–South dispute over market access and the resulting attempts by developing countries to create new trade and development arrangements within a South–South context. Trade issues themselves have progressively moved up the international agenda since the end of the 1960s as the promotion and regulation of trade became extensively politicised through growing direct and indirect governmental involvement, increasing protectionism and other problems such as price uncertainties which have affected a wide range of key commodities.

It is not surprising that the international politics of trade have come to reflect many fundamentally different conceptions of international trade order. The paradoxes and contradictions in national ideas and practice, however, render any attempt at individual classification unprofitable. However, the 1970s were dominated by two broad themes. In the first place there are the attempts to reach multilateral agreements on tariff reductions and codes to regulate restrictive practices. The second is the North–South conflict over economic redistribution and the corresponding efforts to change international institutions. In pursuit of the latter, developing countries sought multilateral rule changes on the basis of the NIEO and calls for global negotiations. Yet by the early 1980s, the results of nearly a decade of intensive multilateral diplomacy, at least within the UNCTAD context, were at best limited with regard to redistribution and revision of international institutions.

This chapter is initially concerned with diplomacy at a multilateral level and examines the work and relationship of GATT and UNCTAD. The second and third sections look at the ways the traditional and newer tasks of diplomacy feature particularly at a bilateral level. The final part of the chapter discusses some of the innovative agreements which have been devised in response to the failure to achieve substantial progress in the NIEO context.

THE GATT

The GATT was formed in 1947, initially with twenty-three signatories, as a result of the failure to bring about an International Trade Organisation (ITO) as envisaged in the Havana Charter. Since then GATT, which is a treaty organisation, and not a UN specialised agency or special body of the UN General Assembly like UNCTAD, has become the major organisation, supported by leading trading countries, with responsibility for the conduct of international trade. The main purposes of GATT are the promotion of freer trade through multilateral negotiation of tariff reductions and the removal of restrictions on trade. These purposes are set out in the GATT preamble as:[4] ' ... reciprocal and mutually advantageous arrangements directed to the substantial reduction of tariffs and other barriers to trade and the elimination of discriminatory treatment in international commerce'.

The central directing body of GATT is the Council, under which are the working parties and panels appointed either by the Council (sixty-six members) or the contracting parties.[5] The day-to-day work is the responsibility of the Director-General and Secretariat. The Director-General also chairs the Consultative Group of Eighteen, established on a temporary basis in 1965 and made permanent in 1979. The Consultative Group, which is composed of high-level representatives from the industrialised countries, developing and centrally planned economies, is concerned with the following major international trade developments: making recommendations to forestall or deal with disturbances which pose a threat to the multilateral trading system and reviewing liaison between the GATT and the IMF. GATT generally operates on the basis of consensus, though there are formal rules on voting and amendments to the articles. An important example of amendments was the introduction of a new Part IV to the articles of agreement in 1964 to reflect the trade interests of developing countries. Overall, the articles deal with not only tariff reduction but a number of other activities constituting barriers to trade. Article II sets out the major principle of non-discrimination on imported goods. Other articles oblige signatories not to use export subsidies or dumping (articles VI and XVI), quantitative restrictions on imports or exports (article XI) or the selective application of quotas (articles XIII). A further important principle in the articles is that tariff reductions are extended on a non-selective or most-favoured-nation (MFN) basis. Parties in dispute are allowed to enter into consultation under article XXII, though this is a serious formal step prior to the issue going before a dispute panel. It has been used by the European Community, for example against Japan. There are, too, a number of special provisions on state trade organisations (article XVII) and economic integration and free trade (article XXIV). Of the exceptions, the most important relate to the use of emergency measures (article XIX), which has proved controversial because of the tendency for temporary measures against imports to remain once put in place.[6]

Limitations on GATT

An important constraint on GATT, especially in the early years, stemmed from its limited membership. Although a fundamental principle underlying GATT was the multilateralisation of world trade, membership remained limited until the late 1960s and early 1970s.[7] In particular, the socialist state trading countries remained outside GATT, with the exception of Czechoslovakia. However, the Polish precedent in 1967 influenced the subsequent application by Romania (1971) and Hungary (1973).[8] Romanian membership was aided by *Ostpolitik* and the lessening of East–West tension, as well by the wish of the Western powers to encourage further reorientation in Romanian foreign policy.[9] More recently, continued textile disputes have influenced Thailand's decision to become a member of GATT in 1982 as a means of securing at least some measure of additional economic security. In the main, Asian states have been generally slow to join GATT. However, in line with its revised economic policies, the People's Republic of China applied for GATT membership in 1986.[10] Important non-members of GATT are the Soviet Union, Taiwan, Venezuela and Saudi Arabia.

A further important constraint on GATT has stemmed from the fact that for the most part agriculture has remained outside the GATT framework to the detriment of less developed countries. The work of GATT has as a result been largely confined to manufactured goods.

Two additional difficulties stem from developments which have occurred in the nature and form of international trade which were not apparent at the time of the drafting of the original agreement. In the first place the growing involvement of governments in the conduct of trade has led to its increasing politicisation and growing numbers of disputes over restrictions, trade credits and other charges of unfair competition. These developments have forced GATT to focus more on measures to counter restrictions, which has inevitably engaged the organisation in greater controversy. Related to this are new developments in the form and conduct of trade, particularly the services sector, including banking and data telecommunications, which some states, such as the United States, have attempted to bring within the GATT regulatory framework, though this has been resisted by leading developing countries such as India and Brazil.

GATT in Operation

The most visible work of GATT has been the series of periodic trade rounds conducted since 1947. The GATT style of operation has been very much one of quiet diplomacy, contrasting with the conference

Diplomacy and trade

style of UNCTAD. The secretariat style, too, reflecting the highly technical nature of much of its work, has been compared with that of a 'confidential boardroom meeting' or club.[11] If anything, the volume of GATT-related negotiations has intensified since the 1970s, as governments have tried to implement tariff-cutting formulae and work out bilateral or longer-term arrangements with other states. Yet GATT trade diplomacy remains almost a private aspect of international relations, receiving only intermittent public attention. In this diplomacy an important role has been performed by successive GATT director-generals, in mobilising support for new rounds of trade talks, bringing together contact groups and, with the Secretariat, promoting both in and outside of formal sessions, compromise proposals.

The trade rounds from Annecy (1948) to the so-called Dillon Round (1960–62) were essentially conducted on an item-to-item basis, with countries bargaining over individual tariff cuts. However, dissatisfaction with product-by-product bargaining led to an attempt to try across-the-board or linear cuts in the Kennedy Round (1964–67), with the objective of obtaining linear tariff cuts of up to 50 per cent. The tendency for a number of states to attach exception lists to bids, meant in practice that the talks reverted to product-by-product bargaining. At the end of the Kennedy Round tariff reductions of around 35 per cent were made by the developed countries, compared with the original objective, though the range varied considerably.

A further and more ambitious round of trade talks, the Tokyo Round, on multilateral tariff reductions and non-tariff measures was undertaken from 1973 to 1979. The Tokyo Round negotiations illustrated two significant features of multilateral trade diplomacy post-Dillon – the role of internal domestic factors, especially in the United States,[12] and the intrusion of external factors arising from the state of the international economy. The preparatory phase of the Tokyo Round was extremely lengthy, due to the need to mobilise domestic and international support. The talks did not properly get under way until 1975 after the passage of the Trade Reform Act by Congress, authorising United States participation. Much of the remainder of the preparatory phase during 1977–78 was taken up with negotiations on the tariff formula, which would act as the bench-mark for the talks. The final stages of the talks were conducted against the deadline, and hence uncertainty, arising from the expiry of American legislation on 3 January 1980. Added urgency was given by the continued deterioration of the international economy, which put the successful outcome of the Tokyo Round increasingly at risk.[13]

163

On the tariff side, cuts of approximately 30 per cent were approved on post-Kennedy rates, on a phased basis over seven years, though, as in previous rounds, these were mainly restricted to non-textiles, manufactured goods and some agricultural products. Although the tariff cuts were not very substantial, eventually bringing the rate on industrial goods down to some 5 per cent post-Tokyo, they nevertheless suggested some commitment to maintaining the idea of trade liberalisation.

More importantly, the Tokyo Round concluded a number of potentially significant non-tariff agreements, or codes as they are generally known, which, like the Tokyo Round,[14] individually take the form of a protocol to the GATT. These include the codes on subsidies and countervailing duties,[15] customs valuation,[16] anti-dumping,[17] government procurement,[18] trade in civil aircraft,[19] import licensing[20] and standards.[21] The fact that the codes were negotiated as agreements and not amendments to the GATT articles continued the practice of avoiding such action where possible, emphasising a particular characteristic of GATT, which is its pragmatism or recognition of the importance of negotiating what is politically possible.

There are of course limitations arising from this form of rule-making. Thus the United States has been prepared to extend the benefits of particular codes only to those states which are signatories to the code in question and not to free riders. The use of agreements therefore introduces selectivity in terms of participation and application.[22] Negotiation of what is politically possible inevitably means that there are gaps or ambiguities in texts. In the subsidies and countervailing duties code, for example, what precisely constitutes 'unjustifiable' use of countervailing measures was left undefined. In the code on government procurement, which aimed to liberalise non-military procurement to competitive bidding, discussions on the inclusion of state-owned authorities such as public utilities gave rise to considerable dispute. The issue was well illustrated in the closing stages of the Tokyo Round, in the dispute between Japan and the United States over the opening up of the Japanese tele-communications market.

But by far the largest gap in the Tokyo Round was the failure to reach agreement on improving the article XIX safeguard system, authorising emergency action against suppliers of disruptive imports. Agreement was prevented because of the fundamental disagreement over European Community demands for the right to apply discriminatory safeguard action with limited GATT surveillance, which was opposed by developing countries, joined in this instance by Japan. The issue was taken up at the November 1982 GATT ministerial conference and remains under discussion. These discussions have centred on the various elements of article XIX, including determination of serious injury, non-discrimination or selectivity, compensation, notification of safeguard measures, the temporary character of the measures and multilateral surveillance. As Olivier Long[23] notes, 'the debate on the safeguard clause reveals a classic dilemma between, on the one hand, insistence on application of the rules at the risk of making the legal instrument and, on the other, a degree of tolerance which weakens the value of the instrument and the protection which member governments expect from it'.

Challenges to GATT post-Tokyo

Since the Tokyo Round several developments have occurred which have posed major challenges to GATT's general aims of liberalising world trade. In particular the principle of non-discrimination has suffered continued erosion. The use of variable import levies and other restrictions, for example, by customs unions and similar economic groupings have become a major source of friction, especially in the context of North–South trade relations. In international trade in textiles, GATT has had, in political terms, to accept the continued operation of the Multifibre Arrangement (MFA). Although GATT monitors the MFA through its Textiles Committee, the agreement can be considered as a further example of a major departure from the fundamental GATT principle of non-discrimination.

A second area is continued protectionism which increased with the deterioration in the climate of international trade after 1979. Protectionist measures of a non-tariff kind have become extremely varied such as orderly marketing arrangements (OMAs) and voluntary export restraints (VERs), for example restraints on Japanese and EEC steel exports to the United States. Other forms of trade restriction in widespread use by both developing and developed countries include import licensing procedures, demands for compensatory exports, currency restrictions, differential taxes to protect newly established industries in newly industrialised countries, such as electronics and tariff switching. At an administrative level qualitative restrictions using standards, certification and import procedures have created entry restrictions on a wide range of less developed countries' (ldc) exports.

The issue of subsidies and corresponding charges of unfair competition, have emerged as major sources of international trade conflict. The main area of export subsidy competition is export credits. Government intervention in export credits has now become highly institutionalised, which has resulted in the blurring of the traditional concept of aid with trade credit, so much so that the former is now almost without meaning except perhaps in a humanitarian sense.

Apart from the subsidies issue, managed trade has become a noticeable feature of international trade practice in the 1980s, in response to increased trade competition and protectionism. Within this category are unilateral import restrictions on goods and services and bilaterally agreed pricing arrangements. Other bilateral arrangements have included greater use of long-term trade agreements and bilateral free trade areas (e.g. United States–Israel). Although some of these arrangements may be of limited economic effect because of their short-term nature, low trade value or the countries involved have little traditional direct trade, taken together they suggest some weakening of multilateralism.

The developments discussed above have created an increasingly complex environment for GATT. Many of the non-tariff restrictions have distorted trade, as in the case of VERs on steel, which have merely led to redirection and the transferences of distortion to other markets.[24] New networks of commercial links have been developed by governments and their commercial entities, with trade diplomacy geared to avoiding restrictions through the negotiation of quota-swapping agreements, relocation of production to non-quota-affected states and agreements with third-party states for transhipment. Inevitably, trade disputes have tended to increase.

Institutionally, GATT has responded to the developments discussed above by broadening its agenda, as we have argued above, into non-tariff areas, including subsidies and anti-dumping, as well as other areas such as counterfeit goods and rules of origin. Negotiations by GATT have also included states which are not members of GATT, leading to the partial extension of GATT rules to non-contracting parties. The continued expansion of GATT membership[25] contrasts with the earlier period and has strengthened the potential collective pressure that the organisation can exert to ensure compliance with GATT obligations.

UNITED NATIONS CONFERENCE ON TRADE AND DEVELOPMENT

The first UNCTAD conference (UNCTAD I) met in Geneva in May 1964, shortly before the formal opening of the Kennedy Round, and was attended by over 2,000 delegates from 119 countries. It began a period of large-scale multilateral conference diplomacy on trade and development issues which was to last for over a decade and a half. The creation of UNCTAD was seen by developing countries as a means of dramatising and addressing the problems of trade and development in a wider and more open framework than GATT, with the aim of bringing about fundamental change in international economic order. In an important way UNCTAD as an institution, set up as an organ of the General Assembly, with a large secretariat, meeting on a four-year basis and inter-sessionally through the Trade and Development Board and other committees symbolised the emergence of the Third World as a potentially powerful diplomatic grouping. Subsequently, North–South issues, particularly after the first oil crisis, were moved to the forefront of the international agenda, adding a layer of increasing dispute, at a multilateral level, between industrialised and developing countries.

The operation of UNCTAD has raised a number of procedural and legal issues. Would UNCTAD develop into a parallel and competing organisation to the GATT, creating institutional duality? What should be the appropriate fora for drafting and revising international rules in such areas as trade, intellectual property rights and shipping? How binding or effective would resolutions and decisions emanating from UNCTAD as a *rule-changing* body be if these were reached by majority voting in which major economic powers either voted against or abstained?

Philosophy of UNCTAD

Underpinning the philosophy of UNCTAD is the view that major changes should be brought about in the structure of economic order, with substantial economic redistribution in favour of developing countries. The development of these ideas falls into two periods. In the first, from 1964 to 1978, the central theme is the restructuring of North–South economic relations. This was largely superseded in the late 1970s by the ideas associated with using diplomacy to develop economic cooperation among developing countries. The early ideas of UNCTAD were strongly influenced by Raul Prebisch, the

Argentinian banker and first Secretary-General of UNCTAD.[26] While a number of features of Prebisch's analysis have been criticised on technical grounds, there is no doubt that the general ideas associated with his work – the relative decline of commodity prices, the existence of trade gaps and the weakness of the developing country 'periphery' caused by limited technological transfer from the industrialised 'centre' – have had considerable impact in colouring the thinking and overall approach of UNCTAD.[27] More generally, UNCTAD has been strongly influenced by the proceedings of the G-77 and the periodic summits of the non-aligned, such as the 1973 Algiers summit, setting out the NIEO. The UN General Assembly has also been extensively used as a vehicle for legitimising UNCTAD ideas through resolutions calling for redistribution and rule changes.

Much of the early work of UNCTAD was of a sectoral kind, preferred by the West, on individual commodities. However, the Integrated Commodity Programme (IPC), launched at UNCTAD IV, marked a shift to a strategic approach to commodity questions and direct confrontation with the West. The IPC called for:

1. The establishment of international stocks of key commodities;
2. A common fund;
3. Price stabilisation through long-term purchases;
4. More effective and less stringent mechanisms than, for example STABEX, to make finance generally available to countries affected by export shortfalls in commodities.

A second theme, developed at the UNCTAD II (Santiago, 1972) and the Algiers summit, identified the need for enhanced technology transfer, restructuring the legal environment and strengthening technical cooperation among developing countries. An inter-governmental group on technology transfer, set up in September 1970, was later transformed into the Committee on the Transfer of Technology in September 1974.[28]

While the ideas discussed above remain key elements in UNCTAD philosophy, a noticeable shift of emphasis occurs from the mid 1970s towards collective self reliance. The ideas associated with enhanced Third World cooperation were developed at two conferences of the G-77, in Mexico City (1976) and Arusha (1979). The scope for Third World cooperation was elaborated further at the high-level conference of the G-77 in Caracas in May 1981, which covered trade, technology, food, agriculture, energy, raw materials, finance, industrialisation and technical cooperation. The shift to promoting economic cooperation among developing countries (ECDC), particularly after the Caracas conference, was to a large extent brought about by the failure to achieve rule changes in the multilateral North–South context, and the corresponding recognition of the need for an alternative strategy of diplomacy for the promotion of South–South relations.

Critique of UNCTAD

The record of UNCTAD in terms of reform of international economic order using large-scale multilateral conferences is limited. Against this it can be put that UNCTAD has played a significant part in both elevating trade and development questions to wider attention and in the process structuring the North–South debate. In this sense UNCTAD has acted as a forum, body of appeal and promoter of the Third World and its interests. In doing so UNCTAD has perhaps inevitably become closely associated with the G-77, and as a result has proved unable to promote diplomatically agreed North–South solutions commanding a broad basis of support.

The influence of UNCTAD can also be seen through the 'spill-over' effect of its work on other institutions such as UNIDO and through the promotion of UN conferences, for example on technical cooperation among developing countries, such as that at Buenos Aires, 1978. Although UNCTAD's mandate remained vague in the early years, it has, in relation to GATT, developed a wide, if in some respects competing, portfolio of interests which, apart from commodities, range from shipping, freight rates, flags of convenience, world food problems and ports to tourism. In these areas UNCTAD committee and expert groups continue actively to promote agreements and supply extensive data. In the trade field, however, the North–South emphasis of UNCTAD has meant that GATT has been more successful in promoting East–West trade. Another noticeable gap in UNCTAD's portfolio is international financial relations, which have tended to remain managed within the G-77's Group of 24.

The extension of UNCTAD's area of negotiating responsibility has owed much to key officials within the secretariat.[29] For example, Wladyslaw Malinowski led much of the UNCTAD Secretariat's work on the Code of Conduct for Liner Conferences, signed in 1974 and which eventually came into force in October 1983.[30] Malinowski's personal diplomacy did much to keep up the momentum of the negotiations. In doing so, he was acutely aware of the need to work not only within the G-77 framework but widen the basis of support in Group B and other countries.

Perhaps one of the major achievements of UNCTAD, negotiated significantly in the early years of its existence, was the Generalised System of Preferences (GSP). By 1971–72, most major preference givers, except the United States, had introduced some form of GSP scheme.[31] In the commodity field the IPC negotiations encountered major difficulties, discussed below, before a weakened version was eventually agreed in June 1980.[32] The course of these negotiations illustrated both the *immobilisme* which develops once issues are transferred to the Trade and Development Committee from plenary sessions, and the fragmented nature of producer groups, especially in tin and cocoa. The Common Fund has not yet entered into force.

A less obvious area of UNCTAD's work, not frequently commented on, is its contribution to rule-making in international development law, through the promotion of multilateral conferences and the negotiation of codes, rules and agreements. Examples of these include the Principles and Rules on Restrictive Business Practices, the International Code of Conduct for Transfer of Technology and its contribution to the revision of the Paris Convention on Intellectual Property Rights. In addition, UNCTAD has tended to have a greater degree of success in certain functional areas such as combating maritime fraud and flags of convenience in that the prospects for successful negotiated outcomes tend to be greater where there are no requirements for the commitment of high levels of finance and support for the issue cuts across group lines.

Constraints on UNCTAD

In the main UNCTAD has tended to have more success in low-level functional areas. Criticism of UNCTAD at a multilateral conference and programme level can be put into four broad areas: (1) the effectiveness of large-scale multilateral conferences; (2) the problem of institutional duality; (3) opposition to centralised solutions; (4) implementation. The UNCTAD system of periodic large-scale conferences using the group system, lengthy clearing processes and extensive agendas has proved excessively unwieldy and generally unproductive. At UNCTAD II, for example, 106 delegations and 27 UN bodies and international organisations participated in the general debate. In 1979 at UNCTAD V, in Manila, the G-77 spent the first two weeks of the conference clearing their positions. Nor has the UNCTAD multilateral style lent itself to the effective breaking down of issues and construction of broadly based packages. Rather, the absence of deadlines[33] and the variable levels of commitment to finding workable solutions, have meant that controversial issues have been moved between the permanent committees and expert groups for study, in effect postponing or shelving their resolution.[34] In this respect, the absence of an impartial secretariat[35] has been a major weakness. The growth of UNCTAD activities has been accompanied by disputes about the appropriate forum for conducting particular negotiations. Western industrialised countries in the main have attempted to keep, for example, discussion on multilateral trade negotiations in a GATT rather than an UNCTAD framework, on the grounds that any transfer or duplication of discussions would prejudice GATT talks. Similarly, the establishment of a negotiating committee for a global system of trade preferences (GSTP), open only to participating members of the G-77, met opposition from Group B countries on competence grounds, and that the restrictive membership infringed the principle of universality of the United Nations.

The issue of competence has arisen on a number of occasions, for example, in the negotiations to revise the Paris Convention. In this instance the United States took the view that the appropriate forum was the World Intellectual Property Organisation (WIPO). A somewhat different set of arguments about the effect of duplication have been put in terms of the impact on bringing about change on trade and development issues. In this context, the Commonwealth Study Group of Experts in an assessment of the North–South dialogue drew attention to the diversion of effort and resources caused by having two major institutions of a competitive nature involved in trade and development.[36]

A fundamental weakness of UNCTAD, however, stems from the low level of relationship between its multilateral conference activities and national government policies. UNCTAD is strong on resolutions but weak on implementation. One reason put forward for this is that many delegations to UNCTAD are composed of foreign ministry officials, rather than finance or economic ministry personnel.[37] Partly for this and other reasons UNCTAD conferences and inter-sessional meetings, acquire a life cycle of their own, with representatives speaking to one another in a form of UNCTAD dialectic and not with their national governments.[38] The conferences are thus divorced from national policies and the immediate preoccupation of most governments.

By far the greatest constraint on UNCTAD is political rather than organisational. The combination of indifference or opposition of Western governments and other states revealed fundamentally different views on international economic order from those of many in the G-77. In the event, the IPC programme and G-77 demands for technology transfer produced increasing North–South confrontation between 1975 and 1981, over such issues as the funding of new commodity institutions and the release of proprietary technology. The United States, as the leading Group B member was essentially opposed to the creation of new institutions, any extension of UNCTAD responsibility, including that over the private sector, and mandatory rules. These main tenets of the overall UNCTAD approach met with varying degrees of opposition from other countries in the Group B bloc. As far as the United States was concerned, many of the main influences on policy direction at a bureaucratic level in the key 1975-81 period came from the cost-oriented EB, which emerged as the State Department's lead department, rather than that of International Organisation on matters to do with North–South relations.[39]

By the Belgrade conference (1983) the impasse in North–South relations, in a multilateral context, was complete.[40] As we have argued above, for the South the so-called 'Northern' option was no longer negotiable. In turn the major industrialised countries, with existing institutions intact, turned their attention to these and other bilateral or associative arrangements.

BILATERAL RELATIONS AND TRADE DIPLOMACY

The legal framework

One of the basic functions of diplomacy in the context of trade at a bilateral level is the establishment of rules and a framework which will enable the parties to conduct commercial and related activities, such as finance and investment, in an ordered manner. The purpose, too, is often to enhance or restructure trade if trading relations – in the absence of an agreement or because a previous agreement has proved inadequate – are either low or distorted. In addition, states frequently consider a formal agreement is important for reasons of economic security, e.g. investment protection agreements (IPAs) to safeguard the assets and operations of their nationals, or to assure security of raw material or commodity supplies.

The style of trade agreements is a matter of both state treaty practice and the political context within which the agreements are negotiated. Trade agreements, which are discussed more fully in Chapter 11, can take a variety of forms, such as economic cooperation agreements, navigation and commerce agreements or long-term trade agreements. Less formal arrangements are sometimes used as between India and Pakistan after the long lapse of the 1978 agreement,[41] or the indicative agreement on trade expansion between the GDR and Austria.[42] Modern practice also suggests that states are widening the range of areas covered by agreements to conclude specific sectoral agreements in such areas as shipping, telecommunications and the supply of nuclear fuels. General trade or cooperation agreements themselves are often accompanied by ancillary agreements which establish rules and regulatory arrangements for scientific, cultural and other forms of cooperation. The conclusion of such packages of agreements is frequently used to mark some important stage or new phase of relations between the parties. The occasion, of course, may be more symbolic than substantive.

While the argument has been put that diplomacy may be used to develop legal arrangements between states (as well as between state and non-state entities) the converse also applies. States may *withhold* the conclusion of a general trade or sectoral agreement to prevent the acquisition of a benefit or use the benefit as leverage to gain concessions on some other issue. For example, Japan has refused to conclude a long-term economic agreement with the Soviet Union until there is progress on the disputed northern islands off Hokkaido, which the Soviets occupied in 1945.[43]

Laying the groundwork

One of the basic functions of diplomacy in trade or any other sector of external policy is the maintenance of friendly and harmonious relations with other states, organisations and individuals. Representatives, heads of state, foreign ministry and other officials are required to carry out a varied and not always compatible range of activities. The most crucial of these are establishing personal links, explaining and defending policy, assessing and making possible commercial opportunities and defusing disputes. In terms of the latter, Japan, for example, has developed a sophisticated form of 'damage-limitation' diplomacy in defence of its trade surplus geared to selected visits and the timings of trade liberalisation or loan measures. Thus, in preparation for the Tokyo Western economic summit in May 1986, visits by the Japanese Prime Minister, Foreign Minister, Finance Minister and Minister for International Trade and Industry were made respectively to Ottawa, Washington, London and Bonn, and quadrilateral talks held with Canada, the United States and the European Commission.[44] Diplomatic groundwork is important too in those instances where there has been a change of regime. Visits are a means of facilitating the re-establishment of confidence, trade continuity and securing financial support, e.g. Guinea and the FRG. New revolutionary regimes often rely on visits by heads of state or foreign ministers to not only acquire international support but lay the basis for innovative agreements with like-minded states, as in the case of Iran's discussion with Pakistan to establish a joint Islamic shipping corporation.[45]

Resolution of trade disputes

Bilateral trade disputes generally occur for one of three main reasons: restrictions on access of goods or over the share of a services market; allegations of dumping or unfair application of countervailing duties; and imbalance in trade. They may be resolved through diplomatic techniques including negotiation and conciliation, judicial means such as arbitration (e.g. International Chamber of Commerce), dispute panels (e.g. GATT), formal legal processes of the European Court of Justice and sometimes by force. Although most disputes are seldom resolved quickly, they do tend to remain sectorally self-contained, with periodic diplomatic efforts to resolve them the norm. Of the 84 disputes brought before GATT under article XXIII:2 or the panels set up under the Tokyo Round, 77 involved either the United States or the European Community. In 26 of these cases the US and the EEC were engaged in disputes with each other.[46] The frequency of trade disputes between advanced industrial countries would seem to suggest a greater margin of tolerance of conflict arising from their trade and other aspects of foreign policy than is the case for minor and other powers, which may be trade dependent on a key export. In the latter cases, disputes can very often have wide foreign-policy implications unless they are quickly resolved through diplomatic means. However, the widening of the range of disputes between the major OECD states, together with increasing use of legal means, could lower the threshold of tolerance and cause greater spill-over into other areas of foreign policy.

In the main, trade disputes tend to be temporarily settled through short-term measures, with the exception of one or two sectors such as

VERs in steel, e.g. long-term US–EEC carbon steel fibre agreements. Yet short-term compromises through, for example, quota adjustment, e.g. United States and Indonesian textile agreements,[47] tend to be no more than essentially holding operations. As such, short-run arrangements generally require renegotiation because of problems of monitoring, commercial pressures from other sources and, in the case of suspension agreements, the backlog of delayed items. On the other hand, such agreements may be the maximum that is politically and commercially possible for domestic reasons. The problem of disputes being reopened is illustrated by the Thailand–United States multi-product dispute involving Thai exports of fabrics (the second largest merchandise export after rice), canned tuna and steel.[48] While Thai diplomacy, through a well-orchestrated lobby campaign undertaken by the former Thai Ambassador to Washington in conjunction with a US law firm, resolved the tuna issue, the reopening of the textile dispute and the initiation by the US steel industry of anti-dumping action against Thai steel widened the conflict. The visit of Secretary Shultz in July 1985, while endorsing good Thai–US relations, did nothing fundamentally, to resolve the dispute, underlining the point that visits with an essentially macro-political purpose (seeking support for multilateral trade talks) cannot easily deal with technical trade disputes.[49]

In some instances of trade conflict, a particular dispute can have general repercussions on the overall level of trade between the two states. For example, the dispute between Spain and Algeria over the level of Liquid Natural Gas (LNG) which Spain should have imported under the terms of a contract cut Spain's exports by a third. The eventual resolution of the dispute was followed by signature of a Spanish–Algerian economic and industrial cooperation agreement.[50]

Trade redistribution disputes arising out of trade imbalances are both frequent and in many instances least susceptible to diplomatic influence. What might be urged politically, and perhaps accepted by a receiving head of government or foreign minister, may not be heeded, supported or considered practical by domestic commercial interests. To prevent or reduce the importance of redistribution disputes, states have established, either separately or as part of a trade agreement, joint economic commissions or similarly titled bodies to review trade distribution and related questions. Occasionally states feel that normal diplomatic methods have been utilized to the full and stronger action is required, including threatening to or actually terminating a bilateral agreement. For example in the Franco-Soviet trade dispute over the balance of trade in favour of the Soviet Union,

France threatened to give notice of termination of the 1967 Franco-Soviet shipping agreement, which it identified as contributing to the trade imbalance through the non-implementation of the equal cargo-carrying provisions.[51] These instances tend to be relatively rare since in general most states prefer to rely on diplomatically agreed solutions, rather than face the breakdown of agreements and retaliatory action.

TRADE AND OTHER POLITICAL OBJECTIVES

Trade is used in a variety of circumstances to support foreign policy.[52] The role of trade and loan agreements is especially evident when a state wishes to direct greater foreign policy attention to another state or region. For example, as part of the general revision of Soviet foreign policy under Gorbachev, coordinated diplomatic visits have been made to several selected non-socialist countries in Asia and the Far East to signal an upgraded Soviet effort. A number of accompanying loan and trade agreements were signed including a trade-promotion agreement with Indonesia.[53] Bilateral agreements can also be used for wider symbolic purposes, such as the Argentine–Brazil aeronautical construction agreement, which was concluded as a means of demonstrating the importance the two countries attached to wider regional cooperation.[54]

The other major area in which trade is used for essentially political purposes is in coercive diplomacy. The use of coercive diplomacy in the form of embargoes, sanctions, trade retaliation and the seizure of assets has now become quite widespread and not limited to East–West relations. It generally serves one or more of four purposes: to influence the economy or political system of the target state; change foreign policy behaviour; demonstrate disapproval; or raise the level of the stakes in a conflict.

In East–West relations the major example of economic restrictions in support of foreign policy is the economic *cordon sanitaire* in strategic goods against the Soviet Union, administered since 1950 through the Co-ordinating Committee (COCOM).[55] Although the embargo was relaxed in the 1970s in line with *détente* on the basis of the concept of 'positive linkage',[56] the breakdown in *détente* in the early 1980s resulted in efforts to tighten the embargo.[57] These have been strongly resisted within Western Europe.[58] The European view that trade justifies itself is in sharp contrast to that of the United States which regards trade as something which can and should be controlled as a form of leverage. The issue has been further complicated by the problem of dual-use technology.[59] The primacy of trade view re-emerged in the course of various efforts to apply economic sanctions. In the follow-up to the Afghanistan and Polish cases, Western alliance response in the cases of Nicaragua, Lebanon, Iran and Libya has been limited or not forthcoming. The reasons for ineffectiveness are several and are well understood. Of these the problems of economic leakage (the 'other suppliers') is a major difficulty.[60] Leakage may occur through the granting of political support to a state facing sanctions. For example in the Nicaraguan case, Canada has given support to Nicaragua including the relocation of its trade representation to Canada.[61]

A further aspect of sanctions, not generally discussed, which makes them problematic is that of transition to normal relations. This is often neither smooth nor easily achieved. In the United Kingdom–Argentina case, the United Kingdom unilaterally lifted the ban on imports from Argentina imposed in the Falklands conflict in July 1985, in an effort to resume normal relations. Other trade-related moves included not opposing proposals in the IMF and Paris Club on Argentina's international debt. However, return to normal economic relations has been held up by the general issue of sovereignty over the Falkland Islands (Islas Malvinas) as well as incidents in the exclusion zone.[62] In general the return to normal relations is a lengthy process, since the placing of sanctions on a country tends to freeze bilateral financial, commercial, political and other problems which have to be eventually taken up as sanctions are subsequently removed or gradually withdrawn.

Coercive diplomacy may take several other forms. In particular, while administrative restraints on goods have become common, these have also been used for non-trade purposes. France, for example, placed administrative restraints on New Zealand trade after the *Rainbow Warrior* affair in order to put pressure on the New Zealand authorities to release convicted French agents.[63] More generally the case brought into sharp focus the conflicts which can arise between legal and foreign policy interests, on the one hand, and trade on the other, when a state faces coercion.

INNOVATION AND DIPLOMACY

As far as the innovative aspects of the relationship between trade and diplomacy are concerned, three developments especially are worth comment: the expansion of counter trade, the growth of bilateral trade agreements and South–South diplomacy. While counter trade, at least in its barter form, has been historically a feature of international trade, it has, with variations, been principally used by the Council for Mutual Economic Assistance (CMEA) countries. In modern diplomacy, the number of countries involved in counter trade and the type of goods has increased. The forms of counter trade too have become more sophisticated both at an intergovernmental level and between governments and non-state agencies. Part of the reason for the changing composition of those involved in counter trade lies in the decline in petroleum prices. Major counter traders are Iran (e.g. with Taiwan (weapons)), Iraq, Nigeria, with other large users such as Algeria, Angola, Egypt, Libya, Mexico, Saudi Arabia and Syria. The other major factor accounting for the increases in number of non-oil-exporting states using some counter trade is foreign exchange shortage.[64]

Counter trade still forms a low percentage of total trade for most developing countries outside Eastern Europe. The Hodara study, for example, on Argentina, Brazil and Uruguay indicated that counter trade accounted for only 2 per cent, 5.5 per cent and 12.5 per cent of their respective total trade.[65] Nevertheless, it is clear that, for reasons of economic and foreign policy, a large number of individual counter-trade transactions are being stimulated by government rather than by commercial action. In a number of instances government agencies and/or state trading enterprises participate directly in concluding the arrangement and carrying it out.[66] A further noticeable feature of governmental involvement is in the promotion of bilateral trade agreements outside the GATT framework. Bilateral agreements have been used by certain developing countries for commencing trade transactions with countries which they had hardly traded with previously, or by countries which are in a state of war and require assured supplies of products in exchange for a guaranteed market for their major export product (e.g. petroleum). Accompanying bilateral trade diplomacy is the general growth in economic relations between developing countries (ECDC). As indicated earlier the framework for ECDC was set out in the shift in development philosophy at the G-77 conferences in Mexico City (1976) and the ministerial meeting in Arusha (1979) in preparation for UNCTAD V. Subsequently the emphasis has shifted from North–South negotiations to concentrate on ECDC in line with the Caracas Programme of Action (CPA) agreed by the G-77 in 1981.[67] The focal point of ECDC, in perhaps a symbolic sense, is the GSTP among developing countries.[68] While tariff reductions and other measures from this are likely to take some time to achieve, the GSTP has come to signify the idea of moving away from the North to enhanced cooperation between developing countries in trade, finance, common production and joint ventures. Since 1981 an ECDC administrative structure has been developed within the G-77 and a growing number of technical meetings held.[69] In July 1985 the ministerial meeting in New Delhi established the negotiating framework for GSTP.[70] In reviewing the progress of ECDC, Ambassador Golov of Yugoslavia, underlined three issues: the need for national legislation to implement ECDC, including preferential tariff arrangements; that ECDC should be self-financing; and that programmes should be implemented within the existing UN structure.[71] The increasing role of the G-77 chairmanship in directing and coordinating ECDC[72] has brought it into sharp conflict with UNCTAD over the overall responsibility for managing ECDC. In part the G-77 leadership have sought to take ECDC out of the framework of UNCTAD because of difficulties encountered with the OECD group in UNCTAD's ECDC Committee.[73] The major issue, remains, however, one of control.[74]

CONCLUSION

A decade of attempts to change economic order through large-scale North–South multilateral conferences has eventually given way to a shift of emphasis to South–South diplomacy. Even so, the institutional layout for the conduct of international trade and development diplomacy remains complex and overlapping. Nor has the shift in emphasis reduced the institutional overlap, rather, if anything, it has intensified the problem, not only between GATT and UNCTAD but created others, including UNCTAD and the G-77 leadership. For GATT itself, new developments in international trade have altered the form and conduct of international trade negotiations, pushing back the boundary line of GATT activities increasingly into non-tariff areas. Continued trade protectionism through tariff and non-tariff measures has itself influenced states to use diplomacy to develop innovatory arrangements with other states and non-state actors to circumvent restrictions, and reach other bilateral agreements. It is clear that of all the sectors of external policy, trade diplomacy has shown the greatest degree of growth.

REFERENCES AND NOTES

1. For a discussion of the role of the China lobby in changing British policy to one of checking Japan and preserving South China as a sphere of influence, see Stephen Lyon Endicott, *Diplomacy and Enterprise: British China Policy* (Manchester University Press, Manchester, 1979).
2. In the trade dispute between the United States and Japan over US exports of beef and citrus products, Japanese farming interests strongly lobbied the Agriculture Ministry and the Liberal Democratic Party's parliamentary farm committee to limit any quota increase. The dispute brought the Japanese Agriculture and Foreign Ministries into dispute. In this instance, the tough line recommended by Agriculture prevailed. See *Financial Times*, 4 April 1984.
3. *Financial Times*, 30 Jan. 1986.
4. *BISD*, Vol. III (Geneva, 1958) p. 3.
5. The Council was established in 1960 and consists of representatives of all contracting parties which request to become members.
6. See Olivier Long, *Law and its Limitations in the GATT Multilateral Trade System* (Martinus Nijhoff, Dordrecht, 1985) pp. 57–61.
7. By 1969 GATT membership had risen to seventy-six, with eleven countries participating in its work without being full members.
8. See M. M. Kostecki, *East–West Trade and the GATT System* (The Macmillan Press, London, 1979) p. 29 *passim*.
9. Romanian membership of GATT did not automatically lead to MFN status. Subsequently Romanian MFN status has been, in the case of the United States, subject to annual review. See *Financial Times*, 5 March 1986 and, GATT L/5915, 18 Oct. 1985, p. 17.
10. *Financial Times*, 13 Jan. 1986.
11. Gerard Curzon, *Multilateral Commercial Diplomacy* (Michael Joseph, London, 1965) p. 51. See also Long, op. cit., pp. 44–56.
12. See Stephen D. Krasner, 'United States Commercial and Monetary Policy: Unravelling the Paradox of External Strength and Internal Weakness', in Peter J. Katzenstein, *Between Power and Plenty* (The University of Wisconsin Press, Madison, 1978) pp. 51–87.
13. See Long, op. cit., p. 29
14. Misc. 31 (1979), Cmnd. 7668.
15. Misc. 21 (1979), Cmnd. 7658; *The Tokyo Round of Multilateral Trade Negotiations* (GATT, Geneva, 1979), and Vol. II, *Supplementary Report* (GATT, Geneva, 1980).
16. Misc. 26 (1979), Cmnd. 7663.
17. Misc. 27 (1979), Cmnd. 7664.
18. Misc. 25 (1979), Cmnd. 7662.
19. Misc. 24 (1979), Cmnd. 7661.
20. Misc. 23 (1979), Cmnd. 7660.
21. Misc. 20 (1979), Cmnd. 7657.
22. See Gary Clyde Hufbauer and Jeffrey J. Schott, *Trading for Growth: The Next Round of Trade Negotiations* (Institute for International Economics, Washington, DC, 1985) p. 21.
23. Long, op. cit., p. 60.

24. See Kent Jones, *Politics v. Economics in World Steel Trade* (George Allen and Unwin, London, 1986) p. 125 on the pressure in the US for control of steel imports from Taiwan, Brazil and South Korea, following the US–EEC steel pact.

25. Membership of GATT had increased to ninety-three by 1986.

26. See Diego Cordovez, 'The Making of UNCTAD', *Journal of World Trade Law* (May–June 1967) pp. 243–328; and Sidney Dell, 'The Origins of UNCTAD', in Michael Zammit Cutajar (ed.) *UNCTAD and the South–North Dialogue* (Pergamon Press, Oxford, 1985); Gamani Corea's Stevenson Lecture at the London School of Economics, 6 Dec. 1976, 'UNCTAD and the NIEO', reprinted in *International Affairs*, Vol. 53, No. 2 (April 1977) esp. pp. 192–8.

27. See Dell, op. cit., pp. 10–19.

28. Transfer of technology was discussed at Nairobi (1976), Manila (1979), Belgrade (1983) and in the special negotiating machinery set up under UNCTAD auspices, the UN Conference on an International Code of Conduct on the Transfer of Technology.

29. See Dell, op. cit., pp. 26–30.

30. See K. H. Khaw 'Postscript on Malinowski and the Code: A Personal Commentary', in Cutajar, op. cit., pp. 230–2.

31. The United States GSP was introduced in 1976.

32. The Yemen Arab Republic became the nintieth government required to ratify the Common Fund on 14 Jan. 1986. The remaining requirement is that the countries which have ratified should represent two-thirds of the Fund's directly contributed capital of $470 million. The ninety countries account for 57.86 per cent of the Fund's capital, i.e. 8.8 per cent short of that required. No socialist country has signed or ratified the agreement. UNCTAD, *Bulletin*, No. 218 (Jan. 1986) p. 8.

33. See John W. Sewell and I. William Zartman, 'Global Negotiations: Path to the Future or Dead-End Street?', in Jagdish N. Bhagwati and John Gerard Ruggie, *Power, Passions and Purpose: Prospects for North–South Negotiations* (MIT Press, Cambridge, Mass., 1984) pp. 110–14.

34. For US policy at UNCTAD V, particularly on this point, see Robert K. Olson, *US Foreign Policy and the NIEO: Negotiating Global Problems 1974–81* (Westview Press, Boulder, Colo., 1981) Ch. 4.

35. See Dell, op. cit., pp. 28–30.

36. *The North–South Dialogue – Making it Work*, Report by a Commonwealth Group of Experts (Commonwealth Secretariat, London, 1982) pp. 51–2.

37. See Iqbal Haji, 'Finance, Money, Developing Countries and UNCTAD', in Cutajar, op. cit., pp. 169–70. See also Surendra J. Patel, in Cutajar, op. cit., p. 142, fn. 3, on the life cycle and high mortality rate of UN documents.

38. For an Australian account see Robert Ramsay, 'UNCTAD's Failures: The Rich get Richer', *International Organisation*, Vol. 38, No. 2 (Spring 1984) p. 391.

39. Prior to the 1973 oil crisis EB interest in North–South relations and the United Nations had been minimal. See Olson, op. cit., pp. 126–7; and Seymour Maxwell Finger, *Your Man at the U.N.* (New York University Press, New York 1980) pp. 250–1.

40. See especially on US policy the statement of Gerald B. Holman to the UNCTAD Trade and Development Board, 5 Oct. 1981, UNCTAD, TD/B/863, reprinted in *Journal of World Trade Law*, Vol. 16, No. 5 (Sept.–Oct. 1982) pp. 455–60.

41. *Financial Times*, 13 Jan. 1986. Total bilateral trade diminished to less than $US50 million after the lapse of the 1978 treaty and application by Pakistan of restrictions. Indo-Pakistan talks were held in Islamabad in Jan. 1986. See also *G-77 Bulletin*, No. 30, (Jan.–Feb. 1986) p. 10.

42. *Financial Times*, 16 Dec. 1985.

43. *The Guardian*, 20 Jan. 1986; *Financial Times*, 31 Jan. 1986. Soviet Foreign Minister, Shevardnadze, visited Tokyo in Jan. 1986 in an attempt to resume the peace talks. Major differences remained over the northern islands issue, but side agreements were concluded on taxation, trade and payments and the 1972 cultural agreement extended.

44. *Financial Times*, 10 Jan. 1986.

45. *Lloyds List*, 16 Jan. 1986.

46. See *Review of the Effectiveness of Trade Dispute Settlement under the GATT and Tokyo Round Agreements*, United States International Trade Commission, Dec. 1985, p. viii.

47. *Financial Times*, 5 July 1985.

48. See, *Far Eastern Economic Review*, 25 July 1985. Apparel exports rose to $US711.6 million in 1984. The United States accounted for 35.8 per cent of total Thai exports in 1984.

49. The United States placed an embargo on Thai apparel exports in Oct. 1985, after the Shultz visit. See *Far Eastern Economic Review*, 7 Nov. 1985.

50. *Financial Times*, 4 July 1985; see also *Financial Times*, 13 July 1984, on origins of the dispute.

51. *Financial Times*, 5 Feb. 1986; and *UNTS*, Vol. 1001, 1976, for the text of the Franco-Soviet shipping agreement. See also, *Financial Times*, 7 Feb. 1986, for the Soviet warning to the EEC not to discriminate against Soviet shipping made at the end of the UNCTAD conference on the Convention on Conditions for Registration of Ships.

52. See Samuel P. Huntingdon, 'Trade, Technology and Leverage', *Foreign Policy*, No. 32 (Fall 1978) pp. 63–80.

53. *Financial Times*, 31 Oct. 1985. Two-way trade is very low at less than $US60 million. See *Indonesian Financial Statistics*, Vol. XVIII, No. 11 (Nov. 1985) pp. 118–19 and 130–1.

54. *Financial Times*, 20 Jan. 1986. The aeronautical agreement was a follow-up to the summit conference between President Raul Alfonsin and José Sarney in Nov. 1985.

55. See J. Wilczynski, *The Economics and Politics of East–West Trade* (Macmillan, London, 1969) pp. 271–89.

56. See Marshall I. Goldman, *Detente and Dollars* (Basic Books, New York, 1975) pp. 50, 71–6.

57. On the tightening of the embargo in the 1980s see Gary K. Bertsch, *East–West Strategic Trade, COCOM and the Atlantic Alliance* (Atlantic Institute, Paris, 1983) pp. 43–52, and 'East–West Trade and Technology Transfer: Toward a Policy of Non-military Free Trade', *SAIS Review*, Vol. 4, No. 2 (Summer–Fall 1984) pp. 101–2.

58. A case which came to symbolise the conflict within the alliance involved the dispute between the United States and Belgium over US efforts to prevent a small Belgian firm, Pegard, which was in financial difficulties, selling computer-controlled lathes to the Soviet Union. See *Sunday Times*, 7 Oct. 1984.

59. See J. Fred Bucy 'Technology Transfer and East–West Trade: A Reappraisal', in Gary K. Bertsch and John R. McIntyre, *National Security and Technology Transfer: The Strategic Dimensions of East–West Trade* (Westview Press, Boulder, Colo., 1983).

60. Community sanctions applied only to contracts which had been concluded after 4 Nov. 1979, and exemptions were made for foodstuffs and medical products. See European Parliament, Working Documents 1982–3, IO/EC/422, Document 1-8312, 8 April 1982, p. 22.

61. *Financial Times*, 11 May 1985.

62. *Financial Times*, 30 May 1986.

63. *Financial Times*, 5 March 1986, and *Financial Times*, 8 July 1986, on the agreement for the transfer of the two French agents.

64. See GATT L/5915, 18 Oct. 1985, p. 44.

65. See UNCTAD/ST/ECDC/27, 11 Sept. 1985, p. 40.

66. GATT, C/W/470, rev. 1, 5 Aug. 1985, p. 39.

67. A/36/333, 26 June 1981.

68. A/37/544, 14 Oct. 1982, Annex II for text of G-77 ministerial declaration on GSTP.

69. See *Economic and Technical Cooperation and Developing Countries*, Vols. 1 and 2 (Office of the Chairman of the Group of 77, Ljubljana, 1984).

70. A/40/762, 18 Oct. 1985, para. 48.

71. See *G-77 Bulletin*, No. 31 (March–April 1986) p. 4.

72. For the coordinating role see the reports of the Follow-Up and Coordination Committee, at Manila, 23–28 Aug. 1982, IFCC-1/G-77/Rpt 1; Tunis, 5–10 Sept. 1983, IFCC-11/G-77/Rpt 1; Cartagena de Indias, 3–10 Sept. 1984, IFCC-111/G-77/84/Rpt 1 and Jakarta, 19–23 Aug. 1985. IFCC-IV/G-77/85/Rpt.

73. See *G-77 Bulletin* No. 30 (Jan.–Feb. 1986) p. 11.

74. See A/40/762, 18 Oct. 1985, para. 49.

CHAPTER NINE
Diplomacy and security

DEFINING SECURITY

The relationship between diplomacy and security is complex and evolving. The question of what constitutes security can be addressed from three perspectives – the international system, nation-state and the individual. Internationally, security can be thought of in terms of the stability of the international system, defined as the level of tension or violence and the corresponding extent to which actor interests can be accommodated through diplomacy, without recourse to violence, on the basis of mediation, rule and norm setting. In the event of violence occurring, the task of diplomacy is ultimately peaceful settlement, through the negotiation of cease-fires, withdrawal and other measures of a longer-term nature. From a quite different perspective violence may be a preferred end in itself and diplomacy the means of orchestrating violence rather than bringing about a negotiated solution.

At a national level, security has traditionally been considered in terms of responses to essentially external threats of a military kind. From this perspective diplomacy features as the state craft of force, involving such actions as deterring aggressors, building up coalitions, threatening or warning an opponent and seeking international support of legitimacy for the use or control of force. The concentration on external threat has in part been a by-product of the so-called 'Golden Age' of Western (largely American) strategic theory, influenced by the cold war and the requirement that strategic analysis provide improved policy advice for dealing with the Soviet Union.[1] However, the advent of large numbers of new states into the international community, many with preoccupying internal problems,[2] underlined the inadequacy of traditional definitions. In fact, national security, that already ambiguous symbol, had to take on an additional dimension. To reflect this, the definition of security needs to be broadened *de minimis* to include, for certain states, regime maintenance as a primary national security objective.[3] The appropriateness of a wider definition of security can be seen from an advanced industrial country perspective in the case of Japan. The Study Group on Japanese Comprehensive National Security identified three politico-strategic objectives, including closer cooperation with the US, increasing Japan's self-defence capability and the improvement of Sino-Soviet relations. In addition the group identified the attainment of energy security, achieving food security and earthquake control as three other central security objectives.[4] It is also useful to add to the conventional classification of states a further category made up of those states with acute external and internal national security problems – the 'dual-security' states.

At a third level, security can be considered from the perspective of the relationship between the state and the individual in terms of the extent to which states incorporate within their national security considerations the interests of individuals. In practice, individuals tend to enjoy varying degrees of state protection depending on state capabilities and conceptions of national security. In consular relations, for example, the link between the individual and the state is often relatively remote, except in periods of crisis. A state may be forced into a more active role in the event of repeated violence against its nationals or diplomatic personnel.

SOME IMPLICATIONS FOR DIPLOMACY

Security interests of states and organisations are seldom static, except for a limited number of core values. New interests are acquired and marginal values are either elevated or discarded. At an economic level, continued access to overseas markets for key exports, the availability of raw materials and the protection of the overseas assets of its nationals are frequently ranked as important security considerations. Conversely, security interests may be downgraded or contracted, as may happen with foreign bases or particular security agreements being allowed to lapse. States generally also face entirely novel and far-reaching threats from, for example, maritime fraud,[5] international economic fraud, narcotics groups and transnationally organised crime.[6] The purpose of diplomacy is to contribute to the process of recognising and identifying new interests at an early stage through continuous reporting and assessments, facilitating adjustment between different interests and contributing to policy implementation.

Secondly, the internal aspect of national security has a number of implications for diplomacy. In those states in which national security is essentially internal, security policy-making tends to be highly personalised around the leader. National security diplomacy, too, is likely to be conducted *internally*, rather than through the country's embassies abroad or other external channels, with representatives of international organisations, non-governmental organisations (NGOs), foreign corporations on such issues as food aid, disaster relief and project implementation. Other non-military national security concerns are likely to involve issues such as financial security, insurgent groups and refugees. Dual-security states tend to encounter problems concerning the balance of emphasis between internal and external security requirements and, in their external diplomacy, the need to compromise on pragmatic grounds with ideological opponents. For example, those states with insurgency problems may find it necessary to attempt policies of political cooperation with an insurgent group's protecting power. Writing albeit largely in an external context, Arnold Wolfers notes: 'security covers a range of goals so wide that highly divergent policies can be interpreted as policies of security'.[7]

A third feature for many weaker states is the problem of establishing suitable regional security arrangements. A noticeable feature of recent diplomacy is the high priority attached by states which perceive themselves weak or vulnerable in a local or regional context to enhancing their security through declarations and treaties, frequently negotiated within the framework of the United Nations.

Finally, it should be recalled that the nexus between security and diplomacy can be broken in a number of circumstances. As we noted earlier, diplomacy may be directed entirely to the execution of violence. In other instances a shift to the use of force may reflect dissatisfaction with the failure of diplomacy. For example, during the Tehran hostage crisis, President Carter terminated the labyrinthine negotiations with Iran and authorised an attempted rescue mission of US diplomatic personnel. He recounts in his memoirs: 'We could no longer afford to depend on diplomacy. I decided to act.'[8]

SECURITY AND THE INTERNATIONAL SYSTEM

The founding concept of post-war international security within the UN framework was intended to be based on the idea of collective security. The UN Charter envisaged collective action to forestall or limit the action of a potential aggressor, through military and other measures. Thus the UN Charter concept of security was one of states acting in concert to control or limit force. Such collective action clearly required universality of membership or something close to that, and the willingness of members to provide appropriate military forces on a suitable scale as envisaged under article 43 of the Charter. Although UN membership expanded rapidly in the 1960s an adequate agreement could not be reached to provide the UN with sufficient military force of a permanent nature. The closest the UN came to a collective security action against an aggressor was in the Korean War (1950–53) with the establishment of a UN force under US command. The Korean crisis provided the context for the wider role of the General Assembly on security matters when it passed the Uniting for Peace Resolution in November 1950 in response to the stalemate in the Security Council caused by the Soviet veto.[9]

The failure, however, to achieve collective security has meant that approaches to security within the UN system have been developed on an *ad hoc* basis, with the negotiation and establishment within the limits of what is politically possible of UN observer, truce and peacekeeping forces. The operating experience of the UN Military Observer Group in India and Pakistan, the United Nations Observation Group in Lebanon (UNOGIL) (1958) the United Nations Emergency Force (UNEF) (Suez, 1956) and Opération des Nations Unies (ONUC) in the Congo (1960–62), however, formed the basis for the subsequent development of the concept of preventive diplomacy set out by Secretary-General Hammarskjöld.[10] Central to the idea of preventive diplomacy was putting UN forces into areas of potential superpower conflict, to forestall direct involvement, with the aim of limiting the scale of the conflict. Writing in 1960, Hammarskjöld noted:[11] 'Those efforts must aim at keeping newly arising conflicts outside the sphere of bloc differences. Further, in the case of conflicts on the margin of, or inside the sphere of bloc differences, the United Nations should seek to bring such conflicts out of this sphere through solutions aiming, in the first instance, at their strict localization . . . .'

Preventive diplomacy, to which the efforts of the United Nations have to a large extent been directed, is of special significance in cases where the original conflict may be said either to be the result of, or to imply risks for, the creation of a power vacuum between the main blocs.

In this way the success of preventive diplomacy depends on the interrelationship between the peacekeeping operation and the related diplomatic efforts to resolve the conflict. Operating experience in the Congo, Cyprus (United Nations Force in Cyprus (UNFICYP), 1964–) and the Lebanon (1978–) suggest that there are a number of particular conditions which influence the effectiveness of preventive diplomacy.[12] In the first place, states must be prepared to put the matter before the UN. Successive secretaries-general have criticised one or more parties to a conflict for their unwillingness to allow UN involvement. Other than this the cases under review indicate the importance of the initial and continued consent of the host government and the primary powers. The operation of ONUC especially brought the UN into major crisis. The United States and the Soviet Union not only had very different views on the legality and mission of ONUC, but the Soviet Union attacked the 'impartiality' of the Secretary-General. In the *troika* proposal the Soviet Union called for substantial changes including the establishment of three secretaries-general.[13] The controversy over the operation directly precipitated the financial crisis over the funding of UN peacekeeping operations. As a result of the dispute over the purposes of the force, the Soviet Union and a number of other states refused to finance the force. Following the Congo experience, subsequent operations have been funded in differing ways, such as voluntary contributions as in the case of UNFICYP. The accumulating debt arising from peacekeeping operations, which had risen to nearly $US400 million by 1985–86,[14] has impaired the capacity of the organisation, both politically and militarily, to undertake or continue preventive diplomacy-type operations. Another important long-term effect on UN diplomacy has been on the increasing tendency for selective funding of UN activities.[15] The growing politicisation of funding has also spilled over into participation in the UN specialised agencies.

The continued financial problems associated with preventive diplomacy have made the condition that smaller members shoulder a disproportionate amount of the burden of providing forces and other resources that much more significant. In those circumstances in which the mandate is particularly ill-defined, as with UNIFIL, the smaller UN member faces difficult diplomatic choices if it wishes to withdraw from a force, as in the case of the withdrawal of the Netherlands from UNIFIL.[16] While a withdrawal may not fundamentally affect a preventive diplomacy operation, it can have potential damaging effects on host country–donor relations and on the morale and political effectiveness of the force.

The overall effectiveness of preventive diplomacy is closely related to the supportive or 'quiet' diplomacy undertaken by the Secretary-General and others. Initiatives by the Secretary-General need to be both politically acceptable and be perceived as having some likely measure of success. In practice, quiet diplomacy appears very often to make no major progress and its overall impact is difficult to gauge. Such advances as are made are often at the margin (e.g. arrangements for prisoner-of-war exchange in the Iran–Iraq War) rather than at a substantive level. Initiatives are likely to become that more difficult as the problem becomes entrenched. Mediation in the Cyprus dispute became progressively more difficult following the Turkish invasion of 1974, which fundamentally altered the UN mission and the Cyprus problem. The *scope* for UN initiatives may, additionally, be limited by other mediatory efforts, e.g. the Haig mission in the Falklands conflict.[17] It is clear that the longer a peacekeeping force remains deployed in a conflict, the more such a force comes to be seen as a built-in feature of the conflict with the result that diplomatic initiatives become *independent* of the operation and purposes of the force. In this way what was initially preventive diplomacy is progressively changed to some other form of general diplomatic activity.

RULES AND INTERNATIONAL SECURITY

Apart from preventive diplomacy as an approach to security in the international system, a further important dimension of internationally derived security is the development of tacit and formal rules. Rules may take the form of treaties or agreements, less formal means including declarations, through to informal tacit arrangements such as customary restraints, or accepting the spirit of an agreement.[18] In general, rule setting involves lengthy procedural and definitional diplomacy, especially within international organisations, in view of the high interests at stake. In the UN extensive diplomatic efforts have been devoted to such issues as definitions of aggression,[19] the legal status of mercenaries[20] and the principles of international law concerning friendly relations.[21] Related to these rule-setting conferences are investigations into, for example, challenges and threats to international security from new sources such as internationally organised crime,[22] or the use of chemical weapons in particular conflicts. These and other similar inquiries and UN special missions frequently form the basis for UN resolutions and formal legal instruments.

A noticeable feature of internationally sourced security are the efforts sponsored particularly, though not exclusively, by weaker states to establish regimes to regulate the status and use of particular territory. For example, the 1959 Antarctic Treaty reserves (article 1) Antarctica for peaceful purposes.[23] Other attempts to neutralise territory or limit the use or placing of weapons include Austrian neutrality (1955),[24] the Rappaki plan for zonal disengagement in Europe (1957–58)[25] and the creation of the Saudi Arabian–Iraq neutral zone.[26] More recently, attempts to designate international areas for peaceful purposes have increased.[27] For example the non-aligned movement discussed the Indian Ocean region at the Lusaka conference in 1970. In December 1971 the issue was taken up by the UN General Assembly, which declared the Indian Ocean a zone of peace and formed the Ad Hoc Committee on the Indian Ocean.[28] A number of regional treaties, including the Treaty of Tlatelolco (1967)[29] have declared nuclear-free zones. In Southeast Asia, ASEAN issued a declaration in 1971 intended to secure recognition of Southeast Asia as a zone of peace, freedom and neutrality (ZOPFAN),[30] while the Valletta declaration of September 1984 made peaceful use claims for the Mediterranean as a closed sea.[31] These and similar declarations suggest that states continue to find value in committing very significant amounts of their diplomatic time to establishing rules, declarations and regimes by international diplomatic conferences despite the remoteness of the objectives.

ALLIES, ALLIANCES AND DIPLOMACY

The foregoing has looked at the scope and limitations on internationally source security in the form of preventive diplomacy and internationally agreed rules. Of the other national actions undertaken by states in the pursuit of security, three broad areas of diplomatic activity have been devoted to the enhancement of security; the redefinition of security interests and the maintenance of freedom of action.

In seeking to *enhance* security, states have traditionally had at their disposal methods such as negotiation of arms supplies and security arrangements with a protecting power. Other options are avoidance of direct involvement in conflicts, maintenance of a low diplomatic profile or, conversely, seeking international political support. Those states which have opted for security through neutrality find it necessary periodically to reinforce the credibility of their orientation by statements or protestations against infringements or erosion of their status.[32] For other states reliance has continued to be placed on bilateral arrangements. Such arrangements have been between local powers, e.g. the Sudanese–Egyptian security cooperation agreement against Libya. More often than not a major external power has featured in an agreement. Between 1970 and 1980, for example, some ten countries signed bilateral treaties of friendship and cooperation or similar arrangements with the Soviet Union.[33]

Relatively few formal multilateral security alliances have been concluded in recent years. The period since 1972 has, outside Europe, been largely one of alliance demise. An exception is the creation of the Gulf Cooperation Council (GCC) in 1981. Diplomatic cooperation among the GCC members (Bahrain, Kuwait, Oman, Qatar, Saudi Arabia and the United Arab Emirates) has increased considerably since then although the security arrangements remain embryonic.[34] It is interesting to note in this context that ASEAN has remained essentially an economic organisation, despite some suggestions of altering its focus following the winding up of the South East Asian Treaty Organisation. A factor working against any formal alliance has undoubtedly been the differing defence arrangements which members have with a variety of external powers, including the US–Philippine arrangements,[35] and, the unusual five-power defence pact combined with semi-non-alignment of Malaysia.[36] In the GCC case existing arrangements with external powers similarly inhibit regional security cooperation. The most important constraints, however, remain the low military capabilities of most individual members in relation to the range of threat, and differing estimates of the significance of internal threats.

While there appears to have been reluctance among states to enter into formal multilateral alliance commitments since the 1970s, interest nevertheless has been shown in regional arrangements of a lesser nature. A good example is the South Pacific Forum,[37] which brings together Australia, the Cook Islands, Fiji, Kiribati, Nauru, New Zealand, Niue, Papua New Guinea, Solomon Islands, Tonga, Tuvalu, Vanuatu and Western Samoa. The grouping has been drawn increasingly together on a number of issues, including problems connected with extended maritime boundaries under the new Law of the Sea Convention, dumping of waste at sea and nuclear testing. The massive extension of the sea space of the smaller members of the South Pacific Forum has posed major problems of development, administration and security. The views of the smaller members of the forum on how best to maximise the benefits, especially from fisheries and other sources,[38] have often been at variance with the revised security perceptions of the larger members of the forum. Australia and New Zealand have been concerned to limit or prevent Soviet hydrographic, fisheries and naval presence in the region. Both countries, for example, have given increased development assistance to Tonga, Western Samoa and the Cook Islands to dissuade them from granting fisheries access to the Soviet Union.[39]

An important area of high diplomatic activity, whether it is in a bilateral or multilateral framework, concerns the acquisition of weapons systems and technology transfer. Very frequently in bilateral arrangements involving a larger external power, demands by the smaller state for advanced weapons systems or replenishment of equipment are invariably the source of diplomatic dispute in that concessions by the primary power on *supply* may sometimes conflict with its other foreign policy interests. Supply remains the essential lever over an ally.[40] The failure of the USSR to refurbish the Egyptian army both before and after the October 1973 War was a major factor in the reorientation of Egyptian foreign policy after 1975.[41] In the NATO context, weapons-system enhancement has been a source of conflict both between West European members, and between Western Europe and the United States. Ravenal, for example, has suggested that the disputes are of a cyclical nature, in that they are patterned as a result of periodic decisions on deployment, upgrading or the introduction of innovatory weapons systems, as illustrated over decisions with Multilteral Force (MLF), Theater Nuclear Forces (TNF) and Strategic Defense Initiative (SDI).[42]

REDEFINING SECURITY

Efforts to redefine the purposes and benefits of security arrangements have now become almost an everyday feature of international relations. In arrangements involving major powers, minor powers have periodically attempted to gain higher economic benefits from allowing their territories to be used as foreign bases. In fact the adequacy of base payment and offset arrangements has become an important cause of alliance 'fraying' in NATO. In the Turkish–United States dispute,[43] for example, Turkey has sought higher levels of military assistance and the modernisation of the Turkish armed forces, which have met with Greek counter-lobbying in the US Congress. Furthermore, Turkey's complex foreign policy orientation has proved both a source of strength and weakness. As a 'crossroads' state, links with European, socialist, Arab and Islamic countries, suggest diversification, mixed with an unwillingness to undertake a fundamental shift in security orientation away from the United States.[44]

In contrast, Greek policy since 1981 offers an unusual illustration of a NATO ally apparently attempting a more ambitious redefinition of its national security interests and alliance relations.[45] Although the incoming socialist government was committed to the removal of American bases and nuclear weapons under a neutralist foreign policy, the 'essentials' of Greek security policy have remained intact. The Papandreou Government subsequently renewed the bases agreement with the United States in September 1983. Greek policy has, however, been modified in several respects. In terms of style, the marginal elements of Greek foreign policy (e.g. the Polish question) have been conducted with a strong anti-Western flavour.[46] Domestically, disputes involving the NATO alliance have been used as foreign policy crises and have served as a diversion from domestic issues. Greek security policy towards NATO has been modified to some extent with limited participation in NATO exercises. Underlying Greek policy is a redefinition of security in which the major threat is seen as coming from the south. The disputes with Turkey over the Aegean and the Turkish occupation of northern Cyprus, along with the associated conflict with NATO over such questions as airspace and the security status of Lemnos have been accorded high priority by the Papandreou Government. The constraints on more substantial redefinition mainly come para-doxically from the requirement for continued US military equipment for the armed forces, and political support in the conflict with Turkey.[47]

Outside of Europe, the issue of the stationing, presence and use of nuclear weapons has been a source of dispute within the ANZUS alliance[48] (Australia, New Zealand, United States) between New Zealand and the United States, while the presence of US warships carrying nuclear weapons in Japanese ports has become increasingly sensitive for Japanese governments.[49]

In ANZUS, New Zealand redefined its security interests in 1985 with the refusal to allow port facilities to United States warships with potential nuclear capability.[50] In response the United States initially cancelled joint exercises, meetings of communications officials and the sharing of joint intelligence. With no modification of New Zealand policy, the United States suspended its security arrangements under ANZUS with New Zealand in August 1986.[51] The New Zealand action underlines the dilemma for smaller alliance members of how to gain diplomatic support for security through conventional rather than nuclear forces. It is a problem to which nuclear guarantor states have yet to develop an effective response. A shift from deterrence to defence if anything enhances the need for transit facilities and sharing nuclear risk, which makes the dilemma more acute.

Redefinition of security has occurred for a number of other reasons. In redefining security, states have sometimes sought to diversify their sources of security. For example, Malta has experimented with various security arrangements with differing countries, including Libya, since the 1970s, and in an exchange of notes with Italy declared itself as having neutralised status in 1981.[52] In other instances, unfulfilled economic and military commitments can lead minor powers to switch protecting states rapidly, e.g. Somalia from the Soviet Union. The arms-supply policies of an external power by definition have security implications for neighbouring states and can create perceptions of vulnerability. Thus the Egyptian abrogation of the Egyptian–Soviet treaty in 1976[53] was influenced not only by Soviet failure to build up the Egyptian armed forces but also by the Soviet rearmament of Libya.[54] In their economic actions external powers are generally sensitive to the security implications of cuts in budgetary and other assistance to former colonies. In some instances reductions in budgetary assistance by an external power have led to efforts to find a new economic *patron*. The Central African Republic and Benin, for example, have attempted to diversify from France. Yet these exercises have generally been short-lived and often led to a *coup d'état*.[55]

In the main, states outside Europe have found it difficult to develop effective regional security arrangements.[56] The contribution to regional collective security of organisations such as the OAU has on the whole been very limited.[57] This situation seems for the most part to have been tacitly accepted and the organisation's role confined largely to political and economic questions. In relatively rare cases some states have taken the step of actually withdrawing from a regional organisation. Morocco, for example, withdrew in 1985 from the OAU.[58] It is clear that withdrawal tends to be an action of last resort because of fears of diplomatic isolation. Although a regional organisation might be ineffective in military terms, it is nevertheless, a diplomatic *milieu* for contact, discussion and lobbying, which are in themselves essential ingredients to continued perceptions of independence, legitimacy and security well-being by the member states.[59]

SECURITY AND FREEDOM OF ACTION

As a matter of *raison d'être*, states are anxious to safeguard their freedom of action as much as possible to conduct what they consider to be appropriate security policies. In the context of international conferences, meetings and other contacts, questions to do with representation, consultation and coordination of policies are seen as especially important. States attach importance to having their positions understood and accepted as far as possible by allies, like-minded countries and others. Reasons of international prestige also make states sensitive to questions of representation. Italy strongly insisted, for example, on the right to participate in the Vienna MBFR talks, although it had little direct interest in the proceedings.[60] In contrast, in the case of the Conference on Security and Cooperation in Europe (CSCE) conference, although a number of countries had only indirect interests, such as Malta and Cyprus, they nevertheless were active in articulating their particular neutralist and non-aligned concerns. Within Western Europe three of the four middle-rank members of NATO (Britain, France and the FRG) regard it as important to maintain separate dialogues through high-level visits and other exchanges with the Soviet Union and selected Eastern European socialist states. Such separate dialogues offset to an extent US–Soviet bilateralism, provide competing assessments, the opportunity to put forward individual views and, on occasion, the chance to act as a third-party mediator.

Within alliances consultation and coordination of policies have become essential features of modern bilateral and coalition diplomacy. Failure to undertake consultation with allies on major strategic issues can have adverse political effects on an alliance relationship, such as occurred as a result of the failure of the United States to consult Japan about the revision of policy towards the People's Republic of China in 1971 (the so-called Nixon 'shock'). At a multilateral level, coalition diplomacy within the Western alliance has involved attempts to clear positions, refine draft texts for international conferences as well as exchanges on everyday international issues. Writing in the context of MBFR, US Ambassador Jonathan Dean estimated that 40 per cent of the time of the MBFR negotiator is devoted to coalition diplomacy, 30 per cent of his total working time to consultation with his national capital, 25 per cent with his own delegation and only 5 per cent for negotiating contacts of all kinds with representatives of the Warsaw Pact.[61]

The use of coalition diplomacy in NATO in the MBFR negotiations has produced improved assessments of risks and possibilities as a result of the exhaustive consultation procedure. The formation of the Ad Hoc Group for clearing positions also meant that each NATO representative had the full right to be heard, improving the prospect of shared responsibility for the talks. Looked at from an East–West perspective, the MBFR talks have provided a setting for consultation within and between NATO and the Warsaw Pact, and an opportunity for exchanges on force levels and strategy of each side, benefits not found as commonly in bilateral superpower talks.[62]

UNCONVENTIONAL DIPLOMACY

The growth in the involvement of individuals who are not formal diplomatic agents in international security negotiations involving states and other actors has become a significant feature of contemporary international relations. Such diplomacy can be described as unconventional in terms of the actors, procedures and outcomes. The growth in unconventional diplomacy has partly come about because of the failure, unacceptability or non-availability of traditional diplomatic methods. As we have argued above, a consequence of the limited success of many traditional techniques has made it possible for individuals to become involved to a much larger extent in resolving conflicts. Other factors accounting for the rise of the individual derive from the specific features of conflicts, such as the nature of the hostilities, urban warfare or hostage crises which preclude or severely limit formal diplomatic exchanges. On the other hand, traditional diplomatic channels, where these exist, are sometimes reinforced by states in conflict through the use of unofficial envoys such as businessmen or journalists. Others involved in unconventional diplomacy, especially mediation, include trade-union leaders, clergy and their envoys, oppostion party leaders and foreign exiles, whose status seems to vary according to the regime in power.

The extent to which an individual is able to operate as a mediator or go-between depends largely on criteria particular to the individual rather than being derived from any formal office or institution. Above all the individual must acquire acceptance either on the basis of neutrality in the dispute or political access. Second, in the absence of formal status, credentials of a cognate nature are necessary. For example, the major go-between in East–West spy exchanges, Wolfgang Vogel, was trained as an East German lawyer. Other possible credentials for mediation include trade-union membership and commercial negotiating experience. In other instances involving the release of foreign workers from rebel-held territory, the political ideology of an opposition party may be a more important basis for influence than neutrality. The credentials need not be of a formal kind, such as political office or diplomatic status, since these would disqualify the mediator and make him too associated with a particular government. The credibility of the individual negotiator is, above all, important. In some instances a mediator, such as the Archbishop of Canterbury's special envoy Terry Waite, was able to build up a successful track record of negotiations before capture.[63]

The method of communication in unconventional diplomacy can be unusual in that one of the parties is not a state. Sources may be unorthodox, as in the Lebanese negotiations to secure the release of Western hostages during 1985–86, and complicated by factionalism within terrorist organisations. Negotiations may be unorthodox also in that, unlike formal negotiations, the credentials stage, e.g. establishing *bona fides*, may be extremely lengthy and highly incremental. A revolutionary organisation may have a number of splinter groups as the *Achille Lauro* affair demonstrated.[64] Formal or informal communication as a result is difficult, before credentials and mutual trust can be established. Above all, in unconventional diplomacy it is highly uncertain as to whether agreements which are negotiated will actually be kept or enforced.

SUMMARY

In modern international relations the nature of security and the security requirements of states have strikingly changed from the kinds of issues traditionally thought of as comprising threats. Many modern threats are of a non-military nature and require diplomatic or other appropriate responses. Diplomacy, too, is an essential element in the continual process of defining, maintaining and enhancing security. In the main, security through United Nations peacekeeping and other quasi-military forces has been a relatively important though declining contribution to national and international security. In contrast, states have placed importance on using the United Nations as a forum for the generation and establishment of rules and regimes such as nuclear-free zones and zones of peace. The economic dimension of security finds its expression in moves outside Europe in the Middle East, Asia, the Pacific and Latin America to increase regional cooperation, and promote stability through the establishment of groupings within which to promote trade, extradition, fisheries and Exclusive Economic Zone (EEZ) management and other cooperation. Many of these are as yet embryonic, but they are an important indication of the differences in perceived needs and emphases of states. Overall, the security threats faced by modern states have become increasingly diverse and continue to pose additional challenges for diplomacy.

REFERENCES AND NOTES

1.   Colin S. Gray, *Strategic Studies and Public Policy* (The University of Kentucky Press, Lexington, 1982) p. 48.
2.   Michael Handel, *Weak States in the International System* (Frank Cass, London 1980), and on internal and external threats in Africa, John M. Ostheimer 'Peacekeeping and Warmaking: Future Military Challenges in Africa', in Bruce E. Arlinghaus and Pauline H. Baker (eds), *African Armies* (Westview Press, Boulder, Colo., 1986) pp. 32–59.
3.   R. H. Ullman, 'Redefining Security', *International Security*, Vol. 8, No. 1 (1983) pp. 129–33.
4.   See J. W. M. Chapman, R. Drifte and I. T. M. Gow, *Japan's Quest for Comprehensive Security* (Frances Pinter, London, 1983) pp. xiv–xviii, for a discussion of the concept of comprehensive security in a Japanese context.
5.   On maritime fraud see for example the UNCTAD studies, *Maritime Fraud* (status of the work of non-governmental organisations to combat maritime fraud) TD/B/C.4/AC.4/9, 22 Aug. 1985, and the UNCTAD Secretariat's report on maritime financial fraud, TD/B/C.4/AC.4/6, 27 June 1985, esp. pp. 6–14.
6.   See Report of the Secretary-General, 'Progress Report on United Nations Activities in Crime Prevention and Control', UN Doc. E/AC.57/1986/3, 28 Nov. 1985, para. 15, Economic and Social Council, UN Doc. E/AC.57/1986/4, 20 Feb. 1986, paras. 51, 72, 80.

7. Arnold Wolfers, *Discord and Collaboration* (The Johns Hopkins Press, Baltimore, 1962) p. 150.
8. Jimmy Carter, *Keeping Faith* (Collins, London, 1982) p. 506.
9. Inis L. Claude Jr., *Swords into Plowshares*, 3rd edn (University of London Press, London, 1964) pp. 245–8; Hans Kelsen, *Recent Trends in the Law of the United Nations* (Stevens and Sons, London, 1951) pp. 953–90.
10. Alan James, *The Politics of Peace-Keeping* (Chatto and Windus, London, 1969) esp. Chs 7 and 8.
11. *Public Papers of the Secretaries-General of the United Nations*, Vol. V (Dag Hammarskjöld) 1960–61 (Columbia University Press, New York, 1975) pp. 131–2.
12. See R. P. Barston, 'Problems in International Peacekeeping: The Case of Cyprus', *International Relations* (David Davies Memorial Institute of International Studies, London) Vol III, No. 11 (May 1971) pp. 928–40.
13. Claude, op. cit., pp. 297–8.
14. The projected deficit as at 31 Dec. 1985 was $US390.7 million, of which $US116.3 million related to withholding, or delay in payments to the regular budget and the balance to peacekeeping activities. See A/40/1102, 12 April 1986, paras. 11 and 15. See also *UN Chronicle*, Vol. XIX, No. 5 (May 1982) pp. 65–70.
15. The United States has indicated that it will continue to withhold its *pro rata* share of the annual UN assessment attributable to the costs of the Preparatory Commission set up under the Law of the Sea Convention. The United States, Turkey and the United Kingdom argued that the costs of the Preparatory Commission should be borne by those states party to the Law of the Sea Convention, since the commission, which deals *inter alia* with deep sea-bed mining is legally independent and distinct from the UN and not answerable to it. See *Oceans Policy News*, Jan.–Feb. 1984, p. 3.
16. *Financial Times*, 10 Oct. 1985; *Report of the Secretary-General on the United Nations Interim Force in Lebanon*, S/17557, 10 Oct. 1985, para. 12.
17. John F. Murphy, *The United Nations and the Control of International Violence* (Manchester University Press, Manchester, 1983) p. 107.
18. Raymond Cohen, *International Politics* (Longman, London, 1981) p. 156.
19. UN General Assembly Resolution 3314 (XXXIX) 29 UN GAOR, Supp. (No. 31), 142 UN Doc. A0631 (1975).
20. *UN Chronicle*, Vol. XIX, No. 5 (May 1982) p. 6.
21. Murphy, op. cit., pp. 89–90.
22. See statement by Giuseppe Di Gennaro, outgoing chairman of the UN Committee on Crime Prevention and Control, and Executive Director of the UN Fund for Drug Abuse Control, in *UN Chronicle*, Vol. XIX, No. 5 (May 1982) p. 60.
23. *UNTS*, Vol. 402, p. 71; *UKTS* No. 97 (1961) Cmnd. 1535.
24. Austrian State Treaty, 15 May 1955, *UNTS*, Vol. 217, p. 223; *UKTS*, No. 58 (1957) Cmnd. 214. The Austrian Parliament promulgated Austrian neutrality as a constitutional law on 26 Oct. 1955.

25. F. S. Northedge, *Descent from Power* (George Allen and Unwin, London, 1974) pp. 244–5.
26. Henry W. Degenhardt, *Treaties and Alliances of the World* (Longman, London, 1981) pp. 3, 6.
27. See *Study on the Naval Arms Race*, Report of the Secretary-General, UN Doc. A/40/535, 17 Sept. 1985, pp. 50–70.
28. Resolution 2832 (XXVI) 16 Dec. 1971; see Philip Towle, 'The United Nations Ad Hoc Committee on the Indian Ocean: Blind Alley or Zone of Peace', in Larry W. Bowman and Ian Clark (eds) *The Indian Ocean in Global Politics* (Westview Press, Boulder, Colo., 1981) pp. 207–22.
29. UN Doc. A/40/535, para. 238, p. 65.
30. Alison Broinowski, *Understanding Asean* (Macmillan, London, 1983) Appendix E, p. 294.
31. See Final Declaration of the first ministerial meeting of the ministers for foreign affairs of the Mediterranean members of the non-aligned movement held at Valletta 10–11 Sept. 1984, UN Docs A/39/526–S/16758; and A/40/535, para. 253, p. 69.
32. See Gerald Stourzh's concept of affinity and credibility paradox in his excellent short essay, 'Permanent Neutrality', in August Schou and Arne Olav Brundtland (eds), *Small States in International Relations* (Almqvist and Wiksell, Stockholm, 1971) pp. 93–8.
33 Zafar Iman, 'Soviet Treaties with Third World Countries', *Soviet Studies*, Vol. XXV, No. 1 (Jan. 1983) pp. 53–70; Grant F. Rhode and Reid E. Whitlock, *Treaties of the PRC 1949–78* (Westview Press, Boulder, Colo., 1980) pp. 15–43 for Chinese friendship treaties.
34. Joseph A. Kechichian, 'The Gulf Cooperation Council: Search for Security', *Third World Quarterly*, Vol. 7, No. 4 (Oct. 1985) pp. 853–81.
35. The initial US–Philippines base agreement was concluded on 14 March 1947, providing for the establishment for a ninety-nine-year period of twenty-three American military, naval and air bases in the Philippines. A mutual defence treaty was signed in Washington on 30 Aug. 1951, as a continuation of the 21 March 1947 Military Assistance Agreement. See *A Decade of American Foreign Policy Basic Documents 1941–8* (Greenwood Press, New York, 1968) pp. 869–81, 881–5.
36. See Murugesu Pathmanathan, *Readings in Malaysian Foreign Policy* (University of Malaya Co-operative Bookshop Limited, Kuala Lumpur, 1980) esp. pp. 126–42.
37. UN Doc. A/40/535, 17 Sept. 1985, para. 254. The observers include Belau, Marshall Islands and the Federated States of Micronesia.
38. *The Times*, 11 Aug. 1986.
39. *The Guardian*, 5 July 1985, *Financial Times*, 12 Aug. 1986.
40. See Ismail Fahmy, *Negotiating for Peace in the Middle East* (Croom Helm, London, 1983) p. 176.
41. Ibid., pp. 145–7, 172, 183–5.
42. Earl C. Ravenal, 'Europe Without America: The Erosion of NATO', *Foreign Affairs*, Vol. 63, No. 5 (Summer 1985) pp. 1020–35.
43. *Financial Times*, 15 Aug. 1986.
44. Kemal H. Karpat, *Turkey's Foreign Policy in Transition 1950–74* (Leiden, 1975).

45. John C. Loulis, 'Papandreou's Foreign Policy', *Foreign Affairs*, Vol. 63, (1984–85) pp. 375–91.
46. Ibid., p. 387.
47. Panayote E. Dimitras, 'Greece a New Danger' *Foreign Policy*, Nos. 57–60 (1984–85) pp. 134–50.
48. See J. G. Starke's discussion of the special issues confronting ANZUS, including the US guarantee, in *The ANZUS Treaty Alliance* (Melbourne University Press, 1965) esp. pp. 228–42. The text of the treaty is at pp. 243–5.
49. See Chapman, Drifte and Gow, op. cit., pp. 120–3.
50. The port access issue came to a head in early Feb. 1985 when the New Zealand Government declined to approve a requested visit by an American warship, USS *Buchanan* on the grounds that it was unable to satisfy itself that the vessel was not nuclear armed. See *Report of the Ministry of Foreign Affairs*, March 1985 (Wellington, 1985) pp. 21–2.
51. *The Times*, 13 Aug. 1986.
52. Exchange of notes on Malta becoming a neutralised state, with Italy, 15 Sept. 1981. See *Italian Yearbook of International Law* (Napoli, Editorial Scientifica, 1983) pp. 352–7 for the texts of the two notes.
53. Fahmy, op. cit., p. 172.
54. Ali E. Hillal Dessouki, 'The Foreign Policy of Egypt', in Bahgat Korany and Ali E. Hillal Dessouki (eds), *The Foreign Policies of Arab States* (Westview Press, Boulder, Colo., 1984) p. 137.
55. I. William Zartman, 'Africa and the West: The French Connection', in Bruce E. Arlinghaus (ed.), *African Security Issues* (Westview Press, Boulder, Colo., 1984) p. 50, and Timothy M. Shaw and Olajide Aluko, *The Political Economy of African Foreign Policy* (Gower, Aldershot, 1984).
56. See, for example, Tom Imobighe, 'ECOWAS Defence Pact and Regionalism in Africa', in R. I. Onwuka and A. Sesay (eds), *The Future of Regionalism in Africa* (Macmillan, Hong Kong, 1985) pp. 110–23.
57. John M. Ostheimer, 'Cooperation Among African States', in Arlinghaus, op. cit., pp. 157–70, and Mark W. Zacher, *International Conflicts and Collective Security 1946–77* (Praeger, New York 1979) pp. 121–60.
58. *The Annual Register 1984* (Longman, London, 1985) pp. 219, 362; *Revue Générale de Droit International Public* (A. Pedone, Paris, 1986) p. 460. Morocco officially ceased to be a member of the OAU on 12 Nov. 1985.
59. On this point see Zacher, op. cit., p. 155. Zacher also notes that the OAU's major function is now more one of creating a consensual African foreign policy on extra-African issues rather than acting as effective agent for collective security.
60. Leon Sloss and M. Scott Davis, *A Game for High Stakes* (Ballinger, Cambridge, Mass., 1986) p. 97.
61. Ibid., p. 92.
62. Ibid., pp. 100–1.
63. See *Sunday Times*, 20 Oct. 1985, on the special envoy's role.
64. See *ILM*, Vol. XXIV, No. 6 (Nov. 1985) pp. 1509–65 for documents on the *Achille Lauro* affair; *Financial Times*, 10 Oct. 1985 and *The Guardian*, 19 Oct. 1985.

CHAPTER TEN

International treaties

INTRODUCTION

Treaties can be defined as agreements which establish binding obligations between the parties, usually though not exclusively, states, and whose terms and provisions are governed by international law.[1] While treaties in the main take a written form, oral exchanges or declarations may give rise to commitments binding on the state or parties concerned.[2]

The Vienna Convention on the Law of Treaties defines treaties in terms of states, in the following way: 'An international agreement concluded between states in written form and governed by international law, whether embodied in a single instrument or in two related instruments and whatever its particular designation' (article 2).[3] The wider definition, however, includes agreements between states and international organisations and between international organisations *inter se*,[4] although for example McNair excluded agreements not in a written form.[5]

The term 'treaty' has in fact come to refer to a wide range of instruments. In its advisory opinion concerning the *Customs Regime between Germany and Austria*, the Permanent Court of International Justice noted *inter alia* that: 'from the standpoint of the obligatory character of international engagements, it is well known that such engagements may be taken in the form of treaties, conventions, agreements, protocols or exchanges of notes'.[6] Two points need to be mentioned therefore with respect to the definition of treaties. In the first place, not all instruments of an international nature are intended to have an obligatory character, as in the case of certain forms of declarations, which may set out aspects of policy or principles.

Secondly, the requirement that the agreement be governed by international law serves to differentiate a treaty from other agreements between states or other subjects of international law, which are governed not by international law *per se* but by the national law of one of the parties (or mutually agreed national law of a third party). An agreement, for example, between two states for the supply of rice or petroleum products, from one of the parties, drawn up on the basis of a standard form of contract relevant to those commodities, would be governed by the terms of the contract, appropriate national regulations, as well as general principles of law, and not internationsl law.

The criteria for determining whether an undertaking, oral agreement, document or set of documents, including an exchange of notes or correspondence, constitute an international agreement have been outlined in recent Department of State provisions and are worth citing as a clear indication of the considerations involved.[7] The four criteria identified were (1) the identity and intention of the parties, (2) the significance of the arrangements, (3) specificity, including criteria for determining enforceability, and (4) the necessity for two or more parties. As regards the first of these, the provisions stipulate that a party to an international agreement must be a state, state agency or an intergovernmental organisation and that the parties, normally two, intend the undertaking to be legally binding and not merely for political or moral purposes. Thus the Helsinki Fact Act would not, according to this view, be considered legally binding.[8] 'Significance' in the provisions is determined according to political importance, the size of grant made by, or credits payable to, the United States and the scale of continuing or future obligations. Under the third criteria, undertakings couched in vague or very general terms containing no objective criteria for determining enforceability or performance are not normally international agreements. The provisions under discussion also concluded that any oral agreement that meets the above criteria is an international agreement, but must be reduced to words.[9]

TREATIES

In international relations treaties are the instruments for many kinds of legal acts ranging from bilateral or multilateral agreements on trade, customs, the creation of international organisations, to the ending of a military conflict and redistribution of territory.[10]

Treaties in the main are concluded in the following forms: (a) heads of state; (b) interstate; (c) intergovernmental; (d) international organisation.

The choice of the type of party may depend on political considerations, such as the degree of symbolic or political importance attached to the matter and constitutional requirements. The choice of form, however, does not affect the binding nature of the obligations. Treaties between states are less formal, and more frequently used than those in heads of state form. Traditionally, treaties were concluded in heads of state form, but in modern practice treaties can be concluded in heads of state, interstate and intergovernmental form. When used in interstate form, the expression 'contracting parties' or 'states parties' is normally used in the text rather than 'high contracting parties', in the heads of state form.[11]

The designation 'treaty' itself has frequently been reserved for international agreements which are considered to be of particular importance, such as a peace treaty, alliance (e.g. North Atlantic Treaty of 4 April 1949, the Southeast Asia Collective Defence Treaty of 8 September 1954) or marking significant changes in relationships, e.g. the Treaty of Amity and Cooperation in Southeast Asia 24 February 1976 signed at Bali; the Montevideo Treaty established the Latin American Free Trade Area, 18 February 1960, the Treaty of Rome establishing the European Economic Community of 25 March 1957 and the Treaty of Lagos, 27 May 1975.[12] However, state practice indicates that the range of issues regulated by treaty are now very wide, including such matters as extradition, navigation, treaties of friendship and setting up international institutions.[13] Treaties may be concluded bilaterally or multilaterally. The decision to use the designation 'treaty', rather than, for example, 'agreement' depends very much on individual state practice, assessments of the issue and the 'style' of conducting external relations.[14]

CONVENTIONS

Multilateral instruments of a law-making or regulative type are generally given the designation 'convention'. Conventions are normally negotiated under the auspices of international or regional organisations or diplomatic conferences involving states and other subjects of international law. Examples of codification conventions include: the Vienna Convention on Diplomatic Relations of 18 April

1961;[15] the Vienna Convention on Consular Relations of 24 April 1963;[16] and the Vienna Convention on the Law of Treaties of 23 May 1969. Law-making or regulatory conventions negotiated through conferences include the Convention on the Prohibition, Development, Production and Stockpiling of Bacteriological and Toxin Weapons, 10 April 1972;[17] the several Geneva conventions dealing with international humanitarian law including the rights and status of combatants and civilians, e.g. Geneva Conventions of 12 August 1949;[18] Single Convention on Narcotic Drugs, 30 March 1961.[19] In the field of civil aviation, the Convention on International Civil Aviation (Chicago) 1944,[20] sets out general principles of air law, such as exclusive sovereignty over airspace above a state's territory, the nationality and registration of aircraft and provisions for establishing a permanent International Civil Aviation Organisation (ICAO). Since 1947, ICAO itself has produced a number of conventions dealing with civil aviation standards and practices, as well as establishing rules on questions such as damage caused by aircraft to third parties (Rome, 1952)[21] and air 'piracy' through the Convention for the Suppression of Unlawful Seizure of Aircraft, The Hague, 16 December 1970.[22]

Treaties of a law-making or regulatory kind produced by the specialised agencies of the United Nations normally take the designation 'convention'. Examples of these are the various labour conventions produced by the International Labour Organisation (ILO), the Universal Postal Union and telecommunication conventions.[23] Conventions have also been concluded by regional and other bodies such as the Council of Europe and the UN Economic Commission for Europe across a wide range of subjects such as human rights,[24] refugees[25] and transboundary pollution.[26] Conventions have also emerged from international and regional organisations in other areas such as maritime regulation and pollution control. The Intergovernmental Maritime Consultative Organisation, the main organisation in this field, was restyled International Maritime Organisation in May 1982 (IMO). It has concluded *inter alia* the 1973 International Convention for the Prevention of Pollution from Ships[27] and the International Convention for the Safety of Life at Sea (1974).[28] The effectiveness, however, of the IMO conventions has been reduced by problems common to many conventions and other treaty instruments requiring ratification – delay in entry into force through slow or insufficient ratification, and conventions not being as widely ratified as is necessary to make them fully effective.[29]

While the above conventions can be classified into a number of general types, such as if the purpose is predominantly codification, institutive or regulative, a great many conventions usually evidence more than one of these features. Modern practice, too, suggests that some of the so-called 'law-making', conventions have developed distinctive legal formats and characteristics which resemble *administrative* law rather than traditional international public law. For example, the United Nations Convention on the Law of the Sea, opened for signature in Jamaica in December 1982,[30] is not simply a codification instrument, but goes much further than the four 1958 Geneva Law of the Sea Conventions in establishing new types of international regulations, rights and responsibilities, for example for the Exclusive Economic Zone and Deep Sea-bed Area. The Law of the Sea Convention of 1982 resembles administrative law in the way regimes are formulated and in the considerable amount of devolution of power and responsibility to international organisation and diplomatic conferences to continue the process of building and developing maritime law.[31]

Although the above sections have discussed conventions as multilateral instruments produced by international and regional organisations, as well as diplomatic conferences, the designation is also used for many different kinds of bilateral treaties, such as on consular conventions and double-taxation conventions. As with other forms of treaties, conventions can be concluded in heads of state, interstate or in intergovernmental form. They can often be simple single-article instruments such as between France and Madagascar of 4 June 1973,[32] on postal and telecommunication matters, which has one article only *(article unique)* in which it is agreed to establish postal and telecommunication services.

AGREEMENTS

Treaties and conventions are the two most formal instruments in the range of various mechanisms available to states and other subjects of international law. Less formal and in more frequent use are agreements and exchanges of notes. Although less formal, the subject-matter covered by agreements need not be routine. Agreements are, in fact, used for a variety of purposes, such as establishing the framework and mechanisms for interstate trade cooperation,[33] land and maritime boundaries,[34] resolving debt questions,[35] fisheries regulations,[36] air services arrangements[37] and many other similar forms of undertaking. However, whatever the subject-matter, for an agreement to be properly considered as a treaty it is necessary to distinguish those agreements which are intended to have an obligatory character from those which do not.

Agreements are distinct from treaties and conventions in a strict sense in that the latter are generally of a more comprehensive kind and have a permanent subject-matter. Agreements normally take the form of a single instrument and tend to be bilateral rather than multilateral. Exceptions to the latter are agreements made by regional groupings or organisations, e.g. ASEAN agreements such as the Agreement on the Establishment of the ASEAN Secretariat,[38] signed at Bali on 24 February 1976, the Agreement on ASEAN Preferential Trading Arrangements, signed at Manila on 24 February 1977;[39] and the ASEAN Cultural Fund.[40]

In general, agreements are usually concluded between governments, rather than in heads of state or interstate form, and take the form of a single instrument.

Finally, it should be noted that agreements can be concluded between respective government departments in different countries. Interdepartmental agreements of this type have become very common, given both the increase in the volume of international business and the growing involvement of departments other than the foreign ministry.

Some examples of the subject-matter of international agreements in British practice are:

Tanzania. Agreement for Air Services between and beyond their respective Territories, 1 July 1980.[41]

Agreement with Sri Lanka for the Promotion and Protection of Investments, 13 February 1980.[42]

Reciprocal Fisheries Agreement between the United Kingdom and United States with respect to the British Virgin and American Virgin Islands, 1983.[43]

Headquarters Agreement International Maritime Satellite Organisation, 25 February 1980.[44]

Agreement with Poland on Certain Commercial Debts, 2 July 1981.[45]

Agreement with Jordan on the International Transport of Goods by Road, 2 February 1981.[46]

Agreement Concerning Interim Arrangements relating to Polymetallic Nodules of the Deep Sea-Bed, 2 September 1982.[47]

Examples of international agreements in Malaysian practice are:

Malaysia–Federal Republic of Germany Loan Agreement, 21 December 1976.[48]

Malaysia–Australia Sugar Supply Contract Agreement, 5 September 1974.[49]

Malaysia–India Air Services Agreement 14 September 1982.[50]

Malaysia–Japan 8th Yen Loan Agreement (M$210 million) 22 March 1982.[51]

Malaysia–Norway Double Taxation Agreement, 9 September 1971.[52]

Malaysia–Belgo-Luxembourg Economic Union Agreement in Encouragement and Reciprocal Protection of Investments, 21 May 1981.[53]

Malaysia–Saudi Arabia Cultural and Scientific Cooperation Agreement, 19 May 1976.[54]

Malaysia–ADB, 10 December 1981 (Batang Ai Hydropower Project).[55]

Malaysia–IBRD, 7 February 1983 (Kedah Valley's Agricultural Development Project).[56]

Malaysia–Pakistan Economic and Technical Cooperation Agreement 9 November 1982.[57]

EXCHANGE OF NOTES

The most common and frequently used treaty instrument for recording agreements between governments is through an exchange of notes or letters. The exchange of notes can be between an ambassador or other appropriate representative and the ministry of foreign affairs of the country to which he is accredited; take the form of a letter between the foreign or other ministers (or their empowered officials) of two respective countries; or be in the third person. The initiating note will set out matters such as definitions, terms and attached schedules, if any, or other provisions. If these are acceptable then the initiating note and the other government's reply accepting these is to constitute an agreement.

In order to avoid the exchange becoming a correspondence through the passing of several notes, the terms of the notes to be exchanged are normally agreed upon through discussion beforehand. If the notes do not bear identical dates then the agreement takes effect from the date of the last note or such other dates as may be specified. Exchanges of notes are usually bilateral and as a general rule do not require ratification. It should not be concluded, however, that the subject-matter need necessarily be routine in nature.

The following example illustrates the main features of an agreement in this form[58]:

NO. 4703. TRADE AGREEMENT BETWEEN THE COMMONWEALTH OF AUSTRALIA AND THE FEDERATION OF MALAYA. SIGNED AT KUALA LUMPUR ON 26 AUGUST 1958

EXCHANGE OF NOTES CONSTITUTING AN AGREEMENT AMENDING SCHEDULE A TO THE ABOVE-MENTIONED AGREEMENT KUALA LUMPUR 25 JULY 1968

Authentic text: English
Registered by Australia on 12 January 1970
I
(EMBLEM)

Kuala Lumpur, 25th July 1968

Your Excellency,

I have the honour to refer to the Trade Agreement between the Federation of Malaysia and Australia, which was concluded at Kuala Lumpur on 26th August, 1958. Paragraph 1 of Article III of the Agreement provides that the Federation Government undertakes to apply to the Australian goods listed in Schedule A to the Agreement, rates of duty no higher than those specified in that Schedule. In this connection, I refer to recent discussions between Representatives of Malaysia and Australia regarding the desire of the Federation Government to levy a protective duty on wheat flour entering Malaysia.

Accordingly, it is proposed that the item 'Wheat flour' be deleted from Schedule A to the Agreement.

If the foregoing proposal is acceptable to the Government of the Commonwealth of Australia, I have the honour to propose that this Note and your reply in the same sense shall be deemed to constitute an agreement between our two Governments to that effect, which agreement shall enter into force on the date of your reply.

Accept, Excellency, the assurances of my highest consideration.

Tan Sri (Dr.) LIM SWEE AUN, P.M.N., J.P.
Minister of Commerce and Industry
Malaysia

His Excellency Mr. A. J. Eastman, C.B.E.
High Commissioner for Australia in Malaysia

In this note paragraph 1 sets out the subject-matter (trade agreement) and the particular discussions held between the parties on the protective levy of wheat flour entering Malaysia. The note then proposes (paragraph 2) that, in the light of these discussions, ' "wheat flour" be deleted from Schedule A to the Agreement'. The following paragraph uses the format by which the initiating note and the reply *in the same sense* constitute an agreement. The agreement came into force on 25 July 1968, the date of the note in reply, in accordance with the provisions. From this example it can also be seen that the exchange of notes was registered by Australia with the United Nations Secretariat on 12 January 1970 in accordance with article 102 of the United Nations Charter.

Exchanges of notes or letters constituting agreements do also occur frequently between states and international organisations in connection with a variety of questions, such as headquarters facilities, arrangements for peacekeeping forces and the arrangements and costs to be borne in respect of an international conference hosted by a member country. In the following example, the exchange of letters concerns the financial and other related matters for the Second General Conference of UNIDO, held in Peru.[59] The exchange of letters between the Executive Director of UNIDO and the Peruvian Deputy Minister of Industry and Peruvian Permanent Representative to UNIDO, amended section V of the Lima agreement of 12 March 1975, on the financial arrangements for the conference to take into account the additional expenditure incurred by the Peruvian authorities. The agreement came into force on 26 March by the exchange of letters.

DECLARATION

Since 1945 declarations have increasingly been used by states, reflecting the growing number of new states entering the international scene, diverse political groupings and the perceived need to demonstrate collective cooperation, as well as project national and regional aspirations. Whether in fact a declaration constitutes a treaty *per se* is open to considerable uncertainty. It was doubtless to overcome this kind of problem that the Mano River Declaration of October 1973, establishing the Mano River development zone between Liberia and Sierra Leone, had six protocols attached to it, providing detailed arrangements for the zone.[60]

While certain declarations can also be properly regarded as treaty instruments as such in view of their law-making function (e.g. Barcelona Declaration of 1921 recognising the right to a flag of states having no sea-coast)[61] or because of specific undertakings in the agreement (e.g. the Declaration on the Neutrality of Laos, signed at Geneva on 23 July 1962)[62] others may not. For example, declarations published after a heads of government conference may partly contain agreements to do or not do something and partly statements of common policy, causing considerable difficulty in determining whether they may be regarded as a treaty instrument.

Two further forms of declarations can be distinguished, both of which cannot be regarded as treaty instruments. Firstly, *unilateral* declarations by states, such as declarations of war, declarations by third states on the outbreak of war that they will remain neutral or declarations during or prior to an armed conflict such as made by the United Kingdom with regard to the total exclusion zone during the Falklands conflict with Argentina in 1982, or the total exclusion zone declared by Iraq in the Iran–Iraq War, do not constitute treaties.[63] Secondly, declarations which take the form of a communication to other states of an explanation and justification of a line of action taken in the past, or explanation of views and policies on an issue such as the Spanish–Argentine Declaration on the Falklands and Gibraltar of 13 June 1984 are not treaties as such.[64]

OTHER FORMS OF TREATIES

Treaties exist in a number of other forms apart from those discussed in the last section. Differences in title derive from a number of factors such as the political context in which the instrument was drafted, the type of subject-matter and others such as the institutional 'style' of the instruments produced by the organisation (e.g. international labour conventions).

Among other forms of treaties are charter (e.g. United Nations Charter, San Francisco 1945),[65] pact, which is used often for an alliance or solemn undertaking (e.g. ANZUS Security Pact;[66] Kellogg–Briand Pact, 1928 on the renunciation of war,[67] properly titled Treaty Providing for Renunciation of War as an Instrument of National Policy, 27 August 1928; or non-aggression, e.g. South Africa–Mozambique Nkomati accord of 1984.[68] 'Pact' is also used as noted above in a journalistic sense to mean a collective agreement, e.g. 'Tin Pact' to refer to the Association of Tin Producing Countries, including Malaysia, Indonesia, Thailand, Bolivia. Other forms of treaties are constitutional, e.g. Constitution of the United Nations Educational Scientific and Cultural Organisation (UNESCO);[69] statute, used to designate an instrument which regulates an international institution or regime, e.g. Statute of the Council of Europe,[70] Statute of the International Court of Justice.[71]

MISCELLANEOUS TREATY FORMS AND OTHER INTERNATIONAL INSTRUMENTS

The term 'act' has widespread use and is distinguished from 'general act' in that the designation 'act' usually refers to an instrument which is part of a complex of agreements. The act usually contains the main terms and provisions of a treaty and takes the form of a *chapeau*, such as the Act of the International Conference on Vietnam, of 2 March 1973, acknowledging the Paris agreement ending the Vietnam War.[72]

A further form of usage of 'act' is the general act, which need not be a treaty in the strict sense, forming rather part of the overall instrument. As a treaty instrument the general act is often of an administrative nature, e.g. the General Act for the Pacific Settlement of Disputes, of 26 September 1928,[73] prepared under the League of Nations, and the subsequent Revised General Act for the Pacific Settlement of Disputes, prepared under United Nations auspices, of 28 April 1949.[74]

Final Act

The term 'final act' *(act finale)* is normally given to a document which serves as a summary of the proceedings of an international conference. A final act is a form of *procès-verbal* and, accordingly, signature does not serve as an indication of being bound by the treaty or mean acceptance of the obligations contained in the treaty, which requires separate signature and ratification. In some circumstances the final act of a conference may contain not only the treaty or agreement itself but also resolutions connected with the treaty or agreement, including interim arrangements before the latter's entry into force. For example, the Final Act of the Third UN Conference on the Law of the Sea[75] provides in resolution I(2) that:

> The Commission (for the International Sea Bed Authority) shall consist of the representatives of states and of Namibia, represented by the

United Nations Council for Namibia, which have signed the convention or acceded to it. The representatives of signatories of the Final Act may participate fully in the deliberations of the Commission as observers but shall not be entitled to participate in the taking of decisions.

In those cases in which a final act is produced by an international conference, the document records *inter alia*, the organisation of the conference, a survey of the texts and conclusions of the main committees and the texts of any resolutions. In the case of the Third UN Conference on the Law of the Sea, the Final Act contained *inter alia*:

1. Record of the prior United Nations' resolutions on the law of the sea;
2. Dates of sessions;
3 Officers and committees;
4. Conference documents and outline of major developments;
5. Resolutions.

Apart from the question of the effect of signature with regard to a final act, a further issue is that of the status of annexes in the main convention.

In the Law of the Sea Convention, for example, article 318 of the Final Provisions of the convention stipulates that, unless otherwise provided, the annexes form an integral part of the convention. In contrast, resolutions contained in the Final Act are not incorporated in the main text of the convention, although there are references in the convention to certain of the resolutions, e.g. article 308(5). In an effort to link the convention and the resolutions, paragraph 42 of the Final Act refers to the convention and resolutions I–IV 'forming an integral whole'.

Protocol

Of the other available international instruments, the protocol is widely used and extremely versatile. Eight main uses can be distinguished in international practice.

In the first place a protocol can be used to *extend* an agreement which is due to run out. International commodity agreements have, for example, been extended in this way: the International Olive Oil Agreement, the International Coffee Agreement and the International Wheat Trade Convention.[76] Second, a protocol may be used to amend or modify an agreement. Protocols are particularly used in this way in respect of agreements which are likely to need quite frequent

213

revision, such as double-taxation agreements (DTAs), e.g. Protocol amending the Agreement for the Avoidance of Double Taxation between the United Kingdom and Trinidad and Tobago, 10 December 1969.[77] If subsequent amendments proved necessary these would normally be termed 'additional protocols' or 'further supplementary protocols'.[78] Protocols can be used for many other types of amendments, such as procedural amendment altering the membership of a technical commission of an international organisation[79] or the substantive provision of a multilateral law-making convention.[80]

Third, a protocol may be pursuant to the main provisions of an agreement. For example, the Protocol to the Franco–Soviet International Road Transport Agreement[81] is concerned with the application of the agreement and provides details of competent institutions and documentation procedures to facilitate road traffic in the two countries. Often a protocol may in fact be a separate instrument or set of instruments for dealing with questions connected with the running of an international organisation, e.g. Fourth Protocol to the General Agreement on Privileges and Immunities of the Council of Europe – Provisions Concerning the European Court of Human Rights.[82]

Fourth, in those instances in which it is necessary to supplement an agreement, a protocol can be used for the additional provisions. For example, a supplementary protocol to an air services agreement may provide for additional fifth freedom landing rights, to allow either or both of the parties to pick up passengers at additional points in order to balance passenger trade between the respective airlines.[83]

Fifth, a protocol may be used to replace or supersede an existing arrangement, e.g. United States–Philippines Protocol[84] on safeguards with regard to the nuclear non-proliferation treaty, which replaced the tripartite agreement with the International Atomic Energy Agency.

Sixth, a protocol may be an optional instrument to a main agreement, concluded with the aim of extending the area of possible substantive agreement, e.g. Optional Protocol to the Vienna Convention on Consular Relations of 24 April 1963.[85]

Seventh, a protocol can be a technical instrument within a general agreement. In this usage, protocols are especially found, though not exclusively, in trade agreements between the EEC and third parties. The agreement between the EEC and Portugal of 22 July 1972[86] has, for example, eight protocols, covering a wide variety of matters such as tariff quotas, product 'ceilings' and detailed provisions on the term 'originating products'. Protocols can also be found within many other types of general agreements, including peace treaties, cease-fire and similar arrangements. The short-lived Paris agreement of 27, January 1973, ending the Vietnam War, contained an attached protocol on the return of captured military personnel and captured foreign civilians.[87] Protocols may sometimes be used in a main agreement to indicate some technical exception or interpretation, though this is more normally done through a side memorandum or agreed minute.

Finally, protocols can be found in use as general instruments quite frequently in some treaty practice, being preferred to an agreement or exchange of notes, e.g. Protocol on Financial Cooperation between the Federal Republic of Germany and Brazil.[88] In the style of the European Community, the financial protocol is used to cover a wide range of economic arrangements with third parties.[89]

Memoranda of Understanding

Memoranda of understanding are now in widespread use by states for regulating many aspects of their external relations in defence, aviation, commerce, education, science, industrial cooperation and other areas.[90] Whether they constitute international agreements in a strict treaty sense varies according to state practice. Much depends on the intentions of the parties and the terminology adopted.[91] Most are not published in official or other series and are not readily available beyond particular government departments, which tend to use the instrument most frequently. Indeed it may be some time before other departments become aware of the existence of an agreement. The latter point illustrates another aspect of the problem of national control over external policy, which was earlier highlighted in the discussion of national financial policy and the debt crisis (see Ch. 7). The main reasons why states use memoranda of understanding instead of treaties are speed, flexibility and confidentiality. Often they are adopted in order to avoid having a formal binding agreement. The delay arising from constitutional procedures is then avoided. Memoranda of understanding are flexible in that they can be brought into force without formal treaty procedures and amended by the respective agencies as appropriate. They are also frequently used by states to protect arrangements they have entered into involving sensitive political, commercial or other economic information.

In addition as a matter of style, certain states and groupings prefer to use informal instruments. For example the Commonwealth practice of using memoranda of understanding is perhaps in keeping with the concept of the Commonwealth as a club, with relations between members being furthered by informal rather than formal agreements.[92] Examples of memoranda of understanding are:

> Memorandum of Understanding between the United States and Soviet Union on the Establishment of a Standing Consultative Commission, 21 December 1972.[93]
>
> Memorandum of Understanding on Second Hydrographic Survey (Straits of Malacca), Malaysia–Japan, September 1970.[94]
>
> Memorandum of Understanding on ASEAN Submarine Cables, Malaysia, Thailand, Singapore, 5 January 1980.[95]
>
> Memorandum of Understanding to Establish a 'Swap' Arrangement, ASEAN, 5 August 1977.[96]
>
> Memorandum of Understanding to provide Yen 400 million to keep the Straits of Malacca Pollution Free, Malaysia, Indonesia, Singapore, Japan, 13 February 1981.[97]

A number of issues have arisen in the use of memoranda of understanding. In the first place there is the question of the status of the instrument. Reference to the title alone of an instrument can be misleading, since some documents although entitled memoranda use treaty language and establish express legal obligations. With regard to the language of an instrument, British practice differs somewhat from that of the United States, in the weight given to the language used, in deciding the status of an instrument. The use of 'shall' rather than 'will', an express indication that the exchange 'shall constitute an agreement between our two governments', rather than 'record the understandings' and 'enter into force' and not 'come into operation' or 'come into effect' are considered consistent with treaty language.

Memoranda of understanding are most often used as subsidiary instruments to treaties. That is they supplement the treaty by providing the framework for subsequent implementation. In air services agreements the main agreement is often accompanied by a confidential memorandum of understanding which contains the generally critical details of flight frequencies and capacities. Difficulties over a subsidiary memorandum of understanding can occur on signature, or after the instrument has become effective, over its status and the interpretation of its provisions. For example, such a memorandum subsidiary to a treaty may contain provisions which purport to amend or are in other ways inconsistent with a treaty. In the case of confidential memoranda, a common problem with civil aviation, arms purchases and similar arrangements, is that the agreements, given their informality, may be challenged or even repudiated by one or more of the parties. Equally, too frequent recourse to the modifying subsidiary memoranda of understanding can undermine the purposes of the governing treaty.

Two further issues are worth comment. As noted above, since memoranda of understanding may be considered confidential by a department or agency, the question can arise over the extent, if at all, the general public should be informed of their contents. For example, in a recent British case only the outline contents of the memorandum of understanding concluded with the United States on SDI contracts were released to Parliament.[98] The frequent use of memoranda of understanding undoubtedly creates another grey area as regards reducing public knowledge about foreign policy. A related aspect, from a governmental perspective, is what has been called the 'retrieval' problem. A general argument earlier in other chapters has been put in terms of the modern problem of internal control over foreign policy. It can be argued that excessive use of memoranda of understanding can create retrieval problems, in that instruments remain unpublished and within the organisational 'memory', such as it might be, of an individual department or agency. Since they may remain unpublished it could be argued it may contribute to inconsistency, low norm setting and poor coordination in foreign policy.

Agreed Minutes

An agreed minute is an informal instrument which may or may not be a treaty. Agreements and conventions are often accompanied by an exchange of side letters or an agreed minute,[99] which serve to provide elaboration on an issue[100] or reflect points of interpretation in a negotiation which do not appear in the main body of the text.[101] The use of signed records of minutes alone frequently reflects the provisional or tentative nature of the exchange or the perception of its level of importance.

Interim Agreements

In those instances when states are unable to reach complete agreement on a problem, a *modus vivendi* may be reached through an interim agreement or arrangement. In such cases the parties are unable to reach a full or final resolution of the issue and seek accordingly to arrive at interim or temporary measures pending a settlement of a particular problem or certain overall aspects of a dispute. In the strategic arms field, the Interim Agreement, for example, between the United States and Soviet Union of 26 May 1972, which accompanied the Moscow ABM Treaty, ran under article 8 for five years.[102]

The style 'interim agreement' or 'arrangement' is often used as a device for reaching a *modus vivendi* or temporary solution in fisheries disputes: for example, the exchange of notes constituting an Interim Agreement between the United Kingdom and Iceland of 13 November 1973.[103] The agreement, which set out fishing areas, time periods for fishing and size of trawlers, was to run for two years. Article 3, in particular, provided that termination of the agreement would not affect the legal position of either party with respect to the substantive dispute. The provision of a time limit on the duration of this agreement is generally found in arrangements of this type – although the actual title 'interim agreement' need not necessarily be used. For example, the agreement between the Government of the Gilbert Islands and the Government of Japan of 26 June 1978,[104] concerning fisheries off the coasts of the Gilbert Islands, entered into force on signature and ran for two years. It is clear that by nature interim agreements, especially of this type, are at best temporary 'holding arrangements' and in consequence the parties face the prospect of almost *continuous* renegotiation of interim arrangements or arrangements to replace them.

The side-stepping of an issue holding up an *interim* solution is well illustrated by the Soviet–Japanese Interim Fishing Agreement of 24 May 1977. The dispute over the 200-mile exclusive fishing zone extension by Japan, was complicated by the long-standing conflict over the disputed northern islands. The Interim Agreement used the manoeuvre of side-stepping the territorial stumbling-block and focused on fisheries only. Article 8 of the Soviet–Japanese Interim Fishing Agreement provided that no provisions of the agreement could be 'construed so as to prejudice the positions ... of either Government ... in regard to various problems in mutual relations'.[105]

Interim agreements can be used in circumstances other than those in which the parties are in considerable dispute over an issue. Thus, a state may wish to establish a temporary framework pending more technical negotiation. For instance, a substantial rise in financial investment in a foreign country by a state's corporation may lead it to consider an interim agreement on investment protection with that country, for reasons of political confidence.[106] Again, pending a comprehensive arrangement, states may seek an interim arrangement, as for example with the United States–GDR agreement,[107] in this case termed an agreed minute on consular matters: 'The two governments agreed that pending entry into force of a comprehensive consular agreement their consular relations will be based on the Vienna Convention on Consular Relations, which they regard as the codification in most material respects of customary international law on consular relations'. In the event that international agreement is seen as either unlikely or the terms possibly unacceptable, states also sometimes safeguard their interests through an interim agreement, as for example the agreement between the United States, United Kingdom, FRG and France, on interim arrangements[108] of 2 September 1982 relating to the regime for exchanging coordinates of deep sea-bed mining operations for polymetallic modules.

FORMALITIES OF TREATIES

The following section examines some of the formal questions concerned with finalising and concluding treaties.

Language

A bilateral treaty drawn up between two countries sharing the same language will be drawn up using that language.[109] A treaty may, however, be drawn up in a language *other* than that of the parties. In those cases in which the treaty is drawn up in the language of the parties and a third language (e.g. French, Korean and English), the third language normally prevails in the event of any divergence of interpretation.[110] In cases in which more than one language is used,[111] particularly in a bilateral treaty, it is important that the languages used in the texts are harmonised by the appropriate drafting group to minimise excessive divergence of meaning.

The languages of treaties prepared under the auspices of the United Nations are Arabic, Chinese, English, French, Russian and Spanish, the official working languages of the United Nations.

Signature

Bilateral treaties are prepared for signature in duplicate in order that each of the two parties may have precedence in the original it retains,

219

in terms of, if appropriate, language and title. Each country will appear first in the title and preamble of the original it retains and the order of signature either above or to the left of the document. The country in whose capital the treaty is going to be signed is normally responsible for preparing the treaty for signature. Unless a treaty provides otherwise, it will come into effect from the date of signature. Exceptions to this are those instruments which make the entry into force of the treaty dependent on ratification. Entry into force is then achieved through an exchange of instruments of ratification.[112]

In exceptional circumstances a treaty, subject to ratification, may come into force provisionally, pending the ratification – for example the Malaysia–Indonesia Trade Agreement, 16 October 1973 (Article VIII).[113]

Initialling and signature

In some circumstances, particularly if there is likely to be some delay before the conclusion of negotiations and signature, a treaty may be initialled as a means of authenticating the text. Initialling itself can be the equivalent of signature if this is the agreed intention of the parties. This is the case with less formal instruments, such as memoranda of understanding. In other cases, initialling may really mark a stage in the negotiating process, for example when a text is referred back to their governments by the negotiators. Further contact or negotiation may be required before a text is agreed for signature.

Entry into force

Entry into force may be made conditional on matters other than the number of ratifications. This is especially so in respect of technical international agreements. In international shipping agreements, entry into force may be made conditional on ratification or accession by states possessing a particular percentage of world gross shipping tonnage in order to give the agreement greater effectiveness. Entry into force after signature (e.g. ninety days) is a device which enables the parties to make the appropriate technical adjustments, or administrative changes (e.g. in civil aviation schedules, visa regulations). In international loan agreements entry into force in multiparty instruments of the World Bank, or ADB, is made conditional on the subsidiary loan arrangements being concluded satisfactorily, and the loan becomes effective at a date specified in the agreement, for example ninety days after signature.

Registration

The concept of registering treaties has essentially been aimed at lessening the effect of secret diplomacy. By requiring states to register their treaties and agreements it was hoped to bring greater openness into international relations. The concept of registration was especially associated with US President Woodrow Wilson (open covenants of peace, openly arrived at). The League of Nations provided for registration under article 18 and in particular that 'no such treaty shall be binding until so registered'. The significant change in article 102 of the Charter of the United Nations from article 18 is avoidance of the principle that unregistered treaties would lack binding force for the parties in question. As for the act of registration itself, registration of an instrument does not confer on that instrument the *status* of a treaty or agreement. In other words, registration cannot validate or make effective instruments which have failed to fulfil the requirements laid down by international law. On the other hand, failure to register a treaty or agreement does not invalidate it, though the position of the parties may be affected before organs of the United Nations. Instruments lodged with the UN Secretariat for registration include treaties and agreements concluded between states, and made by or with the specialised agencies and other organs of the UN, declarations accepting the compulsory jurisdiction of the ICJ and other miscellaneous treaty matters such as termination, ratifications, accessions and details of supplementary treaties. In general, however, most states in practice take a restrictive view of registration out of political preference, for administrative reasons, or the wish to maintain the confidential nature of a transaction. Conversely, there are those high-profile states who selectively use registration – for example of aid or technical assistance agreements – to demonstrate their 'active' involvement in international relations.

Duration

Unless a treaty specifically expresses otherwise, no specific duration is set. In those cases in which it is felt necessary (e.g. visa abolition; investment protection agreement; commodity supply arrangement; technical assistance agreement on training) to limit the duration, a specific provision is required on the length of the agreement and the procedures to be followed upon expiry.

A common device used in certain agreements is the so-called 'revolving formula' by which upon the expiry of an agreement provision is made for the continuation of the agreement for further periods of one year, provided that neither of the contracting parties indicates in writing to the contrary by a specified date prior to expiry.

Reservation

A reservation is a unilateral statement in whatever form made by a state when signing, ratifying or acceding to a treaty, issued with the intention of excluding or modifying the legal effects of particular provisions. Reservations in this sense should be distinguished from interpretative statements made during the negotiation process and declarations made by states on signature, ratification or accession. Such statements or declarations could take the form of clarification on provisions which are unclear or ambiguous. In so far as a declaration seeks to modify the intention of a provision or denounce as non-applicable or unacceptable a provision, then the better view is that it should be considered as a reservation.

Implications of reservations The question as to the effect of reservations becomes acute with regard to multilateral agreements. The issue of reservations can also be relevant in a bilateral treaty context. In a bilateral treaty specific provision may be made in the text for reservations or, alternatively, provision can be made through either an accompanying confidential memorandum of understanding or in an attached protocol.

As regards multilateral instruments, the issues which arise include the effect on: (i) the position of a state which accedes to a treaty with reservations *vis-à-vis* the treaty; (ii) on states objecting to the reservation *vis-à-vis* the reserving state; (iii) on those states who accept the reservations. For example, the issues are illustrated in the case of the separate objections of Hungary, FRG and Belgium, to the individual reservations made by Bahrain, Egypt and Morocco, to article 27(3) of the Vienna Convention on Diplomatic Relations.[114]

In an attempt to overcome those types of difficulties many international conventions adopt a 'no reservations' formula, or a provision to the effect that reservations are not permitted unless otherwise specifically allowed for in the provisions.

The review of the issue by the International Law Commission concluded with recommending that, in those cases where reservations were permitted, it would be a matter for the objecting state as to how it would view its relations with the reserving state. This approach is amplified in articles 20 and 21 of the 1969 Vienna Convention on the Law of Treaties.

Notice of Termination

In considering the question of termination it is important to distinguish termination which is permitted or implied within a treaty from unilateral denunciation or withdrawal. A treaty may be considered to remain in force unless it has been brought to an end by provisions in the treaty relating to expiry or lapse, or the parties have consented, in the absence of such provisions, to terminate it. Many treaties contain provisions of this kind which set a specified period for the duration of the treaty.[115]

The right of termination proper is provided for in modern treaty practice through provisions for denunciation or withdrawal from the treaty upon giving a specified period of notice. Provisions may be drafted to allow for withdrawal or denunciation after an initial period (e.g. three years following entry into force) or withdrawal at any time upon notice, taking effect generally six months after receipt of the notification of denunciation or withdrawal. An exception to the latter is for the withdrawal or denunciation at any time to take immediate effect. An example of this is article XVIII of the articles of agreement of the IMF, 27 December 1945.[116] More difficult is the question of under what circumstances a state may unilaterally withdraw from a treaty which contains no provision for withdrawal or denunciation with or without notice. While in the main unilateral withdrawal under these circumstances is contentious, grounds may exist if there is evidence to indicate the parties intended a right of unilateral termination on notice, or the subject-matter of the treaty implied the existence of such a right.

Article 56 (1) of the Vienna Convention on the Law of Treaties provides that:

> A treaty which contains no provision regarding its termination and which does not provide for denunciation or withdrawal is not subject to denunciation or withdrawal unless:
> (a) it is established that the parties intended to admit the possibility of denunciation or withdrawal; or
> (b) a right of denunciation or withdrawal may be implied by nature of the treaty.

The scope for dispute, however, in instances of unilateral withdrawal from a treaty which does not contain provision for withdrawal or denunciation is considerable. At this point it is sufficient to note that the Vienna Convention on the Law of Treaties nevertheless sets out three possible grounds a party may invoke for terminating or withdrawing from a treaty: a material breach of a bilateral treaty by one of the parties (article 60 (1)); impossibility of performance (article 61 (1)), although this may not be invoked by a party if inability to carry out the obligation is a result of a breach of obligation by that party of the treaty (article 61 (2)); and third, fundamental change of circumstances (article 62). The convention follows a relatively restrictive definition of fundamental change:

1. A fundamental change of circumstances which has occurred at the time of the conclusion of a treaty and which was not foreseen by the parties, may not be invoked as a ground for terminating or withdrawing from a treaty unless:
   (a) the existence of those circumstances constituted an essential basis for the consent of the parties to be bound by the treaty; and
   (b) the effect of the change is radically to transform the extent of obligations still to be performed under the treaty.
2. A fundamental change of circumstances may not be invoked as a ground for terminating or withdrawing from a treaty:
   (a) if the treaty establishes a boundary; or
   (b) if the fundamental change is the result of a breach by the party invoking it either of an obligation under the treaty or of any other international obligation owed to any other party to the treaty.
3. If, under the foregoing paragraphs, a party may invoke a fundamental change of circumstances as a ground for terminating or withdrawing from a treaty it may also invoke the change as a ground for suspending the operation of the treaty.

Procedure for termination

A notice of termination, withdrawal or denunciation is communicated through the diplomatic channel from the relevant authority to the other party or parties, or depositary government or authority.

The notice must follow the manner and procedure provided for in the treaty or in the Vienna Convention. Unless the treaty provides otherwise, conditions cannot be attached, and the notice of termination will apply automatically to any other documents integral to the treaty such as protocols, annexes, agreed minutes and declarations.

The notice takes effect from the period set, if any, from the date of deposit of the notice with the other party. It may be withdrawn or revoked before it takes effect.

SUMMARY

In this chapter we have been concerned to examine the range of modern international agreements. Along with the growth in the volume of treaties and agreements a notable trend is in the diversity of instruments. Of the range of instruments in British practice, exchanges of notes and agreements are the most frequently used.[117] A more important feature of the diversity of instruments is the increasing use of informal instruments such as memoranda of understanding and gentlemen's agreements. Informal instruments are often used for reasons of administrative ease, speed and political or commercial secrecy. Use of such instruments does give rise to a number of issues including the effect on public accountability and the enhancement of bureaucratic power in diplomacy. There are, too, inevitably problems connected with the interpretation and binding nature of informal instruments, particularly memoranda of understanding, in the event of political and administrative change.

A final important change is in the content of agreements. States and other entities conclude agreements in order to manage better particular aspects of their external relations. Thus, greater governmental involvement in the economic sector has seen the emergence of a number of novel government-directed trade agreements. On the other hand, failure to accommodate conflicting interests has resulted in increasing use in many areas of interim-type agreements which in themselves reflect the fragility and incompleteness of the understandings. Apart from using agreements to promote interests and resolve conflict, states seek to reduce risk. In this respect in particular the content of agreements is rapidly altering to reflect the broader diplomatic agenda with agreements on such matters as investment protection, counter-terrorism and the intergovernmental regulation of securities markets. Above all, the expansion in the subject-matter of agreements underlines the growing fusion of public and private interests in many areas of modern diplomacy.

REFERENCES AND NOTES

1. Treaty collections vary considerably in terms of availability and coverage. For treaties deposited with the United Nations, see the Multilateral Treaties deposited with the Secretary-General (ST/LEG SER.E.3) and the *UN Treaty Series (UNTS)*. The *UNDOC* current index

ST/LIB/SER.M/71 (Part II) contains information on texts, reports of conferences and occasionally information on registers of certain treaties, e.g. UNEP. Countries produce information on agreements concluded in gazettes and foreign ministry bulletins while a number have national treaty series. For example, United States treaties are published on a calendar basis in *United States Treaties and Other International Agreements (UST)* and singly in the *Treaties and Other International Acts Series (TIAS)* published by the Department of State. Other relevant sources are *Foreign Relations of the United States, Treaties in Force,* the *Federal Register, Digest of US Practice in International Law* and *Department of State Bulletin.* United Kingdom treaties appear as Command Papers and on entry into force in the UK *Treaty Series (UKTS),* which is indexed annually. For a consolidated index see Clive Parry and Charity Hopkins, *An Index of British Treaties 1901–1968* (HMSO, London 1970). European Community treaties with third parties can be found, along with internal directives, in the *Official Journal.* The external treaties of the Community are in *Treaties, Agreements and Other Bilateral Commitments Linking the Communities with Non-Member Countries* (I/29/84 EN), and *The European Community, International Organisation and Multilateral Agreements,* 3rd rev. edn, (Commission of the European Communities, Luxembourg, 1983). Other sources for agreements and related documents can be found in *International Legal Materials* and the various yearbooks of national international law associations and similar organisations. For example, the Italian *Yearbook of International Law* has a treaty section and the Japanese *Annual of International Law* has a documents section and a chronological list of bilateral and multilateral treaties concluded by Japan. M. J. Bowman and D. J. Harris, *Multilateral Treaties: Index and Current Status* (Butterworth, London, 1984) is a useful general though essentially European-based index of agreements, which does not cover other regional agreements, e.g. ASEAN, trade law or other functional areas. ASEAN agreements are contained in the ASEAN Documentation Series (ASEAN Secretariat, Jakarta); ILO agreements can be found *inter alia* in the ILO *Legislative Series 3/85*; the ICAO in the index to ICAO publications, and Thomas Buergenthal, *Law Making in the International Civil Aviation Organisation* (Syracuse University Press, 1969) pp. 231–6 for a note on ICAO documentation; Chia-Jui Cheng (ed.) *Basic Documents on International Trade Law* (Martinus Nijhoff, Dordrecht, 1986); and M. H. Claringbould, *Transport: International Transport Treaties* (Kluwer, Antwerp, 1986). Council of Europe agreements are published in the *European Treaty Series (ETS).* For agreements on maritime law see R. R. Churchill and A. V. Lowe, *The Law of the Sea* (Manchester University Press, 1985), and R. R. Churchill and Myron Nordquist (eds) *New Directions in the Law of the Sea,* Vols I–XI (Oceana, Dobbs Ferry, NY, 1973–81). The office of the Special Representative of the Secretary-General for the Law of the Sea has begun to collate data on the history of the Law of the Sea Convention, as well as treaties relevant to it. Among these are *The Law of the Sea: Pollution by Dumping* (United Nations, New York, 1985) and *Multilateral Treaties Relevant to the United Nations Convention on the Law of the Sea*

(United Nations, New York, 1985). Charles Rousseau and Michel Virally's, *Revue Générale de droit international public* (A. Pedone, Paris) is a very useful survey of a wide range of current international issues, covering, for example, agreements, territorial claims, disputes and breaks or resumptions of diplomatic relations. A valuable collection of treaty provisions for dispute settlement can be found in *A Survey of Treaty Provisions for the Pacific Settlement of International Disputes* (United Nations, New York, 1966).

2. For discussions of the main issues concerning treaties see Lord McNair, *The Law of Treaties* (Clarendon Press, Oxford, 1961) Ch. XV, pp. 272–305. On rules concerning interpretation of treaties see L. Oppenheim, *International Law: A Treatise*, Vol. I, 8th edn, H. Lauterpacht (ed.) (Longman, London, 1967) pp. 950–8. See also Ian Brownlie, *Principles of International Law*, 3rd edn (Oxford University Press, London, 1979); D. P. O'Connell, *International Law*, 2nd edn (Stevens and Sons, London, 1970); T. O. Elias, *The Modern Law of Treaties* (A. W. Sijhoff, Leiden, 1974); Paul Reuter *Introduction au droit des traités* (Armand Colin, Paris, 1972).

3. UN Doc. A/Conf. 39/27, 23 May 1979, and *UKTS*, No. 58, Cmnd. 7964. The convention entered into force on 27 Jan. 1980. See UN Multilateral Treaties, ST/LEG/SER.G/, 1982, p. 619.

4. See Vienna Convention on the Law of Treaties between States and International Organisations or between International Organisations, which was opened for signature on 21 March 1986. For text see *Revue Générale de droit international public* (1986) pp. 501–44.

5. For further discussion of this point see Lord Gore Booth, *Satow's Guide to Diplomatic Practice* (Longman, London, 1979) p. 236, and McNair, op. cit.

6. Gore Booth, op. cit., p. 238.

7. The provisions are pursuant to 1 USC 1126 (the Case–Zablocki Act) requiring disclosure to Congress of all concluded agreements and consultation by agencies with the secretary of state over proposed agreements. See *Code of Federal Regulations (CFR)* Vol. 22 (1985) pp. 448–54.

8. Ibid., p. 448.

9. Ibid., p. 450.

10. See O'Connell, op. cit., pp. 195–205 on the classification of treaties.

11. Gore Booth op. cit., pp. 240–1.

12. North Atlantic Treaty, 4 April 1949, *UNTS*, Vol. 34, p. 243; South-East Asia Collective Defence Treaty, 8 Sept. 1954, *UNTS*, Vol. 209, p. 23. By a decision of the Council of the Southeast Asia Treaty Organisation on 24 Sept. 1975, the organisation ceased to exist as of 30 June 1977. The Collective Defence Treaty, however, remains in force; Treaty of Amity and Cooperation in Southeast Asia, 24 Feb. 1976, *Foreign Affairs*, Malaysia (March 1976) p. 80; the Latin American Free Trade Area, established by the Treaty of Montevideo, 18 Feb. 1960, was replaced by the Latin American Integration Association, concluded at Montevideo on 12 Aug. 1980, *ILM*, Vol. 20, p. 672. Treaty Establishing the European Economic Community (EEC), *UNTS*, Vol. 298, p. 11. The Economic Community of West African states was set up by the Treaty of Lagos, 27

May 1975, *West Africa* 16 June 1975, p. 679, while the treaty establishing the East African Community came into force on 1 Dec. 1967. The community was dissolved in 1977 and finally wound up on 10 July 1984. See *The Times*, 12 July 1984.

13. See Bowman and Harris op. cit., pp. 481–90.

14. Hans Blix and Jirina H. Emerson, *The Treaty Maker's Handbook* (Ocean Publications, Dobbs Ferry, NY, 1973). On the effect of internal revolution on diplomatic style see Philippe Ardant, 'China's Diplomatic Practice During the Cultural Revolution', in Jerome A. Cohen, *China's Practice of International Law* (Harvard University Press, Cambridge, Mass., 1972) pp. 86–128.

15. *UNTS*, Vol. 500, p. 95. Entered into force, 24 April 1964.

16. *UNTS*, Vol. 596, p. 261. Entered into force 19 March 1967.

17. *UKTS*, No. 11, 1976, Cmnd. 6397.

18. Conventions for the protection of war victims concerning the amelioration of the conditions of wounded and sick armed forces in the field (238); (ii) amelioration of the condition of wounded, sick and shipwrecked members of armed forces at sea (239); (iii) treatment of prisoners of war (240); (iv) protection of civilian persons in time of war (241), *UNTS*, Vol. 75, p. 31.

19. *UNTS*, Vol. 520, p. 151; Vol. 557, p. 280.

20. *UNTS*, Vol. 15, p. 295; Thomas Buergenthal, *Law Making in the International Civil Aviation Organisation* (Syracuse University Press, 1969).

21. *UNTS*, Vol. 310, p. 181.

22. *UNTS*, Vol. 860, p. 105.

23. See Edward W. Plowman, *International Law Governing Communication and Information* (Frances Pinter, London, 1982).

24 European agreement on transfer of responsibility for refugees, 16 Oct. 1980, Misc. No. 3, 1981, Cmnd. 8127.

25. Council of Europe, *Directorate of Human Rights of Aliens in Europe* (Martinus Nijhoff, Dordrecht, 1985).

26. *Convention on Long-Range Trans-Boundary Air Pollution*, 13 Nov. 1979, Misc. No. 10, 1980, Cmnd. 7885.

27. Done at London 2 Nov. 1973; entered into force 2 Oct. 1983; see R. R. Churchill and A. V. Lowe, *The Law of the Sea* (Manchester University Press, Manchester, 1985) pp. 220–1.

28. *UKTS*, No. 46, 1980, Cmnd. 7874.

29. See R. P. Barston and P. W. Birnie, *The Maritime Dimension* (George Allen and Unwin, London, 1980) pp. 116–20.

30. UK Misc. No. 11, 1983, Cmnd. 8941.

31. See Churchill and Nordquist, op. cit.; for further discussion on the evolution of state practice see R. P. Barston, 'The Law of the Sea', *Journal of World Trade Law*, Vol. 17, No. 3 (May–June 1983) pp. 207–23, and 'The Third UN Law of the Sea Conference', in G. R. Berridge and A. Jennings, *Diplomacy at the UN* (Macmillan, London, 1985) pp. 152–171.

32. *UNTS*, Vol. 978, p. 361.

33. Chia-Jui Cheng, *Basic Documents on Internation Trade Law* (Martinus Nijhoff, Dordrecht, 1986).

34. See J. R. V. Prescott, *The Maritime Political Boundaries of the World* (Methuen, London, 1985); Philphot Tansubkul, *Asean and the Law of the Sea* (Institute of Southeast Asia Studies, Singapore, 1982).
35. Lars Kalderen and Qamar S. Siddiqi, *Sovereign Borrowers* (Butterworths, London, 1984).
36. J. E. Carroz and M. J. Savini, 'The New International Law of Fisheries Emerging from Bilateral Agreements', *Marine Policy*, Vol. 3 (1979) pp. 79–98; P. Coper, 'The Impact of UNCLOS III on Management of the World's Fisheries', ibid., Vol. 5 (1981) pp. 217–28; FAO, *Fisheries Technical Paper*, No. 223 (FIPP/T223, 1982); *International Joint Ventures in Fisheries* (FAO, Rome, 1983); Gerald Moore, 'Limits of Territorial Seas, Fishing Zones and Exclusive Economic Zones' (FAO, Rome, 1985); *Coastal State Requirements for Foreign Fishing* (FAO, Rome, 1985).
37. Anthony Sampson, *Empires of the Sky. The Politics, Contests and Cartels of World Airlines* (Hodder and Stoughton, London, 1985).
38. *10 Years Asean* (ASEAN Secretariat, Jakarta, 1977) pp. 125–32; *Foreign Affairs*, Malaysia (March 1976) pp. 21–6.
39. Alison Broinowski (ed.) *Understanding ASEAN* (Macmillan, London, 1982) pp. 283–93; *Foreign Affairs* Malaysia (March 1977) pp. 41–50.
40. Agreement on the Establishment of the ASEAN Cultural Fund (ASEAN Documents, Jakarta, 1980) pp. 76–80.
41. *UKTS*, No. 91, 1981, Cmnd. 8441.
42. *UKTS*, No. 14, 1981, Cmnd. 8186.
43. *UKTS*, No. 32, 1983, Cmnd. 8932.
44. *UKTS*, No. 44, 1980, Cmnd. 7917.
45. *UKTS*, No. 68, 1981, Cmnd. 8374.
46. *UKTS*, No. 43, 1982, Cmnd. 8673.
47. *UKTS*, No. 46, 1982, Cmnd. 8685.
48. *Foreign Affairs*, Malaysia (Dec. 1976) p. 57.
49. *Foreign Affairs*, Malaysia (Sept. 1974).
50. *Foreign Affairs*, Malaysia (Sept. 1982) p. 243.
51. *Foreign Affairs*, Malaysia (March 1982) p. 92.
52. *Foreign Affairs*, Malaysia (Sept. 1970) p. 93.
53. *Foreign Affairs*, Malaysia (March 1982) p. 92.
54. *Foreign Affairs*, Malaysia (June 1976) p. 65.
55. *Kertas Statut*, 43 Tahun 1982.
56. *Kertas Statut*, 116 Tahun 1983.
57. The Malaysia/Pakistan Joint Committee held its inaugural meeting in Kuala Lumpur on 22 Aug. 1983. See *Foreign Affairs*, Malaysia (Sept. 1983) pp. 292–3.
58. *UNTS*, Vol. 325, p. 253.
59. *UNTS*, Vol. 962, p. 399.
60. *UNTS*, Vol. 952, p. 264.
61. *UNTS*, Vol. 7, p. 73.
62. *UNTS*, Vol. 456, p. 301.
63. See R. P. Barston and Patricia Birnie, 'The Falkland Island/Islas Malvinas Conflict: A Question of Zones', *Marine Policy*, Vol. 7, No. 1 (Jan. 1983) p. 20 *passim*.
64. *Financial Times*, 14 June 1984.

65. *UNTS*, Vol. 1, p. xvi.
66. Security treaty between Australia, New Zealand and the United States (ANZUS), 1 Sept. 1951, in J. A. S. Grenville, *The Major International Treaties 1944-73* (Methuen, London, 1974) pp. 337-9.
67. *LNTS*, Vol. 94, p. 57.
68. *The Guardian*, 4 July 1984.
69. *UNTS*, Vol. 4, p. 275.
70. *UNTS*, Vol. 87, p. 103.
71. *UKTS*, Vol. 67, 1946, Cmd. 7015. .
72. *UNTS*, Vol. 935, p. 405.
73. *LNTS*, Vol. 93, p. 343.
74. *UNTS*, Vol. 71, p. 101.
75. UK Misc. No. 11, 1983, Cmnd. 8941.
76. Olive Oil Agreement extended by protocol, 23 March 1973, *UKTS*, No. 58, 1979, Cmnd. 7581; International Coffee Agreement, extended 26 Sept. 1974, *UNTS*, Vol. 982, p. 332, and protocol for the fourth extension of the Wheat Trade Convention, 26 April-17 May 1978, *UKTS*, No. 1, 1980, Cmnd. 7775.
77. *UKTS*, No. 70, 1970, Cmnd. 4444.
78. The Anglo-Swedish Convention for the Avoidance of Double Taxation (as amended) 27 Sept. 1973, *UKTS*, No. 33, 1974, Cmnd. 5607, is a good illustration of this usage, with the protocol being used as the means to bring into effect the several amendments to the convention.
79. See, for example, the modification of Article 56 of the Convention on Civil Aviation of 7 July 1971, extending the membership of the Air Navigation Commission from twelve to fifteen members, *UNTS*, Vol. 958, pp. 217-18.
80. See, for example, the protocol amending the Paris Convention on Obscene Publications, 4 May 1949, *UNTS*, Vol. 47, p. 159.
81. *UNTS*, Vol. 951, p. 187.
82. Paris, 16 Dec. 1971. *UKTS*, No. 58, 1971, Cmnd. 4739.
83. Protocol supplementary to the Air Services Agreement, 13 April 1970, between the United Kingdom and Soviet Union, UKTS, No. 42, 1970, Cmnd. 4388.
84. 21 Feb. 1973, *UNTS*, Vol. 963, p. 267.
85. Vienna Convention on Consular Relations, 24 April 1963. *UNTS*, Vol. 596, p. 262, p. 470, and Optional Protocol Concerning the Compulsory Settlement of Disputes, p. 488.
86. UK Misc. No. 51, 1972, Cmnd. 5164.
87. Protocol to the agreement on ending the war and restoring the peace in Vietnam concerning the return of captured military personnel and foreign civilians, *UNTS*, Vol. 935, 1974, p. 202.
88. 7 March 1974, *UNTS*, Vol. 945, p. 163.
89. See, for example, financial protocol between the EEC and Greece, 28 Feb. 1977. *UKTS*, No. 91, Cmnd. 7389, and between the EEC and Cyprus (with Final Act), 15 Sept. 1977, *UKTS*, No. 31, 1979, Cmnd. 7490.
90. See McNair, op. cit.
91. Anthony Aust, 'Memoranda of Understanding: The Theory and Practice of Informal International Instruments', *The International and Comparative Law Quarterly*, Vol. 35 (1986) pp. 787-812.

92. A number of institutions in the Commonwealth have been set up by informal instruments. The Commonwealth Secretariat was established by an unsigned and undated 'Agreed Memorandum', Cmnd. 2713.
93. The memorandum was part of the large number of agreements at the height of *détente* signed at or subsequent to the SALT I negotiations, *UNTS*, Vol. 944, p. 28. See also the Protocol Relating to Commercial Activities, Pursuant to the October 1972 Trade Agreement, signed 22 June 1973, *UNTS*, Vol. 938, p. 128.
94. *Foreign Affairs*, Malaysia (Dec. 1970) p. 103.
95. *Foreign Affairs*, Malaysia (March 1981) p. 89.
96. *Foreign Affairs*, Malaysia (Sept. 1977) p. 160.
97. *Foreign Affairs*, Malaysia (March 1981) p. 89.
98. *Hansard*, 9 Dec. 1985, Cols. 623, 629, 631, 634.
99. The defence leasing arrangements between the United Kingdom and the United States, for the Turks and Caicos Islands provide a good illustration of the use of a memorandum of understanding and an agreed minute. The memorandum to the main agreement deals with *inter alia* exemption from taxation and the status of local regulations, while the agreed minute refers to article X of the agreement on civil claims, and clarifies the procedures under which islanders can make claims against the United States Government. See *UKTS*, No. 42, 1980, Cmnd. 7915.
100. United States–German Democratic Republic Agreed Minute on Negotiations Concerning the Establishment of Diplomatic Relations, 4 Sept. 1974, *UNTS*, Vol. 967, p. 336.
101. The agreed minute in this case records the main issues and points of interpretation in the negotiations. See *UNTS*, Vol. 953, p. 293. Cf. United States–Philippines agreement of 30 April 1974 (agreed minute) *UNTS*, Vol. 953, p. 161.
102. *UNTS*, Vol. 944, p. 3.
103. *UKTS*, No. 122, 1973, Cmnd. 5484.
104. *Kiribati Gazette*, No. 5, 29 May 1981.
105. See Horoshi Kimura, 'Soviet and Japanese Negotiating Behaviour', *Orbis*, Vol. 24, No. 1 (Spring 1980) p. 67.
106. See the interim agreement between France and the Republic of Korea of 22 Jan. 1975. The agreement entered into force on signature and provided for termination either on the entry into force of the reciprocal convention or within a maximum of three years. *UNTS*, Vol. 971, p. 385.
107. *UNTS*, Vol. 967, p. 336.
108. *UKTS*, No. 46, 1982, Cmnd. 8685.
109. Multilateral socialist treaties are either drawn up in Russian or the language of some of the parties. For example, the Charter of Comecon is in Russian; the Russian, Polish, Czech and German versions are authentic. The other language apart from Russian might be that of the depositary country. For example the 5 July 1962 Customs Convention is in Russian and German, since the GDR is the depository of the convention. See Gyorgy Haraszti, *Some Fundamental Problems of the Law of Treaties* (Akademia Kiado, Budapest, 1973) pp. 174–9.
110. The English text of the 25 June 1971 Soviet-Argentinian trade agreement is specifically designated under the provisions of the

agreement as the text to be used for interpretation and reference, *UNTS*, Vol. 941, p. 14.

111. See F. A. Mann, *Foreign Affairs in English Courts* (Clarendon Press, Oxford, 1986) pp. 107-9 on foreign texts in British courts.

112. In some multilateral treaties the date of entry into force is suspended until some contingent circumstances occur, such as a given number of ratifications is achieved for entry into force.

113. Ministry of Trade, Malaysia, 1973, p. 8.

114. *UNTS*, Vol. 798, p. 341; Vol. 973, p. 328.

115. Under Article VI of the Long Term Agreement between the United States and Soviet Union, 29 June 1974, the agreement remained in force for ten years, *UNTS*, Vol. 961, p. 118. A further example is the 1975 United Kingdom–Poland five-year trade agreement, *UKTS*, No. 64, 1976, Cmnd. 6874. When agreements of this type run out they are frequently kept in force, pending a new agreement, by an exchange of notes. An alternative procedure if there is a time limit set to the duration of the agreement is to include a simple provision in the final section to allow for the continuation of the agreement for further periods (e.g. of twelve months) provided that one or more of the contracting parties does not express objection to the continuation.

116. *UKTS*, No. 21, 1946, Cmd. 6885.

117. A survey of British practice over the period 1972–82 based on the *UK Treaty Series* indicates that exchanges of notes on average account for some 40 per cent of the instruments concluded.

CHAPTER ELEVEN

International agreements: case studies

In this chapter we look at two types of common international agreements – trade and international loans for project finance, with a view to analysing the structure and some of the main issues which arise in the negotiation of these types of instruments.

TRADE AGREEMENTS

States use a variety of means to promote (or regulate) international economic, financial and commercial relations. These include domestic measures, such as taxation and administrative concessions, tariffs, export subsidies, export-free zones, trade-financing loans, anti-'dumping' measures, internationally agreed preference schemes and customs and other economic unions. Trade agreements are but one of the many instruments which are available in this broad range of measures.

In some state practice a trade agreement is styled an 'economic cooperation agreement' (e.g. Romania).[1] However, most economic cooperation agreements tend to cover not only trade matters but a wide range of other items such as industrial cooperation, research and development, scientific exchange with, and the establishment of, economic and scientific joint working committees and commissions e.g. Agreement on Economic, Scientific and Technical Cooperation between Sweden and the USSR.[2] In Soviet and most East European practice, trade agreeements with other states are normally styled 'long-term' (e.g. Hungary and the United Kingdom)[3] although occasionally a time limit is put on the duration of the agreement, e.g. the United Kingdom– Poland five-year trade agreement.[4]

In a bilateral context, the decision to conclude a trade agreement will depend partly on the range of other agreements already in existence between the parties, as well as other considerations such as the level and nature of total trade (e.g. whether it is one-sided, low in overall volume, excessively commodity oriented or limited in the existing range of manufactured or semi-manufactured goods traded).

In other words a trade agreement is usually designed to serve one or a number of specific purposes. In a political sense, a trade agreement might be signed to cement better relations, following, for example, a political visit, or develop relations which have perhaps been dormant for many years. However, not all economic or commercial relations between states are or require the conclusion of an agreement of this type. In these cases, trade exchange is at an acceptable level and content and without any major structural irregularities.

The general purpose of a trade agreement is to establish a legally binding framework within which to promote and conduct economic relations. Among the matters dealt with by an agreement are: MFN and like product treatment.[5] For example the Malaysian–Indonesian trade agreement of 16 October 1973 is pursuant to article II of the Basic Agreement on Economic and Technical Cooperation (same date) between the two countries.[6]

Article 1(2) contains provision for MFN treatment in issuing import and export licences, and in the following subparagraph (2(3)) provides for 'like product' treatment: 'Any advantage, favour, privilege or immunity granted or which may be granted by each Contracting Party on import or export of any product, originating or consigned to the territory of a third country, shall be accorded immediately and unconditionally to the like product originating in or consigned to the territory of either Contracting Party'.

This type of provision is not always provided for, e.g. the Malaysia–Czechoslovak trade agreement, 20 November 1972.[7] Those parts of the MFN clause itself, which make the exchange of goods subject to relevant import and export laws, and foreign exchange controls, may be drafted in a number of ways to strengthen the MFN, for example, so that: 'such laws and regulations shall not invalidate the most-favoured-nation provisions' (Federation of Malaya–Republic of Korea trade agreement, 5 November 1962, article II(2)[8] or it may be weakened by qualification: 'the contracting parties shall, subject to their respective import, export, foreign exchange or other laws, rules and regulations, provide the maximum facilities possible for the purpose of increasing the volume of trade between the two countries ...' (Malaysia–Czechoslovak Socialist Republic trade agreement, 20 November 1972, article 2).

Scope and application of MFN and related provisions

The scope of a trade agreement with another state is often limited by *excluding* from the provisions the preferences, advantages or exceptions that have been or may be granted to generally defined groups of states or named countries. In this exception list might be the preferences granted to:

(a) neighbouring countries in order to improve frontier traffic or regional trade;
(b) countries who are members of a customs union or free trade area;
(c) the Commonwealth;
(d) specified countries;
(e) goods and commodities imported under economic or military aid programmes.

In a separate sense the provisions of a trade agreement may be drafted so as not to preclude the states party to the agreement having the right to adopt or execute measures relating to *inter alia*:

(a) public security, national defence;
(b) public health;
(c) agricultural and veterinary regulations;
(d) trade in specified items, e.g. precious metals, weapons, historical artefacts.

The scope of the trade agreement itself will generally be set out in the form of two schedules referred to in either the first or second articles which are set out as an annex (though still an integral part of the agreement). The respective schedules list the goods and commodities, e.g. rubber manufactures, timber and timber products, machinery and transport equipment, traded for beans, fresh fruit, fish, plywood, cement and bicycles. The schedules can be relatively simple and based on broad categories, as in the example below to the Singapore–People's Republic of China trade agreement of 1979:[9]

SCHEDULE A

EXPORTS FROM THE REPUBLIC OF SINGAPORE TO THE PEOPLE'S REPUBLIC OF CHINA

Industrial Machinery and Transport Equipment and Parts
Industrial and Domestic Electronic and Electrical Equipments and Components
Rubber, Rubber Products and Processed Wood
Chemicals, Petrochemicals, Pharmaceuticals and Fine Chemicals

Medical and Scientific Instruments
Others

SCHEDULE B

EXPORTS FROM THE PEOPLE'S REPUBLIC OF CHINA TO THE
REPUBLIC OF SINGAPORE

Rice and Other Cereals
Foodstuffs and Canned Goods
Tea, Native Produce and Special Products
General Merchandise
Stationery and Sports Articles
Textiles
Machinery and Instruments
Agricultural Implements and Tools
Chemicals and Chemical Products
Steel Products and Non-Ferrous Metals
Animal By-Products
Others

The content of the schedule is a matter for negotiation between the parties. Among the considerations relevant to the content are whether it is considered appropriate to have a detailed list, whether the categories of goods should be broken down according to a classification, e.g. primary products, manufactures, and whether the subcategories themselves need to be broken down so as to refer to detailed items (e.g. industrial machinery and equipment: offshore oil-rig compressor pumps). In some cases the schedule is open-ended, and after listing certain manufactures concludes the list with a miscellaneous category 'other manufactures'. The schedule clause in the main agreement may, if considered necessary, make provision for the parties to hold consultation on any amendment to the list of goods in the future.

Apart from these provisions it is worth noting that additional provisions may be required for trade agreements involving centrally planned or socialist-type economies and market or quasi-market economies. In such cases trade agreements may need to take into consideration and reflect through specific provisions such matters as the legal status of state trading organisations, principles of non-discriminatory commercial treatment, financial subsidy and forms of currency payment. In addition, the question of the treatment of imports of products for immediate or ultimate consumption in governmental use may be an issue for negotiation between the parties.[10]

Miscellaneous provisions

Apart from the above, other provisions of trade agreements normally cover *inter alia*: (a) means of payment; (b) trade promotion; (c) dispute settlement; (d) merchant shipping; (e) commercial aircraft; (f) transit rights; (g) duration of the agreement; (h) entry into force. While some of these items follow a generally standard form, e.g. means of payment (acceptable convertible currency), others can take a number of widely differing forms depending on what the parties seek to achieve or are able to agree in their negotiations as an acceptable outcome. For example, provisions on the treatment of merchant vessels may be extended to provide analagous treatment of each of the parties' commercial aircraft at their respective airports (blanket charge). Again, the merchant shipping clause in the MFN section can be based on MFN provisions for port charges and harbour facilities or the *cargo status* of a ship. If MFN status is granted to vessels without cargoes then this affords wide rights to the MFN party. On the other hand, a state may not wish to see vessels without cargoes frequently using its ports claiming MFN status, on economic and security grounds, and so may seek a more restrictive MFN shipping clause not based on whether vessels had cargo. Article VIII of the Singapore–People's Republic of China trade agreement of 29 December 1979, has for example, a restrictive clause: 'Merchant vessels of each Contracting Party with cargo thereon shall enjoy: in respect of entry into, stay in, and departure from the ports of the other country most-favoured-nation treatment, granted by the laws, rules and regulations applicable to ships under any third country flag'.[11]

In some cases, the shipping provisions section of a trade agreement is used as a means of putting mutual shipping and cargo handling on a firmer basis. For example, article II of the Brazilian–Ghanaian trade agreement provides that: 'the contracting parties agree to promote the preferential participation of Brazilian and Ghanaian ships in the transportation of cargo between ports of both countries'.[12] Apart from this type of general obligation, agreements may, in particular, seek to limit the amount of trade carried by third-party shipping. In the Brazilian–Nigerian trade agreement, for example, article VI, provides that ships of third countries should not carry more than 20 per cent of trade between the two countries. An exception in this agreement is made for full bulk cargoes (article VI(v)).[13] As relatively new states have sought to build up their small merchant fleets, the frequency of shipping provisions in bilateral trade agreements has tended to increase. In fact, this tendency has been enhanced by the growing number of bilateral agreements exclusively devoted to shipping.[14]

Re-export, barter and transit trade

Other miscellaneous provisions worth noting are firstly on transit trade. Transit trade provisions,[15] deal *inter alia* with reciprocal measures for the movement of goods from ports and other facilities of each of the contracting parties to those of third states. The growth in popularity of 'export zones' in or near by the ports of new states has influenced the need for additional provisions to cover the transference of goods to and from export zones and ports.

Secondly, in some trade agreements the form in which the trade is carried out is defined in the general framework. Apart from the questions of schedules and means of payment already referred to, provisions may be included which seek to limit or prohibit certain kinds of trade between the parties, e.g. barter trade. That is, goods directly traded (or involving a third party) between the two parties are prevented from being exchanged on a barter or 'counter-trade' basis, without the prior written consent of appropriate authorities in both countries.[16]

Finally, a common miscellaneous provision found in trade agreements concluded between advanced industrial countries and new states are provisions to protect the national identity and 'integrity' of the product exported. Such provisions may take one of a number of forms. For example an 'origin of goods' clause may be used to facilitate the eradication of origin or prevention of goods and commodities being given false places of origin by including provisions on trade marks, packaging and an agreed definition for export purposes of what constitutes a 'locally'-made product. Thus article V, for example, of the 1974 trade agreement between Canada and Afghanistan provides:

> With respect to trade marks, each of the contracting parties shall protect the trademarks of the other Party to the extent that the national law of each Party permits. Each Party agrees to protect within its territorial scope the products of the other Party against all forms of dishonest competition particularly with regards to the use of false indications relative to place of origin. The contracting Parties undertake to assist one another in the prevention of any practice which might be prejudicial to their trade relations.[17]

In a multilateral treaty context, the question of what constitutes 'locally' made is often difficult to reach agreement on in negotiations of a 'certificate of origin' clause, but also particularly difficult to enforce. This is especially so if, for example, component parts are imported from outside the region and re-exported within it; if there is high regional protectionism; or if one or more of the states in the regional grouping is generally involved in low-value-added re-export trade. Another approach in some international trade agreements to the related question of the end use of goods is to include provision on the re-export of goods. The parties may agree for example to either allow 're-export only by written mutual consent',[18] or 'take steps to prevent the re-export of commodities and goods imported from the other within the framework of the agreement'.[19]

Trade administration

Apart from the above, trade agreements often contain provisions for the establishment of some form of joint consultative machinery, e.g. that of the Australia–People's Republic of China[20] meets annually or semi-annually at official level to deal with the implementation of the agreement, and to review its scope and effectiveness. The agreement may also include provisions on holding regular trade-promotion conferences. Provisions concerned with the establishment of a trade representative office would not normally be included in a trade agreement.[21] Instead, they would be the subject of a separate diplomatic or consular agreement. Such an agreement need not be negotiated simultaneously with the trade agreement, and indeed negotiations for a trade representation office (or additional consular office) are likely to follow quite some time later against the background of the effectiveness and impact of the trade agreement.

Entry into force and duration

In general, trade agreements enter into force on signature, though in special cases entry is provisional, with full entry into force on an exchange of notes. In those cases in which ratification is required, entry into force takes effect on the date of the exchange of instruments of ratification. In the event of the expiry of an agreement, commercial transactions concluded before the date of expiry but not fully executed, are governed by the provisions of the agreement. A common formula for the duration of trade agreements is one which provides for the initial agreement to last for one year with automatic continuation of the agreement for further periods of one year, unless either party notifies the other in writing of its intention to terminate the agreement, at least ninety days prior to the expiry of each period.

INTERNATIONAL LOAN AGREEMENTS

Finance for projects and capital-related activities can be generated from several sources including domestic organisations, international capital markets and international institutions. The purpose of the remaining part of the chapter is to provide a discussion of the legal framework of loans negotiated through international institutions, and highlight some of the broad issues which arise in terms of the construction of the agreement.

We should note first, though, that apart from fund sourcing from international institutions such as the IBRD, IMF and regional institutions such as the ADB, states obtain financial resources from a variety of other sources – some are internally generated through bond issues, others by floating notes in a denominated currency, on the domestic capital market of a foreign country, syndicated foreign loans, as well as bilateral loan and grant arrangements with other states.

Financial loans secured through international institutions for project finance under discussion here differ in a number of respects from funds obtained on the international commercial capital market or through bilateral official arrangements. Among the major differences between international institution funding and inter-national capital market funding are the structure and composition of interest rate spread and external supervision. Commercially acquired funding on the international capital market is generally geared to an internationally accepted lending rate, such as the London interbank rate (Libor). This variable rate is used to form the base point for the loan 'package', the terms of which are then spread at different percentage points above Libor for specific phases or periods of the amortisation. In some arrangements not only a 'mix' of interest levels is used, e.g. ⅜ per cent above Libor for five years, ¾ per cent above for ten years, but agreements too can contain a mix of *base points,* for example a combination of Libor and the US prime rate. The structure then of this type of package is a set of variable interest rates related to one or more base-point systems, which is applied to various tranches or blocks of the loan. The interest rate of the loan, since it is negotiated, provides one of the key differences from the repayment provisions of projects funded by international institutions which tend to be made up of relatively fixed components such as interest rates which are not greatly negotiable. This is not to say that there are *no* areas for negotiation, as we shall point out below. In addition, as far as the IBRD is concerned, from 1982 loans themselves have been based on a variable-rate system, calculated by the Bank, rather than the previous fixed-at-commitment system.

The second major difference between international institution sourced loans and commercial capital loans, is in the role of the international institution in the various phases of the project. This involvement includes project evaluation, tender procedures, monitoring project implementation and, in general terms, the acceptability of projects – reflecting the development philosophy of the institution, expressed in terms of preferences for particular kinds of projects (e.g. ADB agricultural sector development).

Although this chapter, in the loan agreement section, is concerned with project loans since they are commonly used instruments, other types of instruments have developed. Experimentation with differing instruments is particularly noticeable in the IBRD.[22] Included in the range of development finance instruments created in recent years are: sector adjustment lending[23] designed to support specific programmes and institutional development; the more comprehensive structural adjustment loans;[24] and financial intermediary loans for small and medium-size enterprises. These facilities have been augmented by attempts to create new instruments to increase the flows of commercial capital to developing countries by linking the IBRD more directly through IBRD guarantees of late maturities and direct participation in syndicated loans.[25]

Format and structure of international loan agreements

Loan agreements between a government and an international institution, such as the IBRD or ADB, with respect to project funding can be broadly broken down into six areas:

1. General conditions;
2. Terms of the loan;
3. Execution of the project;
4. Other covenants;
5. Effective date and termination;
6. Schedules.

The overall process from initiation to project completion can be put into the following categories:

1. Project identification;
2. Appraisal mission (international institution);
3. Pre-qualifying tenders (if appropriate);
4. Government report (submission) to international institution;
5. Negotiation (with international institution, co-financing partners (if any)) draft subsidiary loan agreement, e.g. between the government (the borrower) and subsidiary political unit (where applicable); draft relending agreement (e.g. to a public utility by the subsidiary political unit) (where applicable);
6. Implementation (signature of agreement; effective date; tender, subcontracting, progress evaluation).

Loan agreements financed through international institutions are governed by the framework or general conditions of the institution, e.g. the IBRD General Conditions Applicable to Loan and Guarantee Agreements, e.g. Ordinary Operations Loan Regulations of the ADB.[26] The general conditions set out certain terms and conditions to any loan agreement or guarantee with any member of the Bank, including such matters as the application of the general conditions, the loan account and charges, currency provisions, cooperation and information, cancellation and the effective date of the agreement. The general conditions may be revised from time to time and are supplemented by guidelines, e.g. ADB Guidelines on the Use of Consultants, or IBRD Guidelines for Procurement under World Bank Loans and IDA Credits. In the event of any inconsistency between a loan agreement and the general conditions, the latter prevail. Some aspects of the general conditions may be omitted or amended as a result of negotiation, which is normally reflected in the first article of the agreement. Frameworks of this type are also used by official (governmental) sources of capital, e.g. General Terms and Conditions of the Japanese Overseas Economic Cooperation Fund which,[27] although modelled on the IBRD, differ significantly in a number of respects both procedurally (e.g. payment based on presentation of letter of credit by the borrower) and substantively in respect to terms and conditions.

Some particular considerations on structure

Interest rate and repayment   Following the provisions relating to the general conditions and definitions (first article), the terms of the loan are set out including the amount, interest rate and repayment schedule. As we have indicated the interest rate and related Bank charges are normally considered fixed items and not negotiable in this type of loan. For example in the loan agreement between Malaysia and the ADB[28] for the Batang Ai hydro-power project the interest rate is set at 10.1 per cent per annum on $40,400,000 in Article 11, Section 2.02, and the repayment of the principal amount of the loan is in accordance with the amortisation set out in Schedule 2. Included in this schedule are the premiums on advanced repayment on an increasing percentage scale (1.5–10.1 per cent).

The system employed in this ADB loan example differs from that used by IBRD for project loans in two respects. The Malaysian–IBRD loan agreement for the Kedah Valleys agricultural development project of February 1983[29] can be used to illustrate the differences. In the first place (the question of different interest rates apart) the premiums on prepayment are calculated differently. In this example they are based on the interest rate (expressed as a percentage per annum) applicable to the outstanding balance multiplied by a factor from 0.2 to 1.

Second, the interest rate in the IBRD example is variable and is determined by applying the concept 'cost of qualified borrowings'. Thus, section 2.07(a) of the Kedah loan (IBRD) cited above, reflects the changes in the IBRD's method of setting interest rates for new loans from July 1982. The revised system replaces the fixed-at-commitment method and has been principally influenced by the increasing exposure of the IBRD to interest-rate risk in recent years. In revising the interest-rate formula the Bank took into consideration that to continue to lend or borrow at fixed rates would have increased its exposure to interest-rate risk. A second influence on the change in lending-rate policy, was that continuation of the practice of making fixed-rate loans blocked the bank from making use of short-term or variable-rate instruments. The combination of the old fixed-rate lending policy, combined with variable-rate borrowing would have ultimately caused severe and unacceptable variability in IBRD net income. Under the revised system the interest rate has been based on the cost of all the outstanding *borrowings* paid out to the Bank after 30 June 1982. These borrowings are called *qualified borrowings* in the agreement. The Bank interest rate is based on the pool of borrowings, made by the Bank ($US9 billion fiscal 1982) to which is added a spread of 0.5 per cent, as in the Kedah Valleys agricultural development project loan agreement, 7 February 1983, or the Jamaica–IBRD second technical assistance project.[30] For interest periods commencing in 1982, the initial rate for the Kedah Valleys project for example was 11.43 per cent (10.93 + 0.50 per cent), paid on a semi-annual basis.

Commitment charge Apart from the above structure, which affects the nominal cost of capital, the brief but extremely important provision in loan agreements – the commitment charge – is a further major variable in evaluating project cost. As already indicated, loan agreements contain, in addition to the interest-rate structure, a number of fixed components such as Bank fees, and, the *commitment charge*. The commitment charge is a percentage rate (in the case under review 0.75 per cent) per annum applied to the principal amount of the loan *not withdrawn* from time to time.[31] In other words, the effect of this provision is to put a premium on meeting deadlines during a project, which are essential in keeping the overall project 'on stream'. A further general difficulty which brings the commitment charge into play results from short-term alterations to the planning framework of the project. This can be caused by many factors such as national budgetary deficits, switch of development emphasis, competing projects and sheer overload within a decision-making unit. These can result in the project either not being taken up for some time or being abandoned, and, in consequence, the incurring of high first and second 'phase' commitment charges.

Co-financing Traditionally, co-financing has involved international institutions such as the World Bank, ADB and certain official sources, such as the Kuwait Fund or the Overseas Economic Cooperation Fund of Japan. However, since the late 1970s, co-financing has been extended to involve commercial sources of capital. The basis of this change lies in two main factors. In the first place international institutions involved in capital and project finance have increasingly come under pressure as their resources became stretched, and correspondingly, access to borrowing became both difficult and costly in a period of high exchange-rate volatility. The involvement of commercial source funding served to stretch resources of regional institutions such as the ADB and the Inter-American Development Bank.[32] Second, apart from increasing calls on the resources of international institutions, the profile of development projects put forward by less developed and newly industrialised countries altered to include more large-scale, cost-intensive projects such as gas separator plants, chemical complexes and public utility schemes.[33] Therefore, commercial source funding became an increasingly important part of loan packages. By 1982, for example, commercial source funding of ADB projects had increased from 5 per cent in the early 1970s to over 14 per cent.

Within the World Bank co-financing has been further developed with the establishment in 1982 of co-financing instruments which link the Bank more closely with the private commercial banking sector. The loan arrangements were informally termed 'B-loans' to distinguish them from the main long-term World Bank loans.[34] Under the scheme the Bank committed $US500 million in order to mobilize $US2 billion for some twenty selected lending operations.[35] The two main objectives of the B-loan programme were to make additional funds available to developing countries from sources not otherwise available and to achieve a lengthening of maturities more suitably matched to the borrower's capacity to repay. In one unusual case, the Bank guaranteed $US150 million of a commercial co-financing of $US300 million for a Chilean highways project in order to assist the borrower in bringing together a much larger overall package of almost $US6 billion in reschedulings and over $US1 billion in new money.[36]

Some implications of multi-party funding The introduction of commercial source funding into international loan agreements sourced by international institutions has a number of implications for both the structure and substance of the agreement. An important element in these arrangements, therefore, is the linkage between the parties, expressed in terms of the separate loan agreements which make up the 'package', which have to be completed to the satisfaction of the international institution, before the commitment (loan amount) and, in consequence, the *overall* loan can become effective. Other issues involved in multi-source funding include *inter alia* the conditions which lead to the suspension, cancellation or acceleration of the maturity of the loan, harmonisation or not of the different interest-rate structures in the loan, and the phase in which an international institution becomes involved in a joint co-financing arrangement.

Finally it can be argued, in terms of B-loans, that the Bank, in providing in effect trigger finance for much larger loans, is taking on a much wider role as guarantor and through economic monitoring than is reflected in its nominal financial involvement. While this may unlock commercial finance and provide some measure of risk relief, it is not clear what the overall effect would be on the Bank and its co-financing policies in the event of major default.

Some additional considerations

So far loan agreements through international institutions have been discussed in terms of structure and issues relating to repayment. The bulk of the remainder of the provisions of loan agreements are concerned with obligations or undertakings with respect to the organisation and management of the project (e.g. accounting records, appointment of personnel, access by the institution to information on, and general, progress, through inspections of the project). In loan agreements these provisions are styled 'covenants' and, as was suggested earlier, constitute one of the important areas of negotiation. Apart from the issues listed above, other areas of negotiation involve, for example, the details of provisions concerning other external debt which the borrower might incur, and conditions relating to the financial capabilities of the party (e.g. a public utility) for whom the loan agreement has been negotiated.

Entry into force

The effective date of international loan agreements is determined by the general conditions, particular modifications to these, and other appropriate conditions in the loan agreement. The procedures for the effective date differ somewhat between types of loan agreements. For IBRD loans, for example, entry into force occurs when the relevant conditions described above have been met, including legal opinions submitted to the Bank, whereupon the Bank despatches to the borrower notice of acceptance. The effective date clause also stipulates a period (e.g. ninety days) by which the agreement should have come into force, otherwise all obligations are terminated unless the IBRD considers the reasons for delay acceptable. Multi-party co-financing loans under the ADB require the subsidiary and relending agreement, and the agreements with lenders other than the ADB, to have been executed and delivered for the effectiveness of the agreement.

SUMMARY

In this chapter we have looked at some of the issues which arise in negotiating the content of trade and loan agreements. Trade agreements, as we have seen in this and Chapter 8, may be concluded for one of a number of reasons. Where the main reasons, however, are other than symbolic, the agreement serves to create a legally binding framework of rights and obligations which has to be turned into commercial reality. Within this framework states are essentially granting privileges and, in most cases, seeking corresponding benefits. The drafting of trade agreements should not be a matter of routine or standard operating procedures in view of the importance and possible long-term repercussions. While facilitating trade, agreements may nevertheless wish to limit it to specific categories, or make special provisions for certain goods or particular types of state-managed economies. Moreover, trade agreements need to be suitably drafted to cope with developments in, for example, communications, transport or the origin of goods which might weaken or call into question the rationale for the agreement.

The acquisition of finance and the management of loan portfolios has become an important and in some instances dominating feature of the diplomacy and foreign policy of a large number of states. The pressure on funds has increased because of changes in the requirements of developing countries to larger-scale projects, shortages of private commercial funds and limitations on the resources of regional and international institutions. In response to variability in net income, regional and international institutions have developed new forms of loan instruments and links with commercial source funding through co-financing. Multilateral and regional institutions, however, continue to be the main sources of co-financing.

REFERENCES AND NOTES

1. For example the Romania–Zambia Agreement on Economic and Technical Cooperation (with annex), Bucharest, 14 May 1970. *UNTS*, Vol. 971, 1975, p. 421.
2. *UNTS*, Vol. 969, p. 222.
3. Budapest, 21 March 1972, in *UKTS*, No. 70, Cmnd. 5016, See also Bulgaria and United Kingdom, *UKTS*, No. 51, Cmnd. 4377, 1970.
4. *UKTS*, No. 64, 1977, Cmnd. 6874.
5. For a discussion of the concept of MFN see John H. Jackson, 'Equality and Discrimination in International Economic Law: The General Agreement on Tariffs and Trade', *The Yearbook of World Affairs* (Sweet and Maxwell, London, 1983) pp. 224–39.
6. Ministry of Trade, Malaysia, 1973.
7. Ibid. 1972, Article 3, pp. 14–16.

8. Ibid.
9. Republic of Singapore, *Government Gazette*, Treaties Supplement, No. 11, 14 March 1980. Trade agreement between the Government of the Republic of Singapore and the Government of the People's Republic of China, 29 Dec. 1979.
10. See trade agreement between the Federation of Malaya and the Republic of Korea, 5 Nov. 1962, article vi(2) and article iv of the trade agreement between Malaysia and Hungary, 2 Feb. 1970; and article iv(2) with Czechoslovakia, 20 Nov. 1972, Ministry of Trade, Malaysia.
11. Singapore–People's Republic of China trade agreement, 29 Dec. 1979.
12. 2 November 1972, *UNTS*, Vol. 975, p. 195.
13. *UNTS*, Vol. 957, p. 174.
14. Malaysia has concluded bilateral shipping agreements with Bangladesh, Turkey and Indonesia and has identified the United States, People's Republic of China, South Korea, Japan and Sri Lanka for future negotiations. *Lloyds List*, 13 June 1984. For the agreements with Argentina and Turkey see *Lloyds List*, 20 June 1984.
15. See for example article 7 of the Soviet–Zambian trade agreement: 'the two parties shall promote the development of transit trade', *UNTS*, Vol. 958, pp. 18–19.
16. For example, in the Soviet Union–Nigeria trade agreement, 29 Oct. 1971, *UNTS*, Vol. 941, p. 24.
17. See, for example, Canada–Afghanistan trade agreement, 27 Nov. 1974, *UNTS*, Vol. 978, p. 151, article v; and Brazil–Nigerian agreement, *UNTS*, Vol. 957 p. 174 (article II); and cf. Protocol 3 to the agreement between Portugal and the EEC, 22 July 1972, Cmnd. 5164, Misc. (51), 1972.
18. See Soviet Union–Costa Rica trade agreement, 26 June 1970, *UNTS*, Vol. 957, p. 342, Article 5; Soviet Union–Nigeria trade agreement, op. cit.
19. Brazil–Egypt trade agreement, 31 Jan. 1973, *UNTS*, Vol. 957, p. 219, article III; and see Soviet Union–Bolivia, trade agreement 17 Aug. 1970, article 4, *UNTS*, Vol. 957, p. 361.
20. Australia–People's Republic of China trade agreement, 24 July 1973, *UNTS*, Vol. 975, p. 59.
21. As an exception see Soviet Union–Bolivia trade agreement, op. cit., and Soviet Union–Costa Rica trade agreement, op. cit.
22. See *The World Bank Annual Report 1985* (The World Bank, Washington, DC) Table 3-1, pp. 50–1.
23. Sector adjustment lending accounted for 14 per cent of total IBRD and IDA commitments during fiscal 1986 ($US2.28 billion up from 1.1 per cent five years previously in 1981 when this technique was first set up). See *The World Bank Annual Report 1986* (The World Bank, Washington, DC) p. 47.
24. See *World Bank Annual Report 1985*, pp. 52–4. Structural adjustment lending in fiscal 1986, made up of IBRD loans, IDA credits and African facility credits remained small at $US777.2 million. These funds were disbursed to programmes in Burundi, Chile, Côte d'Ivoire, Guinea, Malawi, Niger, Senegal and Togo.
25. *World Bank Report 1986*, p. 29.
26. IBRD document, March 1982.

27. *Commitment Procedure* (Overseas Economic Cooperation Fund, Tokyo, 1983).
28. *Kertas Statut*, 43, 1982, Malaysia.
29. *Kertas Statut*, 116, 1983, Malaysia.
30. *Kertas Statut*, 116, 1983, Article 2(07). See also Article 2, Section 2(01), of the technical assistance project agreement between Jamaica and the IBRD, 12 April 1985.
31. *Kertas Statut*, 43, 1982, Article 2(03).
32. See *Financial Times*, 29 Jan. 1986.
33. See *Annual Report 1982* (ADB, Manila, 1985) p. 38.
34. See Harry Sasson, 'World Bank Co-financing with Commercial Banks: The New Instruments', *Arab Banker* (Sept. 1983) pp. 15–16; Harry Sasson, 'Co-financing with the World Bank', *The World of Banking* (March–April 1984) pp. 6–8. *World Bank Annual Report 1986*, p. 29.
35. The countries involved included Thailand, Hungary, Chile, Colombia, Côte d'Ivoire.
36. *World Bank Annual Report 1986*, p. 29.

CHAPTER TWELVE
Conclusion

In the period under discussion diplomacy has changed substantially. The developments affecting methods, content and style can be grouped in four broad themes: the widening content of diplomacy; the decentralisation of the international system; the increasing fusion of public and private interest; and the quest for new diplomatic methods.[1]

As regards the first of these, the content of diplomacy has undoubtedly become more diverse and complex as has the volume of negotiation, mediation and regulation. The major effects have been felt nationally in terms of the engagement of ministries other than those of foreign affairs, trade and defence in international diplomacy. A second implication has been for the ability of states to coordinate and manage their foreign policies. Organisationally, states have attempted to deal with the growing complexity of international business in a number of different ways, although a noticeable general development is a shift to the increased concentration of decision-making at the political centre at the expense of traditional embassy-foreign ministry channels, where these exist. Deciding how best to participate effectively is an increasing dilemma for most states given the increased volume of international business. The continuous overstretching of resources is reflected in the complaints of many smaller and some larger actors about their inability to attend multiple meetings of long-standing international conferences. The problem can be seen in several other ways, such as the turnover of representatives to international conferences or the variability of representatives at regional chapter meetings and specialised technical conferences of the G-77.

An important aspect of the changing content of diplomacy is the attempt by states, international organisations and others to deal with new types of threats such as those posed by qualitative changes in international terrorism, commercial crime and international narcotics dealings. In some of these areas international cooperation through concerted collective action remains embryonic. Thus the release or protection of nationals is perceived by some states as being better achieved through national action rather than concerted collective diplomatic measures. Another feature of the expanded content of diplomacy is the accompanying growth in competitive ideologies. In international trade diplomacy, for example, the great Trader States (United States, Europe, Japan, Canada) have been concerned to focus international attention on issues such as transborder data flows, counterfeit trading and trade in services. This agenda has met with resistance from several of the newly industrialised countries and larger developing countries.

An interesting feature of the response of states and international organisations to new threats and challenges is the attention given to the training of diplomatic and other officials engaged in external policy. By the late 1980s more than fifty states had some form of national diplomatic service training academy. Among these are the long-established continental European academies such as Vienna, or the Rio Branco Institute in Brazil, as well as those of newer states. Regional training centres have also begun to be set up in Southeast Asia (ASEAN) and the Caribbean. Together these developments suggest a recognition of the importance of enhanced professionalism needed to cope with the changing technical requirements of modern diplomacy.

Just as the agenda of diplomacy has diversified, so a second striking theme stems from the growth in the number of state and non-state actors involved in modern diplomacy. Along with the diversification of membership has occurred significant decentralisation in the international system. The superpower-leading, G-77-dominated international system of the late 1960s and 1970s, characterised in part by confrontational North–South diplomacy, has gradually been displaced by new sets of interactions and configurations. A strong feature of these is the growth of regionalism and associative diplomacy, in the wake of the failure of the North–South dialogue. In addition, bilateralism, especially in international trade, has become particularly noteworthy.

Of the several factors influencing the decentralisation of the international system, the influence of developments in the international financial sector are especially important. While certain of these have produced enhanced linkages, such as those resulting from the growth of international capital markets and collective debt rescue operations, others underscore the fragmentation of the modern state and the problems of national financial control. Thus the international role and transactions carried out by para-statal agencies and offshore banking units have brought an added dimension to diplomacy. Para-statals and offshore banks, as examples of the newer actors to emerge in modern diplomacy, play important roles through their linkages with both states and other non-state actors. The extent to which they act autonomously or are only loosely controlled by states also underlines the problems of fragmentation and the central control of external policy.

A third theme, stemming from the above, is the tendency for the greater fusion of public and private interests. In this way the state is assuming or incorporating into its public diplomacy an increasing number of private interests. The argument has traditionally been put in terms of the fusion of domestic and foreign policy, which is manifested institutionally in the external role of what would be regarded as domestic ministries. What is meant here, however, is the acquisition by the state of a stake in both private domestic interests and particularly in the external operations of its nationals and corporate entities. Acquired stakes take the form, for example, of internationally negotiated joint ventures, financial support, trade promotion and the furtherance of international regulation to facilitate and protect economic interests.

In the fourth theme we argue that the international community is above all in a period of transition as it searches to find workable methods for its expanded membership and increasingly complex agenda. The quest for workable arrangements has seen the emergence of new groupings such as the GCC, Southern Africa Development Coordination Conference and the South Pacific Forum, as well as those resulting from associative diplomacy such as Lomé. The emergence of greater bilateralism, mentioned above, in a number of forms including ideological, intra-regional cooperation and trade promotion with new partners, is a further striking development. As regards diplomatic methods, changes have taken place which have reflected attempts to cope with the size of the international community. The expansion of the international community has inevitably brought with it greater conflicts of interests or what James Eayrs referred to as the problem of unmarketable foreign policies.[2] Reaching overarching solutions between major blocs, as well as finding acceptable approaches and solutions *within* blocs has become increasingly problematical. To an extent the institutional conflict, for example, between GATT and UNCTAD, as a manifestation of the North–South divide remains, though it has lessened somewhat. The use and acceptance of consensus decision-making in multilateral diplomacy, especially on technical matters, has had some success. The membership of GATT itself has steadily increased, and although it is by no means universal the composition has become more widely reflective of both developed and developing countries. A final feature of the transition in modern diplomacy is the experimental nature of many of the solutions to problems, especially in international financial debt diplomacy. Stability in this and other sectors remains elusive. It is of the essence of diplomacy, however, to continue the search for orderly change in the international system.

REFERENCES AND NOTES

1. Adam Watson, *Diplomacy* (Methuen, London, 1982) pp. 222-3.
2. James Eayrs, *Diplomacy and Its Discontents* (University of Toronto Press, Toronto, 1971) pp. 75-6.

Index

Index

memorandum of understanding, 215
   issues related to use, 216–17
Merlini, Cesare, 105
Mexico, 17, 144–5
Mexico City, conference at, 168
minute, agreed, 217
Morocco, 73n39, 145
most favoured nation, 161, 180n7, 234–5
Mozambique, 103
   mixed orientation, 38
Multifibre Arrangement, 165

narcotics, 14, 83, 199n22
Nauru, 191
negotiation, 80–3
   characteristics of, 87
   classification of, 77–9
   definition of, 75–6
   dynamic of, 85–7
   financial, 133–4, 138, 141, 143–4
   influences on, 78–80, 93n53
   new types, 87–9
   on commercial crime, 9n29
   procedural aspects, 81–2, 91n27,
      92n37, 92n39, 123n67, 171–2
   process, 80
   relation to bargaining, 90n15, 93n53
   style of, 92n29
Netherlands, 20
neutrality, 19, 38
New International Economic Order, 6,
   160, 168
New Zealand, 23
   concern over Soviet naval activity, 192
   French economic pressure on, 177
   nuclear test site dispute with France,
      46–9
   overseas representation, 23
   Rainbow Warrior affair, 177
Nigeria, trade re-orientation, 39
Niue, 191
Nkomati Accord, 211
notes, diplomatic, 42–5, 89n6
   in protest, 46–54
   other uses of, 54–6

OECD, 103, 107, 138, 146, 155n57, 179
oil crisis, 135, 138, 140–1
Olson, Robert K., 7
Oman, 34, 113
Organisation for African Unity, 29, 194
   security role limited, 194
   and election of secretary-general, 116,
      125n86
Orenburg, gas pipeline, 105

orientation, concept of, 38
ostpolitik, 101

Papua New Guinea, 36, 191
   dependence on copper, 36
para-statal agencies, 21
Paris Club, 145–7
People's Republic of China, 37, 103,
   119, 137
   border dispute with India, 49–50,
      92n37
   conflict with USSR, 37, 102–3
   joins Executive Board IMF, 135
   oil exporter, 39
   pressure over Hong Kong, 86
   reorientation, 38
Peru, 84, 119, 210
Poland, 101
   debt crisis, 145, 155n58
   normalisation of relations with FRG,
      101
Portugal, 12, 85, 214
power, diplomatic, 5
Powers, Francis Gary, 51
Prebisch, Raul, 167–8
protocol, 213–15

Qatar, 191

Rambouillet, summit, 6, 105
Ravenal, E., 192
reorientation, concept of, 37–9
risk, 145, 156n74, 163, 165
   interest rate, 243
   of power vacuum, 188
   provision of capital, 116
   reduction of financial, 152
   use of treaties to lessen, 225
role, diplomatic, 20, 29
Romania, 145, 162, 237
   US annual review of MFN, 180n9

Sadat, A., 8
Saudi Arabia, 113, 162
   importance in IMF, 135, 151
   trade with Thailand, 38
Sierra Leone, 210
Singapore, 97
   trade agreement with PRC, 235–6
South Pacific Forum, 191–2, 252
South–South, diplomacy, 116
   institutions of, 114–15
Soviet Union, 14, 37, 51, 93n40, 176
   approach to treaties, 104
   attitude to *ostpolitik*, 101–2
   bilateral relations with US, 100–1